D1431991

THE AMERICAN SOUTH AND THE GREAT WAR, 1914–1924

THE
AMERICAN SOUTH
AND THE
GREAT WAR
1914–1924

—————————— EDITED BY ——————————

MATTHEW L. DOWNS and **M. RYAN FLOYD**

LOUISIANA STATE UNIVERSITY PRESS ▮▮ BATON ROUGE

Published by Louisiana State University Press
Copyright © 2018 by Louisiana State University Press
All rights reserved
Manufactured in the United States of America
First printing

Designer: Barbara Neely Bourgoyne
Typeface: Adobe Minion Pro
Printer and binder: Sheridan Books

Library of Congress Cataloging-in-Publication Data
Names: Downs, Matthew L., 1980– editor. | Floyd, M. Ryan, 1974– editor.
Title: The American South and the Great War, 1914–1924 / edited by Matthew L. Downs
  and M. Ryan Floyd.
Description: Baton Rouge : Louisiana State University Press, [2018] | Includes index.
Identifiers: LCCN 2018012613| ISBN 978-0-8071-6937-7 (cloth : alk. paper) |
  ISBN 978-0-8071-7012-0 (pdf) | ISBN 9780807170137 (epub)
Subjects: LCSH: Southern States—History—1865–1951. | World War, 1914–1918—Social
  aspects—Southern States. | World War, 1918–1914—Economic aspects—Southern States.
Classification: LCC F215 .A43 2018 | DDC 975/.04—dc23
LC record available at https://lccn.loc.gov/2018012613

CONTENTS

THE AMERICAN SOUTH AND THE GREAT WAR, 1914–1924

INTRODUCTION

The South's Other "Other War"

MATTHEW L. DOWNS AND M. RYAN FLOYD

I n a now-famous essay, the historian Morton Sosna challenged long-held conventional thinking with his contention that World War II was more important to the development of the modern South than the Civil War. He clarified his position in an introduction to Neil McMillen's *Remaking Dixie,* calling the "other war" a "regional watershed" which led to economic growth and change, political "restructuring," and challenges to the region's unequal social hierarchies. Few historians would make a similar case for World War I. The "Great War" casts a much smaller shadow over southern history: the duration was shorter, the investment in economics and manpower was not as great, and the demands of the defense effort were less expansive than in the world war to follow. Nevertheless, the First World War did affect the South, and in many ways, the changes that occurred during and after the conflict laid foundations for the transformative nature of the Second World War.[1]

This collection of recent scholarship on the impact of World War I on the South speaks to that transformation. Specifically, the authors examine how southern participation in the war effort challenged and, in some cases, reshaped the traditional structure of southern life. The essays address a number of specific topics, each of which sheds light onto a particular aspect of southern society during this period. Authors trace the way that the requirements and limitations of a national war challenged southerners to come to terms with their regional and local identities, with discussions of foreign policy, loyalty and security, and the draft and conceptions of patriotism and service. Other contributors address wartime challenges to those groups marginalized by southern life, demonstrating a variety of early attempts to address aspects of civil rights for African Americans (with mixed results) and efforts by young women to assert identities amidst the stereotypes of southern "separate spheres." And finally, authors investigate the way that participation in the defense effort forced southerners to come to terms with a changing economy and the beginnings of industrial modernization. Taken as a whole, this collection provides new insight into an important period in the development of the modern South and suggests that World War I is more important, and more essential, to the South's transformation than has previously been considered by the historical community.

Given the overall interest in early twentieth-century southern history, there is relatively little scholarly discussion of the region's role in World War I. In fact, the Great War has a surprisingly scant American historiography. Of the few notable books investigating the US home front during the war, including David Kennedy's *Over Here,* Nell Irvin Painter's *Standing at Armageddon,* and Robert Schaffer's *America in the Great War,* the South is treated obliquely, subject to many of the larger stresses and changes affecting communities across the nation. There is no stand-alone monograph covering the experience of the South during World War I. George Brown Tindall's *The Emergence of the New South, 1913–1945* comes closest and remains the most comprehensive account of the World War I–era South, despite the fact that the book is approaching its fiftieth anniversary. In a chapter carrying the subtitle "Southern Horizons Expand," Tindall argues that southerners emerged from the war with a larger national and international perspective, inspired to build on wartime changes and facing significant challenges to an existing way of life. The authors included here build on Tindall's conclusions to examine and expand on the extent of those changes, adding to his broader discussion of the transformation of the South while contributing original, new research to show the extent to which the war effort expanded southern horizons.[2]

The work that does exist on the World War I South concerns either individualistic accounts of communities and states or studies of one specific theme covering the broader region. Martin T. Olliff's *The Great War in the Heart of Dixie,* an edited collection covering the war in Alabama, is perhaps the most broad-reaching. The essays included examine a variety of topics, including economic development, military participation, state politics, and the impact on race relations. These essays illuminate the impact of the war on many factors of life in the state, yet the limited scope, focusing just on Alabama, does little to uncover the variety of responses to World War I that occurred throughout the South. Building on the questions asked by these Alabama historians, the contributors to this volume demonstrate that the change was more extensive and more comprehensive than has previously been understood.[3]

Of the variety of topics covered in this collection, the effect of World War I on the lives of African Americans is perhaps the most comprehensively covered by scholars, both in broader histories of the African American response to segregation (such as Leon Litwack's *Trouble in Mind*) and more specific monographs on the World War I era. Historians have discussed the impact of the war on African American soldiers, on the men and women who pursued economic opportunity and freedom in the Great Migration (which began during the war), and the way in which the defense effort encouraged the formation and expansion of organizations dedicated to address racial inequality. Patricia Sullivan's *Lift Every Voice*, the most comprehensive recent history of the NAACP's formation and growth in the years before the civil rights movement, includes a chapter on World War I, suggesting that the organization expanded its reach into the South as the "main battlefront" for civil rights in the nation. For many historians, this period serves as a prelude to the civil rights activity of the Depression and World War II, a time when legal challenges began to bear fruit and organizations dedicated to interracial cooperation (as with groups like the Commission on Interracial Cooperation and the Southern Conference on Human Welfare) created a forum for early civil rights activism.[4]

The Great Migration, too, has attracted much scholarly attention, including recent works like James Gregory's *Southern Diaspora* and Isabel Wilkinson's *Warmth of Other Suns*, which focus on the economic and social dislocation of the movement of African Americans (and in Gregory's case, southern whites) to the North and West. Yet even with the relatively rich historiography outlining the civil rights movement of the World War I years, much about the African American experience is yet to be studied. The authors included in this volume address that need with topics capturing the diversity of the African American experience, including the growth and organization of the NAACP in the South, the impact of wartime rhetoric on civil rights activism in southern cities, the critical debates within black communities over contributions to the war effort, and the reaction to incidents of racial violence, like the East St. Louis Massacre, the "Waco Horror," and others. Considering the African American response to the war effort across numerous topics and several states, this volume suggests a broadness that existing monographs have not yet fully explored.[5]

Fewer historians have tackled the other implications of the war for the South.

For instance, the war challenged the southern economy, depressing cotton exports while encouraging industrial production and development. Prominent agricultural historians, including Jack Temple Kirby (*Rural Worlds Lost*), Pete Daniel (*Breaking the Land*), and Paul Conkin (*A Revolution down on the Farm*), have described the impact of the war on southern farms, but the implications of the decline in cotton for southern development are only recently becoming clearer, as is the role that southerners themselves played in crafting a response to the "cotton crisis" that accompanied the onset of war.[6]

Too, histories of southern textiles in the twentieth century have outlined the ways in which that industry was affected by the conflict, focused largely on the war's effect on mill culture and the prospects for unionization. In Jacqueline Dowd Hall et al.'s *Like a Family*, and in Bryan Simon's *Fabric of Defeat*, scholars note the war as a turning point for mills, or at least the "beginning" of the transformation in the Carolinas. In *Creating the Modern South*, Douglas Flamming notes the war's impact, this time in the manufacturing hub of Dalton, Georgia. Much of this work focuses specifically on the encouragement of labor and unionization at textile and other mills and the way that wartime dislocations affected the labor force.[7]

Beyond these discussions, the larger consequences of wartime economic development have been vastly understudied. While the Great War gets brief mention in classics like James Cobb's *Industrialization and Southern Society*, Gavin Wright's *Old South, New South*, and Blaine Brownell's *Urban Ethos in the South*, historians have largely focused their attention on World War II and the rise of the Sunbelt. The authors included in this work extend this analysis, suggesting how participation in the war worked to restructure the southern economy, and southern conceptions of the economy, in important ways. The war forced southerners to come to terms with the instability of cotton, the promise of industrialization, and the opportunities presented by global commerce.[8]

Even less studied than this early period of economic modernization is the complicated mix of southern patriotism, loyalty, and identity brought to a head during the war by conscription, wartime propaganda, and efforts to control production and consumption. In one of the few books to address such issues, Jeanette Keith's *Rich Man's War, Poor Man's Fight: Race, Class, and Power in the Rural South during the First World War*, the author shows how farmers and workers in the rural South, black and white, dissented and resisted in the face of calls for patriotism and participation in the war effort. Yet such a topic, given its implications for southern identity and a qualified and conflicted nationalism, demands a much broader conversation. Several of the scholars here add to the larger understanding, investigating how southerners responded to appeals for service and patriotism, how they sought to shape and reshape the demands of the war while emphasizing an inherent "southernness."[9]

Southern historians have only begun to understand the true impact of the Great War on the American South. What little work has been done has largely been relegated to the experience of southern soldiers abroad and changes to the lives of African Americans as they began to challenge segregation. The contributions to this collection certainly address these issues, but the variety of topics explored here expand the analysis to suggest that the war brought with it modernization, conflict, and a direct challenge to the southern status quo that had to be addressed, years before the New Deal and World War II inaugurated the era of the Modern, Sunbelt South. This collection speaks to the importance of the war for the South and reckons more fully with the ways that southern participation in the war effort transformed the region in meaningful and lasting ways.

The essays in this book consist of both case studies and broader, more comprehensive works. Some contributors delve deeply into the state-level experience, showing how community-level events speak to broader wartime themes. Matthew Downs's study of economic growth in Mobile, Alabama, for instance, or Kathelene Smith's and Keith Gorman's investigation of women's colleges in North Carolina suggests that a narrow focus yields valuable information about the war's impact across the region. Other chapters cast a wider net. Angela Jill Cooley's discussion of food policies spans several states, and Janet Hudson's study of Carolinians, North and South, speaks to a broader shared war effort and highlights larger themes in the southern experience. All told, the authors collected here cover a number of southern states in terms of both specific research and comparative analysis, including Alabama, Georgia, Louisiana, Mississippi, North Carolina, and South Carolina. The Carolinas are particularly well represented in this collection, with four chapters dedicated to the Great War's impact on state government, on young college women, on conscription and southern identity, and on African Americans and the struggle for racial equality. This focus reflects an abundance of research materials and it demonstrates the centrality of Carolina history to southern history. In fact, the authors' work included here demonstrates the extent to which the variety of experiences embodied in that particular area can stand in for the experience of the South as a whole.

For instance, Janet Hudson's discussion of the impact of World War I–era rhetoric on African American activism focuses on North and South Carolina, yet her conclusion that the war created a foundation for a broader, more successful civil rights movement, is equally applicable to many other parts of the South. In fact, Lee Sartain's discussion of the NAACP shows that African Americans in New Orleans saw the war as a motivating factor in much the same way. James Hall's work on conscription and manhood, drawn from extensive research on North Carolina draft cards and reports, speaks to a much broader idea of southern identity, and his conclusions add to regional conversations about duty, responsibility, and the role of southern "men" during times of national crisis. In his chapter on the South Carolina Council of Defense, Fritz Hamer is careful to note comparatively the work of other councils in other parts of the South; in doing so, he ties his Carolina-centric research to a broader regional history of political change and federal-state relations. In these cases and others, the authors use the local history of North and South Carolina to understand a broader regional story of wartime transformation, and as each of the authors collected here demonstrates, local and regional histories help to highlight the ways in which World War I laid the foundation for the revolutions of the modern South.

This collection is organized thematically. The first four essays illuminate the ways that their participation in the World War I–era defense effort challenged southerners' regional, community, and personal identity. In "'A Diarrhea of Plans and Constipation of Action': The Influence of Alabama Cotton Farmers, Merchants and Brokers on Anglo-American Diplomacy during the First World War, 1914–1915," M. Ryan Floyd investigates the "Cotton Crisis," when wartime policies threatened the continued international trade of southern cotton. Drawing on correspondence between Alabama's congressional representatives and their constituents, Floyd emphasizes that the opinions, threats, fears, and concerns of everyday Alabamians influenced the decision-making of US and British politicians and diplomats and ultimately affected how the two countries approached the Allied naval blockade of Germany. As agriculture entered an irreversible economic decline, southerners sought to use political power to reassert their importance in the nation and its war effort.

James Hall, too, is interested in the intersection between federal power and local interest, and in "Manhood, Duty, and Service: Conscription in North Carolina during the First World War," he pays particular attention to the way in which white North Carolinian men responded to the first draft since the Civil War. Individuals weighed the lingering culture of sectionalism and separateness against the language of honor and duty, and across the state, young men decided to serve and exhibited patriotism. Using draft board records, correspondence, draft cards, and other pertinent sources, Hall shows that for many southerners, the decision to support the war, and the ideals that accompanied the war effort, was a personal one that brought up questions of regional and national identity.

Fritz Hamer's history of the South Carolina Council of Defense (SCCD) approaches the relationship between southerners and the federal government from a different perspective. He describes the work of the SCCD, particularly its efforts to overcome the state's initial opposition to the war and the changes the war effort threatened to introduce. The organization set out to build patriotism in South Carolina through speeches and community organizing, but instead it found significant opposition from key political leaders over American participation in the Allied cause and fears of African American enlistment (and the subsequent challenge to segregation and disfranchisement). Drawing from archival collections and a variety of newspapers, Hamer's essay suggests that the war effort brought struggles for power and influence within southern states as the region considered its position within and responsibilities to the nation.

Finally, in "Food Soldiers," Angela Jill Cooley investigates the interaction between the Food Administration and southern farmers. She shows how federal regulations, designed to address the habits of a growing urban middle class, failed to take into account the nature of southern agricultural food ways. Her work, focused largely on Alabama, Georgia, and South Carolina, demonstrates the extent to which the regulatory apparatus of the Wilson administration both ignored and, conversely, highlighted the plight of rural southerners at a time of change.

Floyd, Hall, Hamer, and Cooley suggest that World War I challenged the South and the people and communities of the region to come to terms with their responsibility to the nation and their identity as loyal, patriotic Americans. Faced with the demand to participate in the war effort, and the demand to forego certain freedoms and privileges for the sake of national defense, southerners had to come to terms with the role of the government (federal and state) in their own lives. While the authors disagree over the extent to which the war caused permanent change in the region's power structure and its relationship to the federal government, their contributions suggest that historians must account more thoroughly for the way that World War I challenged the region's position in the larger nation.

Building on questions of regional identity, section two contains three essays concerning the impact of wartime changes and rhetoric on the traditional gendered and racial hierarchies of the New South. In "The Call to Duty in the Old North State: Women's Colleges and Volunteerism during the Great War," Keith Gorman and Kathelene Smith discuss the response of administrators, faculty, and students at North Carolina women's colleges to the Wilson administration's effort to mobilize the nation. As active participants in the war effort, women drew on an existing culture of volunteerism and service in wartime but, as the authors note, the collegians went further, organizing their own efforts, shaping their own versions of volunteerism, and developing a model for postwar activism. Gorman and Smith posit World War I as a window into the intersection between women's identities and the demands of southern society, and as a turning point in the burgeoning southern women's movement, including campaigns for suffrage, in the early twentieth century.

Where Gorman and Smith trace the war's effect on southern conceptions of the role women should play in society, other researchers suggest that the war was equally challenging for conceptions of race. Given the solidification of segregation and disfranchisement in the South at the turn of the century, World War I came at a crucial time in the struggle for racial equality. In "The Great War and Expanded Equality? Black Carolinians Test Boundaries," Janet Hudson describes how African Americans in North and South Carolina used World War I to address the ongoing inequalities of the South. While some joined organizations expressing loyalty and calling for justice, others acted individually to demand justice, even as they confronted a white power structure determined to weather the conflict and maintain the status quo. Hudson concludes that the war provided a training ground for black activism in the twentieth century as individuals perfected forms of protest, sought new and greater opportunities, and linked core American values with the demand for civil rights. Building on the organizational approach, Hudson adds to the argument that World War I was a crucial time in the struggle for equality.

In contrast to Hudson's holistic view of the wartime freedom struggle, Lee Sartain, in "'The Race's Greatest Opportunity since the Emancipation': The NAACP, the Great War, and the South," approaches the black wartime experience from the perspective of the fledgling NAACP. He argues that the war effort was a turning point, allowing leaders to put the young organization's ideas and plans into practical usage. He pays particular attention to the development of a specific plan for desegregation, using wartime calls for patriotism and morality to mobilize African Americans, embrace a distinct and increasingly dominant voice, and position itself as the central organization for the attainment of civil rights for blacks.

Hoping to mobilize the nation, President Wilson proclaimed that "the world must be made safe for democracy." While his appeal was geared to American participation in an international effort to defeat the Central Powers, many within the United States embraced the spirit of a fight for equality to challenge the traditional inequalities that marked American and southern life. Smith and Gorman, Hudson, and Sartain suggest that the war provided an opening for such a struggle. Young women actively participated in the defense effort, challenging long-held assumptions about women and their role in southern society. African Americans largely supported the Allied cause, but their participation as soldiers and civilians did not preclude efforts to challenge segregation, discrimination, and disfranchisement, whether in groups or in hundreds of individual decisions and interactions. Foreshadowing the determined efforts of the World War II–era "Double V" campaign, some southerners demanded freedom at home, even as their neighbors fought for it abroad.

The final two essays address economic growth and development and the larger impact of the war on the New South. The authors pay particular attention to the modernizing southern economy as the region utilized the defense emergency to press for urbanization and industrial development. For existing industries, this transition could be problematic. According to Annette Cox's "Cotton's Chaotic Home Front: The First World War and the Southern Textile Industry," the Great War challenged southern textile manufactures to address problems with labor scarcity and unrest, a changing global market for goods, and the possibility of growth and expansion. In this detailed account of the state of southern textiles during the war years, Cox suggests that owners took advantage of the chaos and confusion of the war years to grow and assert control over their industry, only to see their efforts evaporate in the postwar years, leading into the Great Depression.

With the South's traditional economies in flux, many southerners saw in the defense effort an opportunity to bring in new growth and development that might draw the region into a more modern, more stable economic future. This was certainly true in Mobile, a city facing the brunt of agricultural decline as the cotton trade that had traditionally buttressed its port fell rapidly in the war years. In "'The Battle of Commerce Is Begun': Building the Port of Mobile, Alabama, after World War I," Matthew L. Downs traces the emergence of a development ethos in the Port City to show how wartime concerns about the state of the city's and region's economy contributed, eventually, to the development of the Alabama State Docks and the revitalization of Mobile's economy in the 1920s. What began as the city's interest in participating in defense industry quickly morphed into a concerted campaign to bring new business to the Gulf, an effort that drew heavily on an active civic and commercial leadership, as well as on the power of state and federal government. On the eve of the Great Depression, Mobile had developed a relatively extensive shipbuilding and trading center, developments directly related to the way in which the city responded to World War I.

Cox and Downs show that World War I was as essential to the economic transformation of the New South as it was for conceptions of southern identity and challenges to longstanding racial and gender hierarchies. Coming at a time when agriculture and traditional industry went into decline, the war spurred modern economic growth and urbanization, setting the stage for the more drastic changes that would accompany World War II. The authors suggest that southern political and economic leaders were cognizant of changes, and that they worked to accommodate them, even as the war brought the kinds of dislocation that profoundly upset the status quo. This final section adds to the overall argument presented in this collection, that World War I marked a period of transformation that ushered in many of the conflicts and challenges that have come to define the modern South.

Few historians would describe World War I as a "regional watershed" for the South. The 1920s saw the region grappling with segregation and inequality, with political conservatism, and with a lack of economic diversification, in other words, the problems that characterized the region after the turn of the twentieth century. And yet, the Great War laid a foundation for changes to such persistent problems. The war effort witnessed some early efforts by African Americans and women to challenge second-class status in southern society. The demands of mobilization challenged the South's reactionary politics and encouraged a reconsideration of the relationship between state and federal government. And as the southern economy shifted to account for the demands of conflict overseas, business leaders embraced the kind of change that would, in the long run, result in profound economic transformation. While perhaps not as transformative as the Civil War or Morton Sosna's "other war," World War II, the Great War encouraged southerners to reconsider their identity and the identity of their region in important and wide-reaching ways. As a result, World War I laid the groundwork for the profound changes of the twentieth century, the changes that created, and are still creating, the modern South.

NOTES

1. Neil McMillan, *Remaking Dixie: The Impact of World War II on the American South* (Jackson: University of Mississippi Press, 1997), xii–xix.

2. David Kennedy, *Over Here: The First World War and American Society* (Oxford: Oxford University Press, 1980); Nell Irvin Painter, *Standing at Armageddon: A Grassroots History of the Progressive Era,* rev. ed. (New York: W. W. Norton and Co., 2008); Ronald Schaffer, *America in the Great War: The Rise of the Welfare State* (New York: Oxford University Press, 1994); George Brown Tindall, *The Emergence of the New South, 1913–1945* (Baton Rouge: Louisiana State University Press, 1967).

3. Martin T. Olliff, *The Great War in the Heart of Dixie: Alabama during World War I* (Tuscaloosa: University of Alabama Press, 2008).

4. Leon F. Litwack, *Trouble in Mind: Black Southerners in the Age of Jim Crow* (New York: Vintage Books, 1999); Patricia Sullivan, *Lift Every Voice: The NAACP and the Making of the Civil Rights Movement* (New York: New Press, 2009); John Egerton, *Speak Now against the Day: The Generation before the Civil Rights Movement in the South* (Chapel Hill: University of North Carolina Press, 1994). Glenda Gilmore's *Defying Dixie: The Radical Roots of Civil Rights, 1919–1950* (New York: W. W. Norton and Co., 2008) traces some of the more radical threads of post–World War I organization and protest, though she, too, is more concerned with the New Deal era. Localized studies of the "long civil rights movement" do a better job of tracing the impact of the war for community-level struggles, particularly Great de Jong's *A Different Day: African American Struggles for Justice in Rural Louisiana, 1900–1970* (Chapel Hill: University of North Carolina Press, 2002).

5. Isabel Wilkerson, *The Warmth of Other Suns: The Epic Story of America's Great Migration* (New York: Random House, 2010); James N. Gregory, *The Southern Diaspora: How the Great Migrations of Black and White Southerners Transformed America* (Chapel Hill: University of North Carolina Press, 2005).

6. Jack Temple Kirby, *Rural Worlds Lost: The American South, 1920–1960* (Baton Rouge: Louisiana State University Press, 1987); Pete Daniel, *Breaking the Land: The Transformation of Cotton, Tobacco, and Rice Cultures since 1880* (Champaign: University of Illinois Press, 1986); Paul K. Conkin, *A Revolution down on the Farm: The Transformation of American Agriculture since 1929* (Lexington: University of Kentucky Press, 2009). For the South's response to the "Cotton Crisis," see Joseph A.

Fry, *Dixie Looks Abroad: The South and U.S. Foreign Relations, 1789–1973* (Baton Rouge: Louisiana State University Press, 2002); Arthur S. Link, *The Higher Realism of Woodrow Wilson and Other Essays* (Nashville: Vanderbilt University Press, 1972); and Bruce E. Matthews, "The 1914 Cotton Crisis in Alabama," *Alabama Review* 46, no 1 (January 1993): 3–23.

7. Jacqueline Dowd Hall et al., *Like a Family: The Making of a Southern Cotton Mill World* (Chapel Hill, University of North Carolina Press); Bryant Simon, *A Fabric of Defeat: The Politics of South Carolina Millhands, 1910–1948* (Chapel Hill: University of North Carolina Press, 1998); Douglas Flamming, *Creating the Modern South: Millhands and Managers in Dalton, Georgia, 1884–1984* (Chapel Hill: University of North Carolina Press, 1993).

8. James Cobb, *Industrialization and Southern Society, 1877–1984*, new ed. (Lexington: University Press of Kentucky, 2004); Gavin Wright, *Old South, New South: Revolutions in the Southern Economy since the Civil War* (Baton Rouge: Louisiana State University Press, 2007); Blaine A. Brownell, *The Urban Ethos in the South, 1920–1930* (Baton Rouge: Louisiana State University Press, 1975).

9. Jeanette Keith, *Rich Man's War, Poor Man's Fight: Race, Class, and Power in the Rural South during the First World War* (Chapel Hill: University of North Carolina Press, 2004).

1

"A Diarrhea of Plans and Constipation of Action"

*The Influence of Alabama Cotton Farmers, Merchants, and Brokers on
Anglo-American Diplomacy during the First World War, 1914–1915*

M. RYAN FLOYD

I n 1914, cotton farmers and merchants across the Deep South anticipated
excellent prices for their product on the international market. However, in
its effort to defeat Germany, Great Britain enacted a naval blockade of the
German coast and redirected many of Britain's merchant vessels for use in the
war effort. The decision created an emergency in the United States as cotton
prices plummeted. People connected with Alabama's cotton industry, like their
counterparts in other southern states, faced serious problems because they were
heavily invested in the state's most popular and problematic crop. The significant
drop in prices threatened their standard of living and their ability to pay back
existing loans to local merchants and banks.

Throughout the first twelve months of the war, farmers and cotton merchants
across the South called on their government to protect their livelihood. Individually, their cries for help appear inconsequential. The concerns of a single
farmer or merchant could easily get lost in the vast pool of letters and protests
sent to public officials across the South and in Washington during the war.
However, these men were not powerless. Collectively, southerners had quite a
loud voice and made a significant impact on American and British diplomacy.[1]
The experience of farmers and merchants in Alabama offers a window into the
crisis and provides a clear picture that is representative of the experience of
cotton men across the South. As in other cotton states, Alabamians wrote letters
to members of Congress, including Senators John Bankhead, Sr., and Oscar
Underwood, to express their opinions and demand that Washington take steps
to improve their lot.

While President Woodrow Wilson opposed providing additional financial assistance directly to the farmers, he and his staff needed political support from the Democratic South and made the cotton trade an important issue for Anglo-American relations. British diplomats, too, recognized the effect that the "Cotton Crisis" could have on the president's administration and how the downturn in cotton prices might pressure the White House to challenge the Royal Navy's blockade, thus threatening the Allied war effort. Consequently, the combined efforts of numerous small farmers and merchants played an influential role in the largest and most devastating war to that point in history.

The outbreak of war in August 1914 caused significant disruptions to the world economy. The belligerents understood that cutting off enemy trade would have a significant effect on the outcome of the conflict. Great Britain in particular understood the importance of economic and naval warfare. For over a century the British had relied on their navy to defend against invasion of the home islands, protect its overseas colonies, and strangle its enemies into submission by cutting off their access to goods made in neutral countries. In addition to being the world's strongest naval power, Britain commanded the largest blue-water merchant fleet and planned to keep its own import trade flourishing.[2] While unintended, their policies had a detrimental effect on the economic conditions of neutral countries, including the United States, because isolating the Central Powers from the outside world meant cutting off the outside world from the Central Powers.

Britons viewed the war as a fight for survival, and on August 5, the Foreign Office distributed to neutral countries a list of goods that London considered absolute contraband, goods that were used solely for military purposes; those considered conditional contraband, goods predominantly for civilian use; and items that remained on the Free List, goods that could traverse the blockade unhindered.[3] It also established a loose blockade of the European coast and redirected the British merchant marine to focus on the Allied war effort. London's decisions caused concern for US businesses. American companies relied heavily on trade with European countries, including nations at war with Britain. Additionally, the American merchant marine was underdeveloped. American merchants relied heavily on British cargo vessels and US ships carried only 17% of the country's exports.[4] For these reasons, there was a lot of speculation about how the war would affect the American economy.

Despite Britain's initial decision to place cotton on its Free List, investors feared that a sudden change to its status would cause the supply to far outreach the demand. This was a serious concern because the 1914 cotton crop was the largest on record and many southerners believed that the region's economy depended on the industry's success. The previous year, cotton states produced 14 million bales and were enjoying gradually increasing prices for their goods. Additionally, the South was dependent on international markets, exporting 60% of the crop overseas in 1913.[5] As historian Gavin Wright asserts, in the years prior to the war "American cotton so dominated the world market that the size of the U.S. crop (in conjunction with world demand) essentially set the price."[6] With the export market in jeopardy during the summer of 1914, cotton's market value plunged, prompting exchanges across the United States to temporarily close their doors and forcing farmers to accept prices below the cost of production.[7]

By mid-October cotton was selling for six to seven cents a pound, which was less than half the prewar value.[8] This price was detrimental to farmers and merchants across the South. They invested heavily in cotton because it could earn them the highest returns and because most merchants would loan money against cotton more often than other agricultural products. This single-crop economy placed farmers and cotton merchants in a precarious position because they were so closely tied to the export market and easily affected by international events.

Farmers and cotton merchants expressed their concerns to public officials. Writing to Alabama senator John H. Bankhead Sr. on August 8, Dothan Bank secretary J. L. Crawford stated that his financial institution would not "under present conditions" be able to manage the crisis. Crawford, like the managers of other state and local banks, was concerned that declining prices would prevent farmers from being able to pay off their crop liens and that financial institutions would suffer losses.[9] Expressing a similar unease, the chairman of the Talladega County Democratic Executive Committee, S. P. McDonald, pleaded with the senator to "put the machinery in motion that will keep the mills of the United States and foreign countries from using the present conditions as a means to buy our cotton crop at less than its value." McDonald, like many, understood the importance that the crop had for the South's economy, adding: "Practically the whole business of the south is dependent upon cotton."[10] Worried about widespread bankruptcies, Cullman attorney M. F. Parker revealed his anxiety when he wrote to Bankhead that "every thing is now getting as tight as 'Dicks hat band' and I fear pressure will start everything to run to cover." If things did not improve, he feared that the bankruptcies would affect the health of the entire nation.[11]

Secretary of the Treasury William McAdoo was well aware of the crisis developing in the cotton market, and southerners were initially hopeful that he could help farmers and stabilize prices. Writing to B. F. Mauldin in Anderson, South Carolina, Senator Benjamin Tillman asserted that he believed McAdoo was "friendly" to the idea of assisting cotton farmers.[12] In early August 1914 McAdoo invited cotton growers, merchants, and manufacturers from across the South to Washington to discuss possible solutions. At the August 24th Southern Cotton Congress, the two hundred delegates, led by the National Farmers Union, concluded that the US government must provide farmers with emergency credit issued through southern banks, as well as purchase large quantities of cotton from farmers. In his memoir, McAdoo claimed that he immediately "issued $68,000,000 of emergency currency to [national] banks in the South," and that he "deposited with them $27,000,000 of government funds." McAdoo also suggested the creation of a government program to warehouse cotton until prices improved.[13]

The administration's other major proposal was the "cotton loan fund." The White House hoped to get national banks and the Federal Reserve to fund a loan of $135 million to farmers, who could borrow the money for one year against warehouse receipts at 4.8% interest. Wilson's staff believed this was the silver bullet that would eventually save the South.[14]

McAdoo noted that prices did improve to 8.5 cents per pound, up from 6.5 cents, but this was still below the cost of production for middling cotton. Additionally, McAdoo funneled money into large national banks across the South.[15] McAdoo's efforts did not satisfy cotton farmers and merchants because they did not trust national banks, and most farmers used state and local banks to obtain credit. Consequently, most farmers were unable to access the limited funds McAdoo provided. Of the $135 million available, farmers borrowed only $28,000.[16]

Fearful about their future, these men did not sit back and wait patiently for a different solution. Instead, they pressured congressmen and the White House to resolve the cotton crisis quickly. This pressure came in several forms, including pleas for help, suggestions on how to resolve the situation, demands that their elected officials support various bills, and political threats.

Opposing the Treasury secretary's plan to place money in national banks, L. J. McConnell, president of the Talladega Chamber of Commerce, expressed to Bankhead that he did not believe that the big banks would use the federal money appropriately. McConnell, like many farmers and merchants, argued that national banks would not come to the aid of southern farmers and merchants: "Common sense (of which you have a very great abundance), will teach you, as experience has taught us that if the peoples [*sic*] money is place[d] in the banks for distribution, the banks will do as they have done in the past." The national banks, he feared, would hold the money and wait until the price of cotton dropped further so that they could "buy the cotton on speculation."[17]

Echoing McConnell, merchants in Prattville wrote Bankhead arguing that money sent to large banks would be "immediately sent to New York, and Eastern banks to pay the larger Southern banks debts there."[18] Writing to senator-elect Oscar Underwood, H. L. McElderry noted that federal funds would not reach the farmers because the money was "placed in large banks who do not handle a shirt tail full of farmers produce in a year. . . . Large banks supply the distributers—wholesale men, cotton buyers, manufacturers but not the producers." He wanted the federal government to put money in the small banks to ensure that it reached the farmers. "If you will get Secty McAdoo to do this," McElderry asserted, "you will relieve the strain [and] you will be the savior of your country."[19]

In addition to espousing the funneling of money to state and local banks, many merchants and farmers supported direct aid to farmers. P. C. Steagall of Ozark, Alabama, asserted that Congress needed to set a "fixed and protected" price for cotton. Urging expediency, he added that if Congress did not provide direct assistance quickly, "then we better meet and go to praying."[20] The editor of the *Progressive Farmer*, Clarence Poe, sent an editorial to Bankhead on August 13 which called for direct support for local farmers. Poe claimed that supplying banks with funds to support the cotton crop was not enough. He asserted that the real need was among the individual farmers: "I believe the government is going to provide money enough to finance the crop, but what I haven't yet seen is satisfactory evidence that this money is going to the man whose sweat made the crop. . . . What we want to know of our Congressmen is 'What are you going to do for this man at the bottom?'"[21]

As a solution to the crisis, some Alabamians suggested offering farmers $40 to $50 loans on each warehoused bale of cotton until prices increased. Merchants in Prattville claimed that this approach was a common practice and that even whiskey producers were able to warehouse their products and receive loans.[22] W. J. Renfroe argued that the South would accept almost anything. He asserted that direct assistance was "not a question of constitutionality but should be taken care of regardless. We put in the grand-father clause (unconstitutional) and dis-franchised the negro, and the South approved it."[23]

As these and other letters indicate, many of the Alabama farmers and merchants who wrote to their senators demanded federal assistance. Looking to Washington for a solution was new for the American South in the early 1900s. In the decades after Reconstruction, southerners focused on local and state support, but two new phenomena occurred in the intervening decades. First, the Progressive Movement made inroads in the South. Many southerners embraced federal participation in Progressive ideals such as business regulation and education reform.[24] Additionally, while southerners opposed government intervention that might supersede state and local authority, their calls for action demonstrate that they welcomed federal assistance in the form of economic stimulus. Alabamians, like other people in the region, favored aid that would help them get the existing economic system moving and then let the private sector take over.

More significantly, southerners were looking to Washington for assistance because of the large southern influence in the White House and Congress. For decades, many southerners felt that they had to depend on state governments because the federal government did not represent them. However, with the election of 1912, this appeared to change. Woodrow Wilson's ascendency to the White House placed a Democrat with southern ties in the nation's highest office. In addition to Wilson, five of his cabinet members, including McAdoo, as well as the president's closest personal and political adviser, Edward House, were from the South. Congress also included many influential southern Democrats who held important political posts and supported much of Wilson's New Freedom agenda. As historians Dewey Grantham and David Kennedy point out, the South was in a position to receive more federal patronage than at any time since 1860.[25]

Numerous Alabamians assumed that this strong Democratic presence in Washington meant that the government would now cater to their needs. L. J. McConnell boasted to Bankhead: "The South is now in the saddle from the President down, why dont [sic] Congress carry out some of the promises made us for the past forty years."[26] On September 19, S. McDonald informed Underwood that at the Alabama Cotton Conference in Birmingham, the local chamber of commerce organized a resolution to send to Woodrow Wilson. The chamber argued that because the cotton crop was an "INTERNATIONAL CROP" and because the "business of the South, and Nation wide prosperity depends upon all sections of the country reaping the benefit of its labors," Wilson should make a proclamation requesting "the entire people of the United States to assist in upholding the price of cotton and the country's prosperity . . . by buying a bale of cotton at no less than ten cents per pound, and holding it until it sells for that price or more."[27] Wilson's presidency gave these Alabamians hope that their economic, political, and social interests would be protected. Consequently, they expected and demanded a lot out of their elected officials, including the president.

Despite their high expectations, farmers and merchants were frequently underwhelmed by what they perceived as the national government's limited efforts to assuage the crisis. T. V. Ballard, a delegate to the State Convention of the Farmers' Union explained to Bankhead that farmers across the state wanted Washington to provide direct aid and circumvent any "middlemen" that might prevent the farmers from obtaining support. Complaining that the government had not done enough, he added, "I hear farmers protesting that you and the other members of the Alabama delegation have thrown them down in this emergency after your continuous profession of interest in protecting and promoting their welfare."[28]

By late August, Alabamians' fear and frustration over the continuing crisis developed into anger. Bankhead and Underwood started receiving letters that expressed indignation and included political threats. Numerous Alabamians accused the Democratic Party of abandoning them in their time of need and threatened not to vote for a Democrat again in the future. When attorney and landowner Jackson M. Young wrote to Bankhead, he complained that he was not getting "satisfaction from anybody" on the matter. He found it aggravating that Congress appeared willing to appropriate funds to purchase transportation for stranded millionaires in Europe. . . . But when the MILLIONS ask for the same treatment accorded the MILLIONAIRES, unexpected difficulties arise. . . . It seems hard for a man from a solidly Democratic district to understand that those men who vote the Democratic ticket are entitled to much. Those millionaires never vote the Democratic ticket, while the silent millions of the South have heretofore been the Party's main strength."[29]

Young then described the plight of a tenant farmer on his property named Henry Stone. The attorney explained that Stone "is a good man and I have hauled him many miles to get his vote in right." Stone, Young noted, sold a 497-pound bale of cotton, "and after paying the fixed charges and the picking, Henry's part was just $8.05." Young used Stone's plight to demonstrate that many people were losing faith in the Democratic Party. He also wanted to threaten Bankhead that southerners might shift their votes. Young asserted that after selling the bale, Stone "went away swearing that he would see the whole lot of you in h-ll before he would ever again quit his work and vote a Democratic ticket." Young noted that if the farmers "'lose this crop' it would destroy the southern economy and that the 'Solid South' will be broken. This is no scare talk." Young asserted that southerners were trying to stay calm, but warned that "we are going to stampede sooner or later, if help comes too tardily. Many of us remember the saying of General Grant, that the Democrats could be relied upon to act the D-d fool at the right time!" Additionally, Young, like many other Alabamians, was tiring of Congress's handling of the crisis, adding that Bankhead and his colleagues "have a diarrhea of plans and a constipation of action." Weeks later, Young again contacted Bankhead, stressing that "we have given up all hope of help from the National Government. We are beginning to think that possibly we have voted Democratic too often."[30]

Alabamians understood that their most powerful weapon was the vote. Like Young, others regularly criticized Bankhead for what they perceived as inaction and threatened to withdraw their votes if he did not fix the cotton situation. Citizens in Alpine sent a letter to Bankhead on September 25 to "ask and demand of you as our delegate and servant of Alabama" to support a bill put forward by Texas representative Robert Lee Henry. The bill, which Henry presented directly to Wilson on October 2, called for the US Treasury to place "several hundred million dollars" in banks across the South that would loan the money to cotton producers. The men asserted that they would demonstrate their "appreciation at the next election." Threatening to vote against him if he did not act in their interests, they stated, "You never have done any thing for the farmer or the laboring class that sent you there. This bill must receive the Presidents [sic] signature if we vote for you again."[31]

Other Alabamians made similar warnings about future elections. W. F. Miller asserted that "congress [h]as been talking of doing something for the Southern cotton grower to finance this crop and talk is all they have done." He wrote to Bankhead explaining that he recently gave his son a "cotton patch" and that his son had produced two bales, which he was going to lose money on because he could not sell it at cost. He expressed that his son had hoped to "sell the cotton to go too [*sic*] school." Frustrated, Miller asserted that he did not feel that the Democrats in Congress had done much to help. He clearly had not received any support from banks and the federal aid had not trickled down to farmers like Miller or his son. Miller was worried and warned that "if congress dont [*sic*] do Something I can tell you the dimocratic [*sic*] party is going To loose [*sic*] in the next National election."[32]

Alabamians also vented their frustration about President Wilson's approach to the crisis. They had assumed that because he marketed himself as a friend of the South, Wilson would focus his energy on saving the region from economic ruin by injecting direct aid. When the president did not react the way that they had hoped, many came out in opposition. L. J. McConnell informed Bankhead that he planned to travel with a delegation to Washington to press for a resolution to the crisis. In a letter to Bankhead he criticized Wilson asserting that he "believed Mr. Wilson to be a 'psalm singing, pecksnifian, damned hypocrite in his professions of friendship for the farmer,' as he had recommended the throwing our markets open to the competition of the world."

Angry at the lack of direct financial support for farmers, McConnell asserted that Wilson would "do exactly what his soninlaw [*sic*] Mr. McAdoo said for him to do." He then accused McAdoo of being in the pockets of the big banks, which, in his opinion, had no interest in helping farmers out of their situation. McConnell described several situations in which he believed that the banks had refused to accept cotton receipts to pay off loans. In one case he claimed that a farmer took his warehouse receipts to the bank to get money for his wife's hospital expenses, but was refused by the bank. He also referenced his belief that the White House was going to sacrifice the cotton South. Such actions angered McConnell to the point that he added, "I say to hell with such an administration."[33]

McConnell stated that he had supported the Democratic Party unwaveringly for decades, but he did not feel that the party was coming to his aid when he needed it most. "I have been a democrat for 44 years," he added, "and in times when the most forceful argument used was a Colt's .44, but I think we have a better friend in the devil than in Wilson. I am sure he is not such a damned hypocrite as is Wilson, and that is what a great many southern farmers believe. Pardon me, but nothing but strong language will *half* convey my feelings in the matter; though I am chairman of a board of Methodist Stewards."[34]

Young and McConnell were not alone in their feelings about the Democratic Party. J. C. Gober wrote to Bankhead in late October that "we of the South expect relief from a democratic administration and if it fails to help us when in position to do so, if it turns a deaf ear to us when in distress we consider we have been sold to the enemy."[35] His sentiments were echoed by G. T. McElderry, who asserted that dissatisfaction with the Democrats was widespread. McElderry informed Bankhead that after attending the "'Hog & Hominy' corn show" in Atlanta he learned from a number of farmers that they were angry with the Wilson administration. McElderry asserted that "there is a *fixed* determination in the minds of nine tenths of the farmers to vote in 1916 for 'the Devil and Tom Bell' against Mr. Wilson and any man the democratic party names with him." McElderry added that he thought that numerous people across the South would do the same. "Senator Bankhead you know from past experience and observation that when you get these old Baptist and Methodist camp-meeting singing farmers 'cussin mad' They will shoot straight and vote together in spight [*sic*] of every thing on earth, and the country alleged to be beneath the earth."[36]

As in other southern states, the Democratic Party dominated Alabama politics. However, this monopolistic position did not mean that Democratic politicians could feel comfortable maintaining their elected positions. While the Democratic Party was the only party in the state of any consequence, it was factionalized. Democrats did not see eye to eye on many hot political issues, and it was common for Democrats to challenge each other in impassioned elections.[37] Consequently, the "solid South" was not as solid as it may have appeared, and the statements made by McElderry and others were not empty threats.

Responding to their constituents' frustration and demands, most state politicians tried to convince farmers and merchants to wait out the drop in prices. Alabama governor Emmet O'Neal and US senator Frank White both encouraged Alabamians to be patient.[38] Nevertheless, Alabama's elected officials did take steps to resolve the crisis. In August 1914, congressmen put forward three bills that were intended to put money in the hands of cotton growers. Representative J. Thomas Heflin went as far as supporting a bill that would require the US government to purchase four million bales of cotton.[39] Their efforts came to naught, in large part because other regions of the country opposed subsidizing the cotton crop. Many businesses in the Northeast liked the low cotton prices and did not want to support any legislation that would increase their costs.[40]

O'Neal organized a governor's conference to bring together leaders of the cotton states in the hopes that they could develop a state-level solution. O'Neal suggested issuing bonds so that states could purchase the cotton, but the idea gained limited support. Most governors wanted federal assistance because they did not think that their states could afford to fix the problem. Plus, several governors asserted that their state constitutions would not allow for the issuance of short-term bonds (under two years).[41]

Bankhead also attempted to calm his constituents' fears and find a solution to the crisis. He replied to numerous farmers and merchants arguing that there was no simple way to remedy the drop in prices. On August 21, he explained to State Farmers' Union president O. P. Ford that Congress and Wilson were doing everything that they could to assist the farmers.[42] Bankhead followed up his note on September 1 with a message that he sent to many people across his district. He asserted that the world was facing a conflict unlike any in human history and that this was going to affect any plan that Congress could create: "The greatest war of modern times is being waged in the whole of Europe. It came like a flash of lightning from a clear sky without a day's warning, and no opportunity was given to prepare for the disastrous results that must necessarily follow." Bankhead claimed that there was no way to predict or prevent the downturn in the cotton market. To him, the war was something that America could not control. He also stressed that financing the cotton crop of "14,000,000 bales, amounting to a billion dollars is a herculean task, and necessarily progress will be slow." Bankhead tried to assure the recipients that Congress was working on a solution but that it did not want to act without thinking the problem through. He warned that the wrong response could make things worse: "If a mistake is made in the beginning it will be fatal in the end."[43]

Addressing the political threats that he received, Bankhead deflected blame for inaction by arguing that the rest of the country liked the drop in cotton prices, resulting in "cheaper cotton and cotton goods." He added that even if southern senators and representatives promoted legislation that offered direct aid, they were outnumbered in Congress: "There are only about ten cotton States with 20 Senators out of a total of 96, and 98 Representatives out of a total of 435." Northern members of Congress, he claimed, were unlikely to pass a bill that would make the mills in New England pay more for cotton: "This is an element of the situation the representatives of the South are coming to recognize, and help, if it comes at all, must be through some other channel."[44]

Bankhead also placed some of the blame on the farmers by asserting that they had relied too heavily on a single cash crop for their livelihood. Writing to a "Mr. Smith," he noted that "when the farmer by his own efforts grows cotton only as a surplus crop, and is able to store it in a bonded warehouse over which he can negotiate loans, he will be independent of the prevailing market quotations; and by the exercise of his own discretion have the last word as to its price." Bankhead stressed the importance of diversifying crops. He did not think that government legislation could force the farmers to change their ways. "It will follow," Bankhead wrote, "as a natural consequence of emergencies such as the planter now faces, and as the business necessities require and demand." He conceded, however, that many farmers were forced to grow cotton because it offered the highest returns: "Cotton is the only sure money crop, and for that reason he is compelled to raise it to obtain cash."[45]

The senator closed by assuring Smith that Congress had considered every viable option. Bankhead did not want to deceive his constituents with the false hope that more could be done, stressing that it was better to be criticized now than censured later. In what appears to be an effort to appease Smith, Bankhead enclosed a check for $50 to participate in the Buy-A-Bale program: "If you can find a distressed confederate soldier, or the widow of a soldier, with a bale for sale I hope you will buy it." He then asked that Smith sell the bale at 12 cents a pound and "turn the proceeds over to the Soldiers Home at Mountain Creek."[46]

After receiving numerous letters from across Alabama asking for or demanding help, Bankhead wrote in a message to the people of Alabama that he was frustrated that at the meeting of southern governors there was no consensus on what to do about the cotton crisis. He expressed annoyance that southern governors continued to press for federal aid. The senator also noted that he did not think that Congress could come up with a plan: "The truth is that if every Senator and Congressman from the cotton growing States should drop every other subject and work every minute of the day for a bill providing that the Government should buy a part of the cotton crop at a fixed price, or loan money directly to the farmer secured by cotton at a fixed price, it would be impossible to secure the passage of such a bill."[47]

To remedy the situation, Bankhead submitted his own proposal for resolving the crisis. He asserted that O'Neal should call the state legislature into session so it could pass a constitutional amendment that would allow Alabama to issue bonds in the amount of $40 million. Bankhead's goal was for the state to purchase cotton at 10 cents per pound on half of each farmer's crop. He then wanted the legislature to create warehouses for the cotton where farmers could store their bales and receive a bond voucher. Farmers could then take the bonds to local merchants and pay off their debts. Merchants, in turn, could submit the bonds to the banks. He suggested that the bonds "bear 4% interest" and expected that the state could sell the cotton at cost in the years to come and pay off the bonds. Bankhead clearly was selling his idea to the people and trying to appear serious about helping farmers when he added, "We are confronted with a situation fraught with disastrous consequences to all our people, if some heroic measure is not resorted to. This is not time for abstract discussions of paternalism and other such doctrines of Government. While we are not actually at war, we have all the business consequences of war. The farmers cannot handle the situation."[48]

His plan met with mixed reviews. Most support came from farmers who pressured the governor to consider the plan. Despite widespread endorsement among farmers, O'Neal refused to back the plan or call a special session to consider it. Bankhead even promoted his plan in the Senate, hoping to convince other southern senators to push similar plans in their states, and sent copies of his speech to southern governors and state newspapers. However, no other state earnestly considered the plan, and by the end of October, his strategy had failed to gain any traction.[49]

Like Bankhead, at no point was Wilson in favor of direct federal assistance to farmers in the South. Offering such assistance was counter to his New Freedom platform and would have created serious financial challenges for the federal government. In a message to a group from North Carolina, the president asserted that the crisis must be resolved "within the limits of economic and safe finance."[50] However, despite the impression that he was turning a deaf ear to the South, Wilson and his staff were aware of the southerners' anger and frustration over the cotton crisis. From the very beginning, officials in the Wilson administration paid attention to the complaints. They worried that southerners could voice their opposition during the 1914 mid-term elections and pressure their congressmen to submit bills that might endanger Anglo-American relations.

Such concerns prompted the administration to make serious efforts to improve the South's economic situation by seeking international solutions. Wilson and his staff worked hard to create a government-owned merchant marine that could reduce American reliance on British shipping and help to open up new markets across Latin America. McAdoo proposed the idea to Congress as early as August 1914, but major business interests opposed the plan because they feared it would result in unfair competition, and the Shipping Bill was eventually voted down in March 1915.

The White House also began pressuring the Allies to limit their interference with US exports to Germany and neutral states in Europe.[51] Britain detained numerous American merchant ships that were headed to and from the European continent, including US vessels traveling to neutral ports within the blockade line. In cases where the Royal Navy determined that the ships' cargoes were ultimately destined for Britain's enemies, it confiscated them. This action challenged the American belief in the Freedom of the Seas, the idea that neutral ships should be able to sail unmolested in international waters. As a result, Wilson publically protested against what he viewed as violations of America's neutral rights at sea.

To assuage southern concerns, the Wilson administration also sought assurances that London would not hinder the cotton trade. Britain had not included cotton on the Absolute or Conditional contraband lists in its August 5 list or the August 20 Order in Council; however, no one knew what the future held and cotton prices dropped in large part because of market speculation. Lack of clarity about the cotton export market convinced many investors that the demand for cotton might go down.[52] The uncertainty created frustration and, as with Bankhead and Underwood, the US State Department received numerous letters and petitions expressing anger over the cotton crisis. Between October 14 and October 24, Acting Secretary of State Robert Lansing received missives from businessmen involved in the cotton trade and senators, including Bankhead, who claimed that despite its Order in Council, Britain was still stopping shipments of cotton and cotton-related goods from reaching neutral ports in Europe.[53]

The letters and petitions concerned Lansing enough that he relayed their contents to the British Foreign Office. In a letter to the US ambassador in London, Walter Hines Page, Lansing asserted on October 24 that "there is an increasing irritation in this country over the fact that Great Britain has not made an affirmative statement to the effect that American-owned cotton exported in vessels of neutral nationality, whatever the destination of the cotton, except to blockaded ports, will not be subject to seizure and detention." Lansing instructed Page to press the Foreign Office for a clear statement about how it intended to treat cotton, adding, "It would relieve present tendency of public opinion which is imputing selfish motives to Great Britain on assumption that cotton shipments, at least those destined for belligerent countries, will be prevented by the British Government. . . . Complaints are increasing on the part of Americas as to interference of Great Britain with commerce which they consider legitimate." He concluded his letter by emphasizing that "this Government feels that it is essential that American public opinion on this matter be quieted and it feels confident that His Majesty's Government will cooperate with it to that end."[54]

In the early months of the war, Britain had no intentions to make cotton contraband. Foreign Secretary Edward Grey understood that Germany used cotton to make uniforms and manufacture munitions parts; however, he also realized that disruptions to US cotton exports could cause serious diplomatic complications. Grey noted to the British ambassador in Washington, Cecil Spring-Rice, that "includ[ing] cotton would certainly provoke a challenge from the United States and would impair the prospect of her agreeing to a list that included copper and rubber." In his memoir, the secretary added that he feared that the United States might consider convoying merchant ships to German and neutral ports and that their cargoes would most certainly not be "limited to cotton." After speaking with Page and Grey, Spring-Rice stressed to Lansing that "cotton will not be seized. [Grey] points out that cotton has not been put in any of our lists of contraband and . . . it is not proposed to include it in our new list of contraband. It is therefore, as far as Great Britain is concerned, in the free list and will remain there."[55]

With the British statement in hand, Wilson asserted at a press conference on October 26 that the cotton crisis was over. However, the president was wise enough to recognize that the British affirmation was not necessarily a long-term guarantee that the cotton industry would be completely insulated from the war. To protect himself and his administration from further criticism, Wilson hinted that some things were outside of his control and that the only way to completely relieve the situation was to end the war.[56]

Two days after Wilson's press conference, Lansing tried to convince Germany to follow suit. He contacted US ambassador James Gerard in Berlin and instructed him to obtain a similar reply from Germany. "Intimate," Lansing wrote, "that such declaration will operate as strong preventative to any change by British Government as to their policy in regard to cotton." In a separate letter on November 8, Lansing explained to Gerard, "There is considerable doubt in certain quarters in this country as to the attitude of the German Government towards the shipments of cotton in neutral bottoms to the ports of the belligerents opposed to Germany. . . . Apprehension in this country would be greatly relieved, and the free movement of cotton encouraged, if Germany and Austria could find it possible to make a public declaration that cargoes of cotton in neutral vessels will not be molested or detained."[57] Gerard replied on November 11 that Germany had no intention to declare cotton contraband.

Lansing also reached out to the French. On December 1, he wrote to French ambassador Jules Jusserand and informed him that the British declaration "has greatly relieved the tension which has prevailed among American planters and shippers, due to a feeling of apprehension and uncertainty as to the policy of Great Britain." The United States, Lansing expressed, would like a similar response from France.[58]

The letters and protests of Alabamians along with similar missives from other southerners clearly influenced the United States' decision to push for a definitive answer from all of the belligerents about the future of cotton. Thus southern farmers and merchants were able to influence Anglo-American relations. Britain took the cotton crisis seriously and agreed to a policy that complicated its plan to strangle German trade. The reaction of policy makers in the State Department and British Foreign Office had, while only temporary, a positive effect on the cotton industry and assuaged the southern populace.

In February 1915, Germany decided to try to break the British blockade by using U-boats (submarines) to sink belligerent merchant vessels traversing waters around Great Britain. London responded in March by increasing the number of goods on its contraband lists, but due to Anglo-American concerns cotton initially remained a protected export. However, military necessity gradually forced Britain to reconsider. As early as March 11, 1915, a number of British scientists complained to the head of the Explosives Supply Department in the War Office, Lord Fletcher Moulton, that Germany used large quantities of cotton in the manufacture of ammunition and argued that Britain must cut off German access to American cotton.[59] In addition, the Foreign Office continued receiving US complaints about the blockade but recognized that American shippers were smuggling copper and rubber (two items that were considered absolute contraband) to Germany by hiding it under cotton bales in the hulls of ships. Consequently, by the summer of 1915 Britain chose to change cotton's status.[60]

These issues convinced British prime minister Henry Asquith and his cabinet to stop all cotton shipments destined for Germany. The challenge was to accomplish this task without creating major problems with the United States. Grey reminded the cabinet that the reason that they initially kept cotton on the Free List was to avoid American action against the British embargo on copper and rubber, "articles which we considered really important to Germany for supplying her army."[61]

The foreign secretary also feared that changing the policy could push more southerners to support a ban on weapons sales to Britain and its allies in retaliation. This was an unlikely result, considering the economic benefits that the United States gained from trade with the Allies, but his concerns were not unfounded. Many southerners did favor an arms embargo. Leading the charge in Congress, Georgia senator Hoke Smith asserted to Lansing in May 1915 that if Britain did not change its naval policy, "the exportation of munitions will be stopped, and the action of Congress may go much further."[62]

Observing the situation in Congress, Spring-Rice warned that changing the status of cotton could create a "bad political situation." The ambassador was concerned that a ban on cotton sales to Germany might force the president's hand because Congress could override a veto. He also cautioned that such a cotton situation would certainly anger the South, "which is dangerously strong, and would bring most southern senators and representatives into line against [the] export of arms and ammunition."[63]

Once rumors of Britain's decision reached the South, Alabamians again called for action. With cotton prices improving by mid-1915, however, the focus was less on obtaining direct assistance for farmers and more on a diplomatic resolution. In a message to Bankhead, R. Mayer wrote that the federal government needed to ensure that the United States could sell cotton in neutral European countries: "As cotton has never been declared contraband, it is simply ridiculous that the South cannot export a crop to neutral countries without the consent of a country that has no interest whatever in our welfare."[64] Mayer did not care if cotton ended up in the hands of Britain's enemies. Demonstrating his frustration over Britain's effort to prevent the reexportation of US cotton from neutral European states to Germany, he asserted, "Whose business is it if Norway, Sweden, Denmark and Holland buy two or three times the amount of cotton from us that they usually consume? They are neutral people, and we have the right to sell them our goods without consulting the English government or anyone else." Mayer finished his letter to Bankhead by demanding a resolution to the ongoing confrontation over the blockade. "We are not at war with anyone," he stated; "we do not want to go to war with anyone, but we want to protect our Southern people who have borne the burden of this conflict up to now, and who will be bankrupt unless their government has enough backbone to insist upon the rights of free markets for our cotton crop with neutral countries."[65]

To many Alabamians, protecting the cotton trade had to be Washington's first priority. Some asserted that defending American commercial rights was more important than addressing the May 7, 1915, sinking of the British ocean liner *Lusitania*. M. M. Rosenau wrote to Bankhead, "We are all Democrats and admirers of our President, but we feel that enough has been said and done about the Lusitania and what we want now is to see something done about the wrongs we are and have been suffering for a time much longer than the Lusitania affair.... There were only 100 or so Americans on the Lusitania, whereas millions of people all over America and especially in the South are being wronged by England and nothing is being said or done about it." Along with the letter, Rosenau sent a petition with over one hundred signatures demanding that Bankhead and Underwood do something to protect cotton.[66]

Like Rosenau, numerous Alabamians were more frustrated over British naval policy than over Germany's use of submarines against passenger ships. For them, the German U-boat attacks were a distant problem that had very little to do with the United States. Rather than spend time challenging German naval policy, many Alabamians preferred that Washington focus its attention on Britain. They wanted Bankhead to force Wilson and Lansing to find a diplomatic solution. "I think you should without waiting for Congress to convene," wrote J. J. Willet, "bring pressure to bear on the President and Secretary of State to cause them to bring pressure to bear upon England to modify its rules relating to cotton." He added that "England has used us to her advantage long enough, and it is time we were asserting our rights. I am not a belligerent and my sympathies are pro English, but I know from experience that as long as you lay down and let others run over you they will continue to do it." Days later, Willett sent Bankhead a copy of a letter that he mailed to Wilson. In his letter, Willett argued, "While it is the duty of our government to protect our citizens who ride the seas, even in the war zone of danger, it is much more the duty of our Government to protect the toiling millions who stay at home and raise the crops needed for clothing the world." Bankhead took such letters seriously and replied that he appreciated Willett's concerns and explained that he was planning to meet with the president in the near future.[67]

In a separate letter to the president, Willett called on Wilson to take action by emphasizing the president's responsibility to his party:

We beg to remind you that when the Republican Party is in power at Washington the South expects nothing and gets nothing, but with the Democratic Party it is different; the South is Democratic and it is not too much to say it is the heart and back bone of the Democratic Party. . . . We do not think we are selfish and we do not think we are sectional when we say we have claims upon the Democratic Party and this Administration and when that claim is merely to prevent us from being sacrificed to England's cold blooded greed.

Willett then stressed that "the thoughtful people of the South are rapidly coming to the conclusion that so far as the South is concerned, England's navalism is a greater menace to us than Germany's militarism. We therefore, ask that you use the whole power of your Administration to lift the embargo upon cotton."[68] Willett was not the only person to contact the president directly. Representatives of the Farmers Educational and Co-Operative Union of America in Pike County sent a resolution to Wilson demanding that he and the State Department press for an end to the embargo at once.[69]

The letters and petitions sent by Alabamians and other southerners had the intended effect on the government. In numerous messages to his constituents, Bankhead explained that he had met with President Wilson and that the White House was doing everything it could to resolve the crisis. Replying to G. S. Barksdale, who argued that the South was "being shamefully BETRAYED, and sacrificed by the Democratic party" by its apparent inaction, Bankhead stated that he was "satisfied that [Wilson] is thoroughly alive to the situation, and is doing everything he can, in connection with the State Department, to reach an agreement with England that will largely tend to open our cotton market." Bankhead expressed that the situation was delicate because the United States needed to maintain good relations with Britain: "A misunderstanding with England of a serious nature would completely destroy it. It seems our finger is in the trap, and it is the part of wisdom to work with the spring rather than jerk it out of the trap, but I am persuaded there is relief not a great ways in front of us." Bankhead added that "the president is receiving a great many letters from bankers, cotton merchants and prominent business men all over the South, and I am sure that he is doing everything that can be done to relieve the situation."[70]

As Bankhead noted, Wilson was well aware of the situation. The president was also mindful of the stress that congressmen were under to find a resolution. In mid-August, frustrated over the pressure he was receiving, Wilson asserted to his fiancé, Edith Galt, "[Washington] is beginning to fill up with men of the restless, meddling sort. . . . Some of them are congressmen with wild schemes, preposterous and impossible schemes to valorize cotton and help the cotton planter out of the Reserve Banks or out of the Treasury—out of anything, if only they can make themselves solid with their constituents and seem to be 'on the job.'"[71] Wilson, too, wanted a resolution; however, as Bankhead indicated in his letters, Wilson understood the delicate nature of Anglo-American relations. He clearly knew, better than most, that pressing Britain too much could backfire because it was America's largest market. Thus, diplomacy had to be handled very delicately.

Previously, in July, when Wilson learned about London's plan to ban all cotton shipments to Germany, he expressed to Edward House that Britain's decision might turn public opinion against the Allies and stir Congress to push for the arms embargo.[72] Lansing also noted that the change in policy would anger many Americans and certainly result in demands for retaliation that "will embarrass us seriously." Americans, he asserted, would feel that Britain had violated its promises.[73]

Washington was not the only place where southerners' demands for a resolution had an effect. In July when Britain informed the White House that cotton would likely be on the Absolute Contraband list, US ambassador Page explained to Lansing that he had warned the British government that "such action would embarrass the Administration and especially would be harmful to pro-British feeling in the United States. I made plain the political bearings of the subject and the danger of adding southern members of Congress and the southern press to the forces of the anti-munitions campaign."[74] Britain heeded the warnings and on July 15, Spring-Rice contacted Grey with a possible solution. He wrote that Americans sold 2,700,000 bales of cotton to Germany and Austria-Hungary annually. The ambassador argued that Britain should develop a consortium of banks that could purchase all of the cotton that the Central Powers normally purchased and warehouse it until the conclusion of the war. He also advised

Grey that before announcing the ban, the Foreign Office should convince Britain's allies to buy the stored cotton.[75]

A week later on July 21, Spring-Rice informed Grey that he did not think an arms embargo would pass but emphasized that London needed to handle the issue with velvet gloves. The ambassador asserted that his government needed to appease the South and reminded Grey that the president had to consider the demands of the American people, regardless of Wilson's personal feelings. Spring-Rice was still convinced that Germany could take advantage of tension in Anglo-American relations and turn "important interests against us. . . . The dollar against honour;—and, after all, the passengers on the Lusitania are dead and the cotton people are much alive. Dead people have no votes and no pockets. We have not threatened either the honour or the lives of Americans but we have threatened and are threatening their pockets."[76]

Asquith's government took Spring-Rice's warning seriously. The following day, Grey circulated a draft declaration to the cabinet. In the pronouncement, the foreign secretary stressed that Britain understood cotton's importance to the American South and emphasized that his country was "most anxious not to take any step that would cause disaster to the material interests in those States." For that reason, he noted that Britain planned to enter negotiations to purchase all of the cotton that would customarily go to Germany and Austria-Hungary. The following day, Page informed Lansing that "the [British] commercial attaché at Washington is instructed to confer with cotton interests and to [come] to some satisfactory working arrangement whereby this country [Britain] will buy large quantities at a good price."[77]

Initially the Wilson administration was wary of the British proposal. However, on July 31, Spring-Rice informed Grey that Lansing had changed his view of the situation. The secretary of state admitted privately that as long as Britain made sure that cotton interests in the United States did not lose money, the ban would probably face little opposition. He also concluded that enacting the ban would prevent American merchants from creating problems for Anglo-American relations by shipping goods illegally.[78] Two weeks later, Spring-Rice informed the White House that his government planned to purchase enough surplus cotton to ensure the market price remained at least 10 cents per pound and had ensured that neutral countries would be allowed to purchase enough cotton for domestic consumption.[79]

In addition to Britain's announcement, Alabamian and chair of the Cotton

Committee of the Federal Reserve Board William P. G. Harding noted that the 1915 crop would be much smaller than the previous year. He also indicated that US demand for cotton was on the rise because American manufacturers needed more for the munitions industry. Spring-Rice wrote to Grey that Harding assumed that the US market would "absorb every bale that is likely to be cultivated." Moreover, the British munitions industry needed more cotton. In a letter to Lansing, the US consul-general in London, Robert Skinner, noted that it "cannot be said, therefore that the war had been disadvantageous to American cotton interests since it has caused an enormously increased consumption of cotton for the manufacture of explosives, whereas up to the beginning of the war, the cotton manufacturing business had been dull and the general demand, at least as far as Great Britain was concerned, far below normal."[80] With such information in hand, the Wilson administration did not oppose Britain's decision to ban cotton shipments to Germany.

Britain's efforts worked, circumventing serious repercussions from the South. Following London's announcement, the *Birmingham Age-Herald* reported on August 24, 1915, that the decision to place cotton on the contraband list "appeared to attract very little attention." With a smaller crop in 1915, and with greater stability in the export market, prices began to rebound. By the close of the day on August 27, contracts for December sold as high as 10.02 cents per pound. Seeing the rise in prices the *Age-Herald* reported that the "outlook for the cotton belt is even brighter than the most optimistic had forecast a month ago." Southerners across the region expressed similar sentiments. The *New Orleans Times-Picayune* editor asserted that there was "no reason why the south . . . should not obtain prices that will make those of last autumn look unreal."[81]

Individual voices of Alabama farmers and merchants may not have had a serious impact on the people in Washington or London; however, their collective voice made a significant impression on people in diplomatic circles on both sides of the Atlantic. Alabamians, like other southerners, had a common cause and thus influential power over the Wilson administration and southern senators and congressmen. In the heat of the crisis, Mississippi senator John Sharp Williams noted to Wilson: "I am perfectly aware of the fact that it is dangerous to tell my constituents that I can see anything else besides cotton."[82] Like Williams, southern Democrats needed votes to remain in office and were under pressure to satisfy their constituents' demands. While the White House was opposed to direct assistance to farmers, Wilson and his staff did recognize the farmers' and merchants' influence and sought diplomatic solutions to the cotton situation. Pressure on the White House in turn placed pressure on Great Britain, which adjusted its policies to appease the southern farmers and merchants and prevent a major disruption to Anglo-American relations.

NOTES

1. Most historians of Anglo-American relations during the First World War focus on the interaction among high-ranking diplomats, national leaders, and commanding businessmen; see, for example, Charles Beard, *The Devil Theory of War: An Inquiry into the Nature of History and the Possibility of Keeping out of War* (New York: Greenwood Press, 1977); Charles Tansill, *America Goes to War,* reprint ed. (New York: Little, Brown & Company, 1963); Sidney Bell, *Righteous Conquest: Woodrow Wilson and the Evolution of New Diplomacy* (New York: Kennikat Press, 1972); Jeffrey J. Stafford, *Wilsonian Maritime Diplomacy: 1913–1921* (New Brunswick, NJ: Rutgers University Press, 1978); Ross Gregory, *The Origins of American Intervention in the First World War* (New York: W. W. Norton, 1971); John W. Coogan, *The End of Neutrality: The United States, Britain, and Maritime Rights, 1899–1915* (Ithaca, NY: Cornell University Press, 1981); Arthur Link, *Wilson: The Struggle for Neutrality* (Princeton, NJ: Princeton University Press, 1960); Kendrick A. Clements, *The Presidency of Woodrow Wilson* (Lawrence: University Press of Kansas, 1992); John Milton Cooper Jr., *Woodrow Wilson* (New York: Alfred A. Knopf, 2009); Lloyd E. Ambrosius, *Wilsonian Statecraft: Theory and Practice of Liberal Internationalism during World War I* (New York: Scholarly Resources Inc. 1991); Robert W. Tucker, *Woodrow Wilson and the Great War: Reconsidering America's Neutrality 1914–1917* (Charlottesville: University of Virginia Press, 2007); and Robert Ferrell, *Woodrow Wilson and World War I, 1917–1919* (Bloomington: Indiana University Press, 1985).

While these works are essential to understanding foreign relations, it is important to recognize that there were other people and groups that had an impact on the direction of US and British policies during the early stages of the conflict. One such group was the Alabama farmers and merchants who dealt with the cotton crisis of 1914–15. In *Abandoning American Neutrality: Woodrow Wilson and the Beginning of the Great War,* I address the major international issues that drove President Wilson to intentionally aid the Allies in mid-1915. This chapter expands on one such issue, the cotton crisis. However, instead of focusing on US and British statesmen, this chapter concentrates on the efforts of Alabama farmers and merchants to force a change in US and British policy. See M. Ryan Floyd, *Abandoning American Neutrality: Woodrow Wilson and the Beginning of the Great War, August 1915–December 1915* (New York: Palgrave Macmillan, 2013).

2. Arthur J. Marder, *From Dreadnought to Scapa Flow* (New York: Oxford University Press, 1961), 367–69, 382–83.

3. "The Ambassador in Great Britain (Page) to the Secretary of State," August 5, 1914, *Papers Relating to the Foreign Relations of the United States: 1914 Supplement, The World War,* (Washington, DC: Government Printing Office, 1928), 215–16 (hereafter cited as FRUS).

4. "New Shipping Bill Will Be Pushed through Today," *New York World,* August 2, 1914, in Arthur S. Link, *Papers of Woodrow Wilson* (Princeton, NJ: Princeton University Press, 1979), 30:325–26; Elizabeth Greenhalgh, *Victory through Coalition: Britain and France during the First World War* (Cambridge: Cambridge University Press, 2005), 104.

5. Arthur, S. Link, *The Higher Realism of Woodrow Wilson* (Nashville: Vanderbilt University Press, 1971), 309; John J. Broesamle, *William Gibbs McAdoo: A Passion for Change* (New York: Kennikat Press, 1973), 172.

6. Gavin Wright, *Old South, New South: Revolutions in the Southern Economy since the Civil War* (New York: Basic Books, 1986), 56.

7. Link, *The Higher Realism of Woodrow Wilson,* 310; Robert Hoyt Block, *Southern Opinion of Woodrow Wilson's Foreign Policies, 1913—1917* (Ph.D. diss., Duke University, 1968), 115.

8. Link, *The Higher Realism of Woodrow Wilson,* 309–10.

9. J. L. Crawford to Bankhead, August 8, 1914, Bankhead Papers, Cotton Crisis, LPR 49 Container 29 Folder 5, Alabama Department of Archives and History.

10. S. P. McDonald, Chairman of the Talladega County Democratic Executive Committee, to Bankhead, August 12, 1914, Bankhead Papers, Cotton Crisis, LPR 49, Box 29 Folder 5, Alabama Department of Archives and History.

11. M. F. Parker to Bankhead, August 27, 1914, Bankhead Papers, Cotton Crisis, LPR 49, Box 29, Folder 5, Alabama Department of Archives and History.

12. Benjamin Tillman to B. F. Mauldin, August 8, 1914, Tillman Papers, Outgoing, Box 24, Folders 9–14, Clemson University Libraries Special Collections.

13. William G. McAdoo, *Crowded Years: The Reminiscences of William G. McAdoo* (New York: Houghton Mifflin Company, 1931), 299–300; John J. Broesamle, *William Gibbs McAdoo: A Passion for Change* (New York: Kennikat Press, 1973), 174; Joseph A. Fry, *Dixie Looks Abroad: The South and US Foreign Relations, 1789-1973* (Baton Rouge: Louisiana State University Press, 2002), 151; Link, *The Higher Realism of Woodrow Wilson,* 317; Bruce E. Matthews, "The 1914 Cotton Crisis in Alabama," *Alabama Review* 46, no. 1 (January 1993): 3–4.

14. McAdoo, *Crowded Years,* 299.

15. Ibid., 300.

16. Ibid., 299.

17. L. J. McConnell to Bankhead, August 22, 1914, Bankhead Papers, Cotton Crisis, LPR 49, Box 29, Folder 5, Alabama Department of Archives and History.

18. Petition from merchant and businessmen in Prattville, August 22, 1914, Bankhead Papers, Cotton Crisis, LPR 49, Box 29, Folder 5, Alabama Department of Archives and History.

19. H. L. McElderry, president of the Talladega National Bank, to Underwood, September 4, 1914, Oscar Underwood Papers, LPR 29, Box 35, Folder 4, Alabama Department of Archives and History.

20. P. C. Steagall, cashier of the Dale County Bank in Ozark, Ala., to Bankhead, Bankhead Papers, LPR 49, Box 29, Folder 5, Alabama Department of Archives and History.

21. Clarence Poe, "Cotton Legislation Must Be Framed for the Producer," sent to Bankhead on August 13, 1914, Bankhead Papers, LPR 49, Box 29, Folder 5, Alabama Department of Archives and History.

22. Petition from merchant and businessmen in Prattville, August 22, 1914, Bankhead Papers, LPR 49, Box 29, Folder 5, Alabama Department of Archives and History.

23. W. J. Renfroe to Bankhead, September 7, 1914, Bankhead Papers, LPR 49, Box 29, Folder 5, Alabama Department of Archives and History.

24. Edward L. Ayers, *The Promise of the New South: Life after Reconstruction* (New York: Oxford University Press, 1992), 413.

25. Dewey W. Grantham, *The South in Modern America: A Region at Odds* (Fayetteville: University of Arkansas Press, 2001), 65–67; David Kennedy, *Over Here: The First World War and American Society* (Oxford: Oxford University Press, 2004), 241.

26. L. J. McConnell to Bankhead, August 22, 1914, Bankhead Papers, LPR 49, Box 29, Folder 5, Alabama Department of Archives and History.

27. S. McDonald, representative of the Talladega County Democratic Executive Committee, to Underwood, September 19, 1914 (resolution enclosed September 18), Oscar Underwood Papers, LPR 29, Box 35, Folder 5, Alabama Department of Archives and History.

28. T. V. Ballard to Bankhead, August 25, 1914, Bankhead Papers, LPR 49, Box 29, Folder 5, Alabama Department of Archives and History.

29. Jackson M. Young to Bankhead, August 27, 1914, Bankhead Papers, LPR 49, Box 29, Folder 5, Alabama Department of Archives and History.

30. Jackson M. Young to Bankhead, August 27, 1914, and Jackson M. Young to Bankhead, September 17, 1914, Bankhead Papers, LPR 49, Box 29, Folder 5, Alabama Department of Archives and History.

31. Officers of the E. E. Union in Alpine, Alabama, to Bankhead, September 25, 1914, Bankhead Papers, LPR 49, Box 29, Folder 5, Alabama Department of Archives and History; Memorandum presented to President Wilson by Robert Lee Henry, October 2, 1914, in Link, *Papers of Woodrow Wilson*, 31:119–20.

32. W. F. Miller of Georgiana, Alabama, to Bankhead, September 26, 1914, Bankhead Papers, LPR 49, Box 29, Folder 5, Alabama Department of Archives and History.

33. L. J. McConnell to Bankhead, October 4, 1914, Bankhead Papers, LPR 49, Box 29, Folder 5, Alabama Department of Archives and History.

34. Ibid.

35. J. C. Gober of Arab, Alabama, to Bankhead, October 26, 1914, Bankhead Papers, LPR 49, Box 29, Folder 7, Alabama Department of Archives and History.

36. G. T. McElderry, Chairman of the Talladega Chamber of Commerce, to Bankhead, December 3, 1914, Bankhead Papers, LPR 49, Box 29, Folder 7, Alabama Department of Archives and History.

37. Wayne Flynt, *Alabama in the Twentieth Century* (Tuscaloosa: University of Alabama Press, 2006), 53–54; V. O. Key Jr., *Southern Politics in State and Nation* (New York: Random House, 1949), 17–18.

38. Matthews, "The 1914 Cotton Crisis in Alabama," 8–9.

39. Ibid., 11.

40. Bankhead to Ballard, September 1, 1914, Bankhead Papers, LPR 49, Box 29, Folder 5, Alabama Department of Archives and History.

41. Matthews, "The 1914 Cotton Crisis in Alabama," 5.

42. Bankhead to O. P. Ford, August 21, 1914, Bankhead Papers, LPR 49, Box 29, Folder 5, Alabama Department of Archives and History.

43. Bankhead to Ballard, September 1, 1914, Bankhead Papers, LPR 49, Box 29, Folder 5, Alabama Department of Archives and History.

44. Ibid.

45. Bankhead to Mr. Smith, n.d., Bankhead Papers, LPR 49, Box 29, Folder 5, Alabama Department of Archives and History.

46. Ibid.; in September 1914, seeing limited federal relief, Alabamians started participating in and promoting a strategy to get private investors to purchase cotton through the Buy-A-Bale (of cotton) program. This plan was intended to help farmers sell some cotton at 10 cents a pound so that they could meet their immediate debts. The program was mildly successful because people in urban areas such as Birmingham, Montgomery, and Mobile purchased large numbers of bales. However, the Buy-A-Bale movement was short-lived and did not provide enough assistance to make a real difference. Matthews, "The 1914 Cotton Crisis in Alabama," 13–15.

47. Bankhead statement to the people of Alabama (intended for publication in state newspapers), October 3, 1914, Bankhead Papers, LPR 49, Box 29, Folder 6, Alabama Department of Archives and History.

48. Ibid.

49. Matthews, "The 1914 Cotton Crisis in Alabama," 18–21.

50. "President Opposes the Valorizing of Cotton," *New York Times,* October 8, 1914, 15.

51. Link, *The Higher Realism of Woodrow Wilson,* 318–19.

52. Ibid., 310.

53. Acting Secretary Robert Lansing to Bankhead, October 21, 1914, Bankhead Papers, LPR 49, Box 29, Folder 7, Alabama Department of Archives and History; President of the Galveston Cotton Exchange and Board of Trade I. H. Kemper to Lansing, October 20, 1914, in *FRUS: 1914 The War Supplement,* 285–86; President of the New York Chamber of Commerce Seth Low to William Jennings Bryan, October 24, 1914, in *FRUS: 1914 The War Supplement,* 287.

54. Lansing to Page, October 24, 1914, in *FRUS: 1914: The War Supplement,* 288–89.

55. Grey of Fallodon, KG, *Twenty-Five Years 1892–1916,* Volume 2 (New York: Frederick A. Stokes, 1925), 109, 114–15; Spring-Rice to Lansing, October 26, 1914, in *FRUS:1914: The War Supplement,* 290.

56. Remarks at a Press Conference, October 26, 1914, in Link, *The Papers of Woodrow Wilson,* 31:233–35.

57. Lansing to Gerard, October 28, 1914, in *FRUS: 1914: The War Supplement,* 290; Lansing to Gerard, November 8, 1914, in ibid., 291.

58. Gerard to Lansing, November 11, 1914, in *FRUS: 1914: The War Supplement,* 291; Lansing to Jusserand, December 1, 1914, in ibid., 292–93.

59. Letter to Lord Moulton from numerous signers, March 11, 1915, Bonar Law Papers, Parliamentary Archives, London, UK.

60. Grey to Spring-Rice, December 22, 1914, FO 115/1771, National Archives, Kew, UK.

61. Grey to Cabinet (No Date), David Lloyd George Papers, D/25/8/3.

62. Quoted in Dewey W. Grantham Jr., *Hoke Smith and the Politics of the New South* (Baton Rouge: Louisiana State University Press, 1967), 285.

63. Spring-Rice to Grey, July 6, 1915, in David Stevenson, ed. *British Documents on Foreign Affairs: Reports and Papers from the Foreign Office Confidential Print. Part 2, From the First to the Second World War. Series H. The First World War, 1914–1918*, Volume 5, *Blockade and Economic Warfare, 1: August 1914–July 1915* (Frederick, MD: University Publications of America, 1989), 333–35; Spring-Rice to Grey, July 7, 1915, in ibid., 334.

64. R. Mayer to Bankhead (?), June 28, 1915, Bankhead Papers, LPR 49, Box 29, Folder 7, Alabama Department of Archives and History.

65. Ibid. Nations, particularly the Netherlands, purchased large quantities of American goods with the intention of selling them to the Germans, just across their border; in fact, the Netherlands was one of Germany's only real lifelines to the outside world. Knowing that Germany relied on trade with its neutral neighbors, the Royal Navy monitored the quantity of goods that were sold to these states. Once it was clear that they purchased much more than the nation could consume, Britain sought to prevent the importation of excess cargo. Spring-Rice to Grey, November 3, 1914, FO 800/84.

66. M. M. and D. L. Rosenau, of Athens, Alabama, to Bankhead, July 21, 1915, Bankhead Papers, LPR 49, Box 29, Folder 7, Alabama Department of Archives and History.

67. J. J. Willett of Anniston, Alabama, to Bankhead, July 3, 1915; Willett to Bankhead (letter to Woodrow Wilson enclosed, July 8, 1915), July 8, 1915; and Bankhead to Willett, July 12, 1915, Bankhead Papers, LPR 49, Box 29, Folder 7, Alabama Department of Archives and History.

68. J. J. Willett to Bankhead, July 19, 1915, Bankhead Papers, LPR 49, Box 29, Folder 7, Alabama Department of Archives and History.

69. Representatives of the Farmers Educational and Co-Operative Union of America in Pike County to Wilson, July 5, 1915, Bankhead Papers, LPR 49, Box 29, Folder 7, Alabama Department of Archives and History.

70. G. S. Barksdale to Bankhead, July 20, 1915; Bankhead to Barksdale, July 30, 1915; and Bankhead to R. L. Bradley, July 29, 1915, Bankhead Papers, LPR 49, Box 29, Folder 7, Alabama Department of Archives and History.

71. Wilson to Edith Boling Galt, August 13, 1915, in Link, *Papers of Woodrow Wilson*, 34:180.

72. Wilson to House, July 19, 1915, in Link, *Papers of Woodrow Wilson* 33:526.

73. Lansing to Wilson, July 28, 1915, in Link, *Papers of Woodrow Wilson*, 34:34–35.

74. Ambassador Page to Lansing, July 15, 1915, U.S. Government, *Papers Relating to the Foreign Relations of the United States, 1915, Supplement to the World War* (hereafter, *FRUS, 1915 Supplement*) (Washington, DC: Government Printing Office, 1928), 192–93.

75. Spring-Rice to Grey, July 15, 1915, FO 800/ 85; Link, *The Higher Realism of Woodrow Wilson*, 327.

76. Spring-Rice to Grey, July 21, 1915, FO 800 / 85.

77. Grey to Asquith Cabinet (n.d.), David Lloyd George Papers, D/25/8/3; Page to Lansing, July 22, 1915, in *FRUS, 1915 Supplement*, 193.

78. Spring-Rice to Grey, July 31, 1915, FO 382/464.

79. House to Wilson, August 14, 1915, in Link, *Papers of Woodrow Wilson*, 34:200.

80. Spring-Rice to Grey, August 3, 1915, FO 382/464; Spring-Rice to Grey, August 9, 1915, ibid.; Robert Skinner to Lansing, July 28, 1915 (Received August 9), *FRUS, 1915 Supplement,* 502–3.

81. *Birmingham Age-Herald,* August 24, 1915, August 28, 1915, and August 27, 1915; *New Orleans Times-Picayune,* August 23, 1915, as cited in Sue Jones Pearson, "The South and the European War, 1919–1917" (M.A. Thesis, Samford University, Birmingham, 1967), 44–45.

82. John Sharp Williams to Wilson, June 29, 1915, in Link, *Papers of Woodrow Wilson,* 33:457–58.

2

Manhood, Duty, and Service

Conscription in North Carolina during the First World War

JAMES HALL

The First World War affected North Carolinians in many ways, particularly the men who eventually served their country in uniform. These individuals, in addition to their families and the communities from which they came, experienced the war primarily through the efforts of the state and the nation to induce them to serve. Many of them, civilians all, saw as their first duty the need to stay with their families. Their communities generally agreed with them and worked to exempt many of them from service. North Carolina had the highest percentage of dependency deferments in the nation. But the men who did not get deferments largely came forward when called, becoming a distinct second group, and thousands of them eventually served in uniform. Those who served often found compelling reasons to do so, joining a larger community of their fellow soldiers fighting for the nation. Communities supported both the soldiers and the "stayers," thereby maintaining both the war effort and their own local home front at the same time. The ability to steer this seemingly divided course was possible only by appealing to principles the members of these communities held in common. These ideals embodied a set of character traits expected of men: honor, duty, service, virtue. Such values guided these communities and individuals as they navigated the demands placed on individuals during the crisis of war.

Inhabiting a landscape of obligation and principle not far removed from that described by Bertram Wyatt-Brown in his classic work *Southern Honor: Ethics and Behavior in the Old South,* these men lived within a system of shared values and core beliefs in which an individual's character was greatly influenced by the expectations of the community.[1] Furthermore, in this environment, one's

manhood was intertwined with his sense of honor and shame, and in negotiating the draft and service in the war, each of these men felt a unique pull on
his individual sense of right and wrong based on his perceived duty to those
around him. When tested, the men looked to fulfill their roles within the larger
group, first to their families and the social order in their individual hamlets and
hometowns, and later to the army and to the nation that asked them to serve.
Appeals to their duty and honor, to their manhood—concepts central to their
core values—confronted those who stayed and those who served with difficult
choices. As sons, as husbands and fathers, and eventually as soldiers, these men
navigated the draft while attempting to keep their principles and their place in
the community intact, even as that community evolved around them. Whereas
those receiving deferments stayed home, largely with the sanction of the community, the drafted men went to war, also with the support of their neighbors.
Governed by the shared sense of principles and community each man held,
serving in a way they believed worthy of their individual notions of manhood,
these men could inhabit these distinctly different stations with their individual
concepts of duty and honor intact.

Historians are increasingly interested in exploring the United States and the
Great War, given the ongoing centennial of the American war effort, but many
of the essential works exploring the war and the home front examine the South
only as a part of the author's larger focus. When these broader studies discuss
conscription, even when critiquing the inequalities and prejudice of the draft
overall, they conclude reasonably that the goal of the draft was to raise a fighting force, something the draft did accomplish. As David Kennedy writes, "the
administration's approach to the distasteful business of military impressment
was largely successful."[2]

More recent scholarship on the Great War has studied the experience of
individuals and the war effort. These include exceptional studies on the war
and the experience of individual soldiers, from training camp to the battlefield
and back again. The works include an examination of the effects of the war on
southern men, as well as the change in relationship with a government that
asked them to serve, what Christopher Capozzola labels "the wartime state."[3]
But these studies too, engage the South—and conscription—only as part of their
larger emphasis.[4] The exception to this historiography is Jeanette Keith's *Rich
Man's War, Poor Man's Fight*. Keith's study describes the level of resistance to the
draft in the South, and the struggles of the state to compel loyalty and service

from southerners. North Carolina was, in fact, the site of armed resistance, as well as of instances of desertion and delinquency. However, many North Carolinians responded to the call to arms and served in the military, and many others received deferments based on the demands of family and community life. This chapter examines more closely how those citizens of North Carolina experienced the draft, from the draftees themselves to the board members who decided their cases, and how their experience, considered broadly, evolved over the duration of the war.[5]

Germany's return to unrestricted submarine warfare in February of 1917 was the beginning of the end for US neutrality. Stating that "neutrality is no longer feasible or desirable," Wilson asked Congress for a Declaration of War on April 2 and Congress quickly approved the measure.[6] But many people opposed Wilson's call for war including North Carolinian Claude Kitchin, speaker of the House of Representatives. Kitchin made an impassioned speech before the House in which he argued against US entry into the conflict. Among other arguments, he posited that the country was not threatened by Germany, and that "nothing in that cause, nothing in that quarrel, has or does involve a moral or equitable or material interest in, or obligation of, our Government or our people."[7] The remainder of the North Carolina congressional delegation voted to support the war, and Wilson and his advisers began considering how the country would go about managing its participation in the conflict.

There was initially some question as to whether the United States would actually send more than a token force to Europe. There were those in Congress and the administration that believed the United States might not actually have to send soldiers to fight in Europe. In the early months of 1917, visiting British and French delegations called for more economic aid than for military support; in March 1917, for instance, the French ambassador in Washington described the aid needed from the United States as "mainly on the sea and with credits and supplies." The only American soldiers needed were "a detachment for sentimental reasons." Yet the ever-changing political and military landscape eventually convinced the Wilson administration to send a substantial American army.[8] Wilson initially favored a volunteer force, as did the majority in the House of Representatives, but recruiting numbers fell woefully short. According to Frederick Palmer, the army signed up 4,355 men in the first ten days after the declaration of war, and only 32,000 men by April 24. The totals were "poorer than . . . in the Spanish War or the Civil War." Clearly, volunteerism would not be enough.[9]

Congress passed the Selective Service Act on May 18, 1917. Kitchin voted against it, hoping still to field a volunteer army, but vowing to support Wilson if Congress passed the measure.[10] Wilson stated that conscription was the "most equitable way to raise a force," a feeling echoed by others in the higher levels of the administration, most especially Newton Baker and Josephus Daniels, the secretaries of war and the navy respectively. Wilson had avoided premature talk of a draft, but there was a plan for such an eventuality, and while there was some support for an amendment to continue the volunteer system before turning to conscription, Wilson visited Congress and scotched the idea. Secretary of War Baker knew of the army's support for conscription, and he had a bill ready when the president made his request.[11] The bill called for an increase in the size of the regular Army and the National Guard to around 900,000 men, obtained through the enlistment of volunteers. In addition, the act directed the army to raise a force through a selective draft, the new "National Army," with 500,000 men authorized immediately (a number later revised upward to 687,000).[12]

With the passing of the Selective Service Act, the Wilson administration had the legal means for raising the army, and the plan formulated in Washington was initiated. The draft as instituted was primarily the work of Judge Advocate General Enoch H. Crowder, soon to be appointed provost marshal general (PMG), the officer responsible for overseeing the draft from his headquarters in Washington, DC. Historian John Whiteclay Chambers later wrote that Crowder, "more than any other individual . . . created the modern American Selective Service System."[13] The plan was to register all the men within the given age group, select the men to be drafted, and ship them to camps for training.

The first step was to register the estimated 10 million or so men in the nation that fell within the ages of twenty-one to thirty.[14] Election precincts were used to register the men at some eight hundred sites across North Carolina, after which registration boards were set up either by county or for units of population of thirty thousand or above where needed.[15] The broad outlines were relayed from Crowder's office in Washington; he served as the national executive for Selective Service and assigned quotas, forwarded directives, and sometimes interpreted the finer points of the draft legislation to pertinent officials. The details, however, were largely left to the states, represented by the state governor on one side and the local boards on the other. This effort to draft an army, to harness the state's scattered communities, required at its head someone with a special mix of administrative energy and rhetorical charm, a post suited for North Carolina's recently elected governor, Thomas Bickett.[16]

Bickett, elected into office in 1916, was a skilled orator and speechwriter who took to the task of supporting the war, and conscription itself, with enthusiasm. Bickett's statements are studies in how to use the language of duty and honor to call men to serve their country. In a proclamation shortly after the passage of Selective Service, he harkened back to the past, writing, "I appeal with confidence to the patriotic manhood of the State; and I expect a response worthy of the sons of the fathers who laid down their lives in order that we might be free."[17] His appeal to the state before the first registration, entitled "The Day and Its Duties," describes a "day whereon a mighty nation is to register its consecration to selfless service in the cause of universal justice and abiding peace. The day is destined to loom large in history, and will be forever linked with a world wide acceptance of the rights of men first declared at Philadelphia and made secure at Yorktown." He continued, noting that men who registered would record their names as "champion[s] of justice to all men and of peace for all time."[18] Such language, underlining the connection between service to one's country and the responsibilities inherent in young male citizens, informed a community definition of duty and embodied a concept of honorable action. Bickett remained an ardent supporter of the war effort, supporting war bond and liberty loan drives, always filling his addresses with the notions of duty and sacrifice.

The first countrywide registration for the draft, scheduled for June 5, 1917, saw the introduction of the first widespread piece of public media designed to ensure that all eligible men did, in fact, register. In this appeal lay one of the key tenets of manhood, the concept of duty. The office of sheriff in each county issued posters to inform the populace of the coming registration. The posters were designed locally and differed from county to county, but were typically plain, most measuring 11×17 inches and printed with black script on white stock. They reminded readers of the upcoming registration, describing who had to register, when, and the penalty for failing to do so. Some posters named the members of the local registration board. But, while the placards issued in each county varied, the overwhelming majority did not emphasize a patriotic need to spread democracy, nor did they encourage bravery and sacrifice. Rather, the thrust at this early stage was on the need for conforming to the letter of the law. The notice from Stanly County is representative of the tone of most: "Registration is a public duty. For those not responsive to the sense of this duty, the penalty of imprisonment, not fine, is provided in the draft act."[19] Every man of draft age was to register on the given date at a given place.

The fact that these early notices focused primarily on the legal aspects of conscription, and not on the cause for which these men might eventually have to fight, is hardly surprising. After all, none of them, neither the officials tasked with implementing the draft nor those men who were within the range of eligibility had experienced anything like this before. Reminders of the penalty for not registering, rather than seconding the much loftier notions for which the president requested the country to go to war, would certainly have a better chance at achieving the desired result of a successful registration. Registering was the first of many steps. In order to field an army, men first had to be assembled, and the newly appointed draft officials were focused primarily on that task at this point. Convincing the draftees that they were fighting for the right cause could wait until later.[20]

In practice, registration was a voluntary procedure. That is, the law said that these men had to register with their local boards, but the government had no easy way to force them to do so. The failure to register was punishable by imprisonment, but as long as the boards were able to fill quotas with men doing their duty, the need to track down those who failed to register was low on the priority list. The success of the registration process hinged upon whether these scattered communities and the people within them obeyed the directives issued from Washington and announced by the responsible state and local authorities. In his proclamation before the sign-up, Woodrow Wilson described June 5 as "nothing less than the day upon which the manhood of the country shall step forward in one solid rank in defense of the ideals to which this nation is consecrated."[21] Governor Bickett sounded a similar note when he labeled registration day as "the day whereon a mighty nation is to register its consecration to selfless service in the cause of universal justice and abiding peace."[22] The local board for Anson County echoed the sentiments of Wilson and Bickett with a statement before the registration: "Let us see to it there shall not be one single dodger, shirker, or slacker in Anson County, June 5 1917."[23] Still, no one knew for sure what the response would be.

When the results were tabulated from this first draft, the boards in North Carolina, like those across the nation, reported that their local registrations were largely without incident. This initial step, as Jeanette Keith writes, "went marvelously well in the rural South as it did throughout the nation."[24] The board from Beaufort County later recorded that "with a very few exceptions, men registered willingly and gladly at the first registration." Another wrote that the "registration passed off quietly . . . lines quickly formed at all registration points."[25] The newspapers, posters, and declarations had done their jobs, and the easy part was complete.

Drafting an army from the first registrants was a massive effort. The men had to be examined, classified, and either sent to camp or deferred from service. The local men who made up the boards were, of course, key to this, but they often needed temporary help during the rush of registration and classification. The draft boards were paid for the duration of their service, but citizens were asked to donate their time to assist the boards, to "patriotically [offer] their services free of charge."[26] The boards were charged with examining each registrant and deciding as to whether the man was fit to serve or had grounds for deferment. Serving on the board, or on the supporting clerical staff, could take a great deal of time. After the war, the board chairmen reported that time spent dealing with board work had been considerable. One chairman replied that he devoted "every day during week about six hours while board meetings were held." He added that "frequent Sunday trips . . . were necessary."[27] The other respondents gave similar replies. Members of the boards, the support staffs, and all the auxiliaries felt compelled to do this to support the overall effort, but choosing which of the registrants to send to camp was a difficult task, made especially so by the families of the would-be soldiers. Widespread support for registration did not necessarily mean support for military service.

Possible induction into the army was not embraced by everyone. Many of the men felt a responsibility to stay with their families instead of going off to fight, and the exemption boards and the locales they served often made every effort to exempt them from service. The largest group exempted was husbands requesting to stay and care for wives and children. In North Carolina married men made up over half of the total number of registrants, and of these over 90% were deferred from the draft for dependency.[28] Most draft boards did everything they could to defer married men if they thought them deserving. Some were even able to exempt all married men under their jurisdiction. The board of Franklin County, for example, noted proudly that "in no instance did the . . . Local Board send a married man with dependent wife [and] children to camp—even when pressed between Washington and the District Board."[29]

Questionnaires completed for the PMG by local boards after the first draft stated essentially the same thing: husbands who supported wives, and especially wives and children, should be deferred from service whenever possible. Most boards could not exempt *every* husband, but almost all answered "yes" to the query "Did your Board discharge virtually all married men?" The written explanations were universally the same: husbands needed at home should be taken last, if at all. Able to fill their given quotas, the boards used the power given them to keep husbands at home, at least during the earliest stages of the draft.[30]

Some boards saw these deferments as essential to continued community support for the war effort. One board replied that they were holding married men from induction "for harmonious adjustment to the prevailing uniformity of actions by other boards," rather than "send out a greatly dissatisfied soldiery, as well as a disturbed community from whence they came."[31] That the boards wanted to fill the ranks with single men should not be surprising. The boards were, after all, reflections of the overall populace, and an upset citizenry held no benefit for them whatsoever. They heard from draftees, family members, volunteer helpers, and each other, and their duty as they saw it was to supply men for the army while also keeping the community as tranquil and as stable as possible in the midst of the war. Where able to supply single men, the boards did so. Later, they chose men without children, and then those with children last. And while in hindsight we know there were to be further calls for draftees, they did not know this at the time. For all they knew, the boards had fulfilled their requirements for numbers, and might not be asked to supply more.[32] The boards made it their primary goal to register the men needed while not upsetting the community, and they worked to accomplish that.

When the actual induction of men into the army began, the inductees arrived for entrainment to camp dutifully but largely without undue fervor. The question regarding mobilization on the PMG's 1917 questionnaire simply asks for "recommendations . . . as to method of mobilization of men into cantonments" and how to treat individuals "who report tardily."[33] The question regarding late replies netted many responses, all telling essentially the same story, that where tardy men existed they were few in number: "Have had no willful tardiness" answered one response, and "very few violations" reported another.[34] From inside the local draft boards, the appeals to duty and patriotism seem to have worked. Most of the respondents told a similar story, that while some of the men called to serve were less than enthused, they performed their duty. The statistics of

48

the first call-up supports these responses. Some 63,599 men were called before the boards in the state, and of that number, 3,122 failed to show up when summoned, making them delinquents. Of the men called to camp, North Carolina had less than 5% fail to appear, solidly near the bottom in the country.[35]

Some, as noted, did fail to appear before the board when requested, but almost invariably the local boards gave the same reason for this: ignorance. The 1917 questionnaire asks boards to respond to the question "How can the Government best reach registrants who fail to appear for physical examination?" Most responses provided specific advice related to recommendations for reaching absentees, but those that mentioned numbers almost uniformly stressed the fact that the amounts were negligible, resulting from lack of communication. "We have not yet found a man who was willfully absent," writes one chairman, stressing that "they have invariably come immediately upon receipt of notice, and their absence is caused by ignorance."[36] The postwar questionnaires echo these sentiments. The chairman for Halifax County describes an atmosphere in which men had migrated in search of war work and could not be reached by examination notices. He reported that "we believe that this can be accounted for on grounds of ignorance, rather than pre-meditated evasion."[37] Officially, these men were delinquent, but to reporting officials most failed to show up because they did not know to come in, not because of willful resistance. While this may seem a convenient explanation, nearly every draft jurisdiction had similar situations, and many were resolved when these missing individuals eventually reported.

Accepting late registrants for service was the simplest form of resolving the issue of delinquents. As noted earlier, the boards really had no effective local enforcement arm to go after these men, and with quotas filled, there was often no urgency to reach them. The official policy of the War Department, as forwarded by Governor Bickett, was to "report the name to the nearest United States attorney or Marshal, and the delinquent will be arrested at once." However, the same notice stated that men "whose failure to register is due to inattention or to lack of information or of understanding shall be released as soon as they have registered."[38] Local boards were quite lenient, and men reporting with a viable excuse were almost always accepted as a matter of course. By the end of the draft late registrants were noted on reports just as any other category.[39] This surely was the easier course for all concerned.

Men who had been accepted and sent to camp sometimes decided to desert from the army, and North Carolinians were no exception. While the aforementioned records cite a small number of deserters in the state, the reports from the draft boards themselves ask readers to imagine that there were almost no deserters at all. The 1917 questionnaires speak little to the issue of deserters, but the postwar reports address this question directly. The third section of the query contains questions about deserters, resistance, attempted evasion, and enforcement of the draft laws. The reporting counties replied universally that there was no open resistance, and where deserters were mentioned, the number was either "few" or "a few." Of the seventeen respondents to the postwar questionnaires, ten answered "no" for open resistance, one answered "none," and two answered "never," while the other respondents left this question unanswered. Regarding deserters, the answers range from "no deserters" to "only five deserters" on the nine questionnaires that gave a reply.[40] Moreover, according to the respondents, deserters were often simply ignorant. One chairman labels the deserters in his county as "ignorant men whose prejudices had been played upon and inflamed by people even more ignorant than themselves."[41]

Clearly, the communities themselves had an interest in labeling deserters as somehow unaware of their obligation, and ignorance may have been the most convenient label. Each of the draft boards, whether they represented counties or cities, had a stake in how members acquitted themselves in responding to the draft calls. While pride was surely part of it, each community had also had other interests with regard to their handling of the draft. Leaders were tasked with assigning men where they were needed, and just as some were left to stay, others were asked to serve. Not answering the call, in this case deserting from the ranks of the army, was shirking more than one's duty as a soldier, it was rejecting the shared principles of the community from which one came, principles enunciated in the speeches of state and federal officials and enumerated in calls to serve.

This shared interest in full participation made community members the primary tools for convincing delinquents and deserters to change their minds and report in. The statewide effort was eventually directed from the North Carolina Council of Defense, which applauded the efforts of the local boards with regard to "fine results . . . reported in the counties as to deserters and delinquents."[42] The chairman of the Council, D. H. Hill, highlighted the local aspect of the effort to bring in both delinquents and deserters, asking that parents of these men be informed by the board chairman, or better yet by "pastors and family physicians . . . assuring them of the friendly interest of their fellow citizens . . .

to urge them before it is too late, to save their sons from disgrace and punishment."[43] The argument was the same as those of the respondents in the board questionnaires, that appeals from within the community, from people they knew, would have the greatest effect. If they clearly knew what they were fighting for, these men would do their duty and either return to the ranks or appear for examination, whichever was the case. If everyone made the effort, writes Chairman Hill, "Such activity . . . will soon free our State of all these men, and will save many a good father and mother from the shame of having a son sent to the penitentiary."[44] The honor of the individual was inextricably wedded to the honor of his family.

North Carolina was the scene of two separate instances of large groups of deserters. In both cases, these deserters eventually responded to personal appeals made to them and they were allowed to report to the exemption board or return to the ranks.[45] The first of these took place in Mitchell County in the spring of 1918. There, thirteen deserters and nine delinquents returned to the army after an appeal by the local draft board chairman and the assistance of an agent from the Department of Justice. When one of the deserters surrendered himself voluntarily, the county board chairman, John McBee, communicated through this deserter to the rest of the group that he would attempt to get them "lenient treatment in view of their voluntary surrender." McBee described the events leading to the return as a community effort, and he stated that "Sheriff Burleson and many citizens of the county aided greatly in inducing both deserters and delinquents to come in."[46] This plea, according to the chairman, eliminated all such men in the county "except one" and "several outside of county and State."[47] The option of lenient treatment had the desired effect, and they returned to the colors.[48]

The second example of a larger group of deserters occurred in June 1918 in Ashe County. Governor Bickett made a personal appeal directly to the deserters' sense of honor and duty, eventually persuading them to surrender and rejoin the army. When efforts to bring the men in by force were met with gunfire, the governor traveled to the county seat in Jefferson and spoke to a large assembly that included friends and relatives of the deserters. In a speech lasting over two hours, the governor wove a history lesson that cited the Revolution, the Civil War, the Spanish-American War, and the genius of Woodrow Wilson and the Selective Service Act. He painted America as a reluctant belligerent that fought because it had no choice. "Peace is entirely too dear when it comes at the price of honor," stated the governor. According to Bickett, and in keeping with the overt narrative regarding men forsaking their duty, men desert because "they have not been told the truth about this war. . . . Ignorance and misinformation are at the bottom of all this trouble and all this shame."[49]

The governor, too, thought that North Carolina men, when they understood the reasons behind and importance of the conflict, would show up when called, and the numbers compiled by the PMG support this view. On the eve of the last registration, North Carolina had registered 228,844 men, and deserters in the state averaged 2.67%, the lowest percentage in the South. The PMG's *Final Report*, after accounting for men enlisted elsewhere and those wrongly labeled as deserters, concludes that deserters accounted for only 1.20% of the total number registered in North Carolina. The only southern state with a lower percentage was Texas, with 1.11%.[50] Such records imply that the governor was successful, and as the PMG later reported concerning deserters in Ashe County, "[In] less than two weeks practically every deserter known to be in Ashe County surrendered and returned to camp."[51]

As the United States became an active participant in the war, the message of shared sacrifice and duty in the eyes of the local community began to evolve into one based also on the duty of the individual within a national group. The local tenor was not gone, as evidenced by the events in Mitchell and Ashe counties, but the men needed less convincing that the war was worth their service. American soldiers, including some from North Carolina, were now fighting and dying in the conflict. The early quota of 687,000 soldiers was long passed, and by August of 1918 there were over 1 million US soldiers in France.[52] The German offensives of the spring of 1918 underlined the need for "the largest possible American contingent" in France, and the PMG planned for an additional 2 million men.[53] By the advent of the third major draft call of September 1918, much of the "official" rhetoric was centered on the concept of a larger group, most notably the American army. Some of the best examples of these are the instructions to the public speakers known as "Four Minute Men." Products of the Committee on Public Information, also known as the Creel Committee after director George Creel, the "Four Minute Men" were men and women sent across the country to appear at public events, theaters, fairs, and other community events. They were volunteers, typically chosen from the community in which they would be speaking in order to reassert the connection between local and national duty.[54] Issued in the summer of 1918, the talking point suggestions reflect the increasing awareness that American men would recognize that duty. "Americans will hear the call and meet the test like men," states one. Another notes, "[The recruit] offers everything. No man can do more."[55] Another passage suggests using the phrase, "Trust American manhood to come forward and identify itself."[56]

These instructions were not unique to North Carolina, but state bodies adopted the language in their own communiqués to local chapters. As the PMG urged in a letter to the Four Minute Men, the nation was "relying upon the conscience and manhood of the American people . . . to inspire every man with the resolution . . . to come forward and do his duty."[57] The core belief was the same, that duty and honor compelled the men to serve, but the community had grown larger. Whereas before the men felt their duty was to the local community, now that duty was amplified by the pull from the nation and the army, from the men who had gone before them and were already serving. While this sort of appeal did not exist early in the draft when the army was not yet engaged in active combat, it was in full evidence by this stage in the war.

Again, postwar questionnaires suggest that these latest appeals worked. In an atmosphere colored by the emotional pull of a nation fully at war, the draft boards and the draftees found their way more readily. The system having been established, registration was straightforward, war news more easily reached the men in rural areas, and the response was no longer the solemn appearance before the board of the early draft calls. Local reports describe an upbeat population and a more willing soldiery. Nearly every respondent answered in the same manner, that local opinion of military service "grew more popular as the war progressed."[58] Perhaps the most telling is the response from Halifax County: "A decided change took place during the spring of 1918. . . . Applications made frequently to the board to advance date of call without reaching order number." In other words, individuals whose lottery number had not yet been called sought to volunteer before their call-up. The response continued, noting that "the percent of [exemption] claims filed was very small and it became necessary for the board to defer men who presented no claim."[59]

In the wake of the fighting, the country assessed the draftees' service in the war and the state did the same. The prose describing this service relied upon two main themes: community and patriotism. The tenor of these postwar accounts remains essentially the same throughout. Nearly all describe the ability and willingness of North Carolinians to respond in the war. All herald examples of the state's great effort and sacrifice in meeting and often exceeding the requests of the country. Granted, some may be embellished, and others silent in regard to the failures they experienced, such as deserters and delinquents, but when examined in conjunction with the official record, they largely stand up to scrutiny.

The Local Board Questionnaires provide some of the best examples of these accounts of the fitness and ability of the state's men and communities in terms of their responses to the draft. One respondent asserted that "men have heard the call and responded with unaanimity [sic] never before approached."[60] Another described "a sincere desire to serve the community, the state and the nation, in any way possible."[61] In general, all portray a populace that was more than willing to respond to the nation's call, the direct effect of the draft in this case, something made possible only by the war and the request from the government. One person stated that the uniting of the community "would have been impossible under any other conditions; it has taught the community that it owed a debt to the Government which seemed hard for the people to understand at the start."[62]

Local communities, as well as soldiers, responded to the notion of patriotism as the war progressed. Their own accounting portrayed a sense of increased patriotism through the shared obligations of the draft. Some of the statements were rather mundane: "I think it made the people more patriotic" and "The people were able to meet the demands of the law in the name of patriotism."[63] There were also the descriptions of people who had a "spirit of patriotic zeal" and who were "greatly enlightened and stimulated in all matters relating to patriotism." Finally, the respondents averred that the draft "increased the patriotism of the community 100% and has made all of the people look upon the flag as the symbol of Americanism."[64]

The dual allegiance that animated soldiers, the idea of Americanism, that one is a resident both of the United States and of one's state, also echoes through the accounts of wartime service and through the institution and operation of the draft. Nearly all of the respondents to the draft questionnaires adopted President Wilson's line that the draft was the only fair way to man an army. The chairman of the Local Board for Randolph County wrote that the effect of the draft on the people in his county was "to make better—more American." In Robeson County, the chairman wrote that "selective service was the only right way to select an Army" and that the county's residents were "American to the core." And finally, the questionnaire from Halifax County used language more succinctly than any of the others, and is worth quoting at length: "[The] effect of operation of selective service system in connection with the world war has give[n] this generation in America a larger vision of personal relation to Government. . . . The opportunity came and America was found fit."[65] These opinions, recounted in the summer and autumn of 1920, a full year after the peace conference at Versailles, are evidence to the lingering effect that the war had on these men, and also to the extent to which the war shaped their respective communities.

The demands of conscription eventually touched all North Carolina men between the ages of eighteen and forty-five. Most did not serve in uniform and even fewer saw combat. But, whether they served or obtained a deferment to stay home, these men and their communities followed the principles of duty and sacrifice as set forth for them by a society that placed a premium on one's deeds, and they held true to their principles, even as the nature of World War I and the demands that the conflict placed on participants at home and abroad changed. That sense of duty, of honor, based on the responsibility they felt to their family, their community, and eventually, their country, shaped the way that young men responded to the draft. That same conception of duty shaped the way that community leaders oversaw the requirements of conscription, how they chose to distribute deferments, and how they appealed to those who, willingly or otherwise, failed to respond to the call for service. Thus, questions of the duty that men owed to their community shaped North Carolina's response to the war effort and ensured that, with the end of the conflict, those soldiers would return as dutiful members of a community that recognized their wartime sacrifices.

NOTES

This essay is dedicated to Barry Mitchell Hall (1939–2017).

1. Bertram Wyatt-Brown, *Southern Honor: Ethics and Behavior in the Old South,* 25th Anniv. Ed. (Oxford: Oxford University Press, 2007).

2. David Kennedy, *Over Here: The First World War and American Society* (New York: Oxford University Press, 1980), 154.

3. See Christopher Capozzola, *Uncle Sam Wants You: World War I and the Making of the Modern American Citizen* (New York: Oxford University Press, 2008).

4. For studies examining expansion and overreach of the state during the war, see the previously mentioned work by Capozzola. For an examination into the soldiers who fought the war, and the expectations of soldiers and veterans and their relationship with the government and expectations

in return for their service, see Jennifer Keene, *Doughboys, the Great War, and the Remaking of America* (Baltimore: Johns Hopkins University Press, 2001). On the soldiers' experiences and expectations see Edward Gutierrez, *Doughboys on the Great War: How American Soldiers Viewed Their Military Experience* (Lawrence: Kansas University Press, 2014). On the draft and the change in military/civil relations because of the war, see Joshua Kastenberg, *To Raise and Discipline an Army: Major General Enoch Crowder, the Judge Advocate General's Office, and the Realignment of Civil and Military Relations in World War I* (Dekalb: Northern Illinois University Press, 2017).

5. Jeannette Keith, *Rich Man's War, Poor Man's Fight: Race, Class, and Power in the Rural South during the First World War* (Chapel Hill: University of North Carolina Press, 2004).

6. Unrestricted submarine warfare convinced the administration that war was inevitable, but the Zimmermann Telegram, the message from the German foreign secretary ordering the German ambassador in Mexico City to incite Mexico to "make war" on the United States, was the key to convincing the nation that Germany was a threat to the United States. Wilson's message to Congress in *Congressional Record,* 65th Congress, 1st session, April 2, 1917, 102–4.

7. Quoted in Alex Arnett, *Claude Kitchin and the Wilson War Policies* (Boston: Little, Brown, 1937), 234. Arnett includes the text of the full speech: See ibid., 227–35. The key source for the national debate over the draft is John Whiteclay Chambers's *To Raise an Army: The Draft Comes to Modern America* (New York: Free Press, 1987). Numbers vary slightly depending on the source, but the US Army of the time numbered some 180,000 men when the National Guard units were included.

8. Frederick Palmer's *Newton D. Baker: America at War* (New York: Dodd & Mead, 1931), 1:108–9, 120; Arnett, *Claude Kitchin,* 191; Josephus Daniels, *The Wilson Era: Years of War and After* (Chapel Hill: University of North Carolina Press, 1946), 25, 52. As late as May the discussion in Washington still centered on a small number of soldiers. See Chambers, 144–48.

9. Palmer, *Newton D. Baker,* 1:145. The army continued to accept volunteers until December of 1917, after which time all manpower needs were met by conscription. By war's end drafted men made up over 2.8 million, or about 67% of the total of 4,185,220.

10. Congressman Edwin Yates Webb was the only other representative from North Carolina to oppose the measure.

11. Palmer, *Newton D. Baker* 1:184–85; Chambers, *To Raise an Army,* 180; and Arnett, *Claude Kitchin,* 247–48. For Daniels' support of the draft, see Daniels, *The Wilson Era,* 160–61.

12. John Dickinson, *The Building of an Army: A Detailed Account of Legislation, Administration and Opinion in the United States, 1915–1920* (New York: Century Co., 1922), 57–58.

13. Chambers, *To Raise an Army,* 180.

14. Population estimates were derived both from the Census Bureau and from statistics provided by private insurance companies. See example of table in US Provost Marshal General, *Second Report to the Secretary of War on the Operations of the Selective Service System* (Washington, DC, 1919), 181. (Hereafter cited PMG *Second Report.*)

15. North Carolina formed 109 boards in its 100 counties.

16. For a brief summary on the general makeup of the local boards see Chambers, *To Raise an Army,* 181–82. Also see PMG *First Report,* 6–9. Most of the registration details were in place before

the act became law, so much so that the PMG stated in his report that the registration could have taken place as early as May 25, 1917. The PMG estimated that nationwide the boards themselves comprised 12,000 members with a supporting staff of around 125,000. The first registration of men aged 21–31 (inclusive) saw 9,586,508 (later amended to 9,925,751) registered across the nation and territories, with 208,430 in North Carolina. PMG *Second Report,* 396. Bickett was elected in 1916 with roughly same margin as Wilson: 58%.

17. "A Proclamation by the Governor." May 21, 1917. Sarah Lemmon, *North Carolina's Role in the First World War* (Raleigh, 1975), 19.

18. "The Day and Its Duties: An Appeal by the Governor," May 26, 1917, Military Collection, WWI- # 3, Box 5, Folder 14, North Carolina State Archives (hereafter NCSA).

19. Registration Day Posters, Military Collection, WWI # 3, Box 5, Folder 20, NCSA.

20. Registration Day Posters, Military Collection, WWI # 3, Box 5 Folders 20—23, NCSA.

21. E. David Cronon, ed., *The Political Thought of Woodrow Wilson* (New York: The Bobbs Merrill Co., 1965). Quotation is from statement penned on May 18, 1917, regarding upcoming first registration for draft.

22. "The Day and its Duties: An Appeal By The Governor," WWI # 3, Box 5, Folder 14, NCSA.

23. Craighead-Dunlap Chapter, Daughters of the American Revolution, *Anson County in the World War, 1917–1919: A Compilation of the Various Activities and Services Performed during This Period of Stress* (Raleigh, 1929), 326.

24. Keith, *Rich Man's War, Poor Man's War,* 59.

25. Local Board Questionnaire, Beaufort County, Military Collection WWI #3, Box 1, Folder 10, NCSA; and Craighead-Dunlap Chapter, DAR. *Anson County in the World War,* 326. North Carolina eventually counted 208,430 registrants in this first attempt. PMG *Second Report,* 396. The number given in the PMG *First Report* was 197,481; the difference accounts for late registrants, tabulating errors, and the like. PMG *First Report,* 78.

26. Circular # 2, April 28, 1917, Adjutant General's Office, WWI #3, Box 5, Folder 13, NCSA. The chief secretary of the Winston-Salem local board estimated that to register 10,000 men in a single day he would need a clerical support staff of 266 to assist in the process. Local Board Questionnaire, Forsyth County, 2, Military Collection WWI #3, Box 2, NCSA.

27. Local Board Questionnaire, Halifax County, Military Collection WWI #3, Box 3, Folder 9, NCSA. Other replies from questionnaires align with this.

28. While the majority were in fact deferred because they had a wife and children, potential draftees could be deferred by the local board because any relative depended upon them for financial support. PMG *Second Report,* appendix, 401.

29. Local Board Questionnaire, Franklin County, Military Collection WWI #3, Box 3, Folder 2, NCSA.

30. Ibid. The state quota was set by the PMG, and the number was apportioned throughout the local boards by the governor, assigning local quotas based upon numbers already in the service, exempt occupations, etc., so that the burden was theoretically spread evenly throughout the state.

31. Chatham County Local Board Experience file, 5, States File, Records of the Selective Service System, 1917–1919, Box 35, Record Group 163, National Archives, Washington, DC (hereafter RG 163).

32. As previously noted, the first call was for 687,000 men, and the first registration was sufficient to reach that number. In general, each local board had to call for examination twice the number needed to supply their quotas, reducing the pool through deferments for dependency, physical defects, etc. PMG *First Report,* 38.

33. Question from Section XI, "Mobilization," Local Board Experience file, RG 163. Copies of these questionnaires are found throughout the States File, RG 163.

34. Polk County Questionnaire and Stanly County Questionnaire, Local Board Experience File, Box 35, RG 163.

35. PMG *First Report,* appendix table 4, p. 81. In draft parlance there were three categories of resistance: slackers, or men who failed to register; delinquents, or men who registered but failed to show up when called before the board for examination or failed to show up for induction; and deserters, or men who were enlisted and abandoned their units. For this first registration, the percentage of no-shows (delinquents) for North Carolina (4.91%) was behind only Iowa (3.67%), Missouri (4.80%), Rhode Island (4.47%), and Nebraska (4.79%).

36. Local Board Experience File, Columbus County, Box 35, RG 163. This theme, of men not showing up due to ignorance, is found throughout the official reports of the draft.

37. Local Board Questionnaire, Halifax County, Military Collection WWI #3, Box 3, Folder 9, NCSA.

38. Letter from Governor Bickett to county sheriffs, June 1, 1917, Military Collection WWI #3, Box 5, Folder 13, NCSA.

39. Local Exemption Board Report, City of Winston-Salem, Military Collection, WWI #3, Box 2, NCSA.

40. The Local Board Questionnaires are found throughout the Military Collection WWI #3, NCSA.

41. Quotation is from Local Board Questionnaire, Beaufort County, Military Collection WWI #3, Box 1, Folder 10, NCSA.

42. Councils of Defense were established in each state to help coordinate assistance to the state governments during the war. Letter from North Carolina Council of Defense, July 30, 1918, Military Collection WWI #3, Box 6, Folder 17, NCSA.

43. Letter from North Carolina Council of Defense, July 16, 1918, Military Collection WWI #3, Box 6, Folder 17, NCSA.

44. Letter from North Carolina Council of Defense, July 30, 1918, Military Collection WWI #3, Box 6, Folder 17, NCSA.

45. Just as the local boards enjoyed a great deal of leeway in dealing with delinquents and slackers, army officers in charge of the training camps also had a great deal of discretion in how they handled deserters. Draftees from North Carolina were assigned to one of two camps, and in each one of these instances the governor contacted the commanders of the individual training camps and asked that the men be allowed to rejoin their units.

46. U.S. Provost Marshal General, *Final Report on the Operations of the Selective Service System to July 15, 1919* (Washington: GPO, 1920), 288. (Hereafter, PMG *Final Report.*)

47. Ibid., 287–88.

48. Ibid., 287–89. McBee's report on the incident mentions that each of these men was returned to camp at their own expense and rejoined their old units, whether those units were still in camp or had already shipped out. The specific appeal used to encourage the deserters to return was unrecorded.

49. *Public Letters and Papers of Thomas Walter Bickett: Governor of North Carolina 1917–1921,* (Raleigh, 1923), 172–81. Quotations are from pp. 174–75. The North Carolina Council of Defense also sent a letter to each county, dated July 16, 1918, to the effect that each deserter who now gave himself up voluntarily would "be included in the number of those whom the Governor has asked to treat as leniently as possible." Copy of the letter in Military Collection WWI #3, Box 3, Folder 17, NCSA.

50. PMG *Second Report,* 460; PMG *Final Report,* 52, table 18.

51. PMG *Final Report,* appendix C, 288.

52. Quota from first call in PMG *First Report,* 38. Monthly table of soldiers in United States, France, and elsewhere in Dickinson, *Building of an Army,* 116.

53. PMG *Second Report,* 23–24.

54. The most recent publication on the Creel Committee is Alan Axelrod's *Selling the Great War: The Making of American Propaganda* (New York: Palgrave Macmillan, 2009). Also see Creel's own work, *How We Advertised America* (New York: Harper & Brothers, 1920). The CPI memoranda and instructions sent to the state are the sources I have especially drawn from for this section. See Four Minute Men instructions, Military Collection WWI #3, Box 3, Folder 17, NCSA. The September 1918 call was the last of the war, taking younger and older men than the previous drafts. There are references throughout the instructions from the PMG about precedence for such a move, and much is included in the Four Minute Men instructions for use in rebuttals of citizens questioning the "right" of the government to make such a request. Registration on September 12, 1918, would be for ages eighteen–forty-five, inclusive, and numbered over 13 million men throughout the nation.

55. The instructions warn to "cut out 'Doing you bit.' 'Business as usual.' 'Your country needs you.' They are flat and no longer have any force or meaning." Four Minute Men instructions, Military Collection WWI #3, Box 3, Folder 17, NCSA.

56. Ibid.

57. Letter from PMG, "To All Four Minute Men" August 16, 1918, Military Collection WWI #3, Box 3, Folder 17, NCSA.

58. Local Board Questionnaire, Robeson County, Military Collection WWI #3, Box 4, Folder 14, NCSA.

59. Local Board Questionnaire, Halifax County, Military Collection WWI #3, Box 3, Folder 9, NCSA.

60. Local Board Questionnaire, Halifax County, Military Collection WWI #3, Box 3, Folder 9, NCSA.

61. Local Board Questionnaire, Beaufort County, Military Collection WWI #3, Box 1, Folder 10, NCSA.

62. Local Board Questionnaire, Guilford County, Military Collection WWI #3, Box 3, Folder 8, NCSA.

63. Local Board Questionnaire, Stokes County, Military Collection WWI #3, Box 4, Folder 20, NCSA; and Local Board Questionnaire, Chowan County, Military Collection WWI #3, Box 1, Folder 21, NCSA.

64. Local Board Questionnaire, Robeson County, Military Collection WWI #3, Box 4, Folder 14, NCSA.

65. Local Board Questionnaire, Halifax County, Military Collection WWI #3, Box 3, Folder 9, NCSA.

3

World War I and South Carolina's Council of Defense

Its Campaign to Root out Disloyalty, 1917–1918

FRITZ HAMER

n spring 1918, Chalmers Wessinger, superintendent of Lancaster grade schools in South Carolina, faced charges of disloyal conduct to the state and nation. According to sworn statements by local citizens, Wessinger defended Germany's right to carry out U-boat attacks on American vessels. Furthermore, he had discouraged his brother from joining the US military in the midst of the nation's great crisis. Although he was a native of Lexington County, a graduate from South Carolina College, and well regarded by his peers, he was still singled out by the powerful chair of the South Carolina Council of Defense as a German sympathizer who must be removed.[1]

Wessinger represented one of thousands of Americans during World War I who suffered accusations of disloyalty or pro-German feelings, sentiments antithetical to those who considered anything but patriotic support for the war treasonable. Even if the evidence brought against many Americans seemed more hearsay than reality, the hysteria that enveloped the nation during the United States' second full year in the war more often than not caused the accused disgrace, if not prosecution and even imprisonment.[2]

Wessinger's prosecution and conviction exemplifies the extent to which authorities across the country sought to enforce patriotism and loyalty during World War I. This approach stemmed, ultimately, from President Woodrow Wilson, who feared that if too many Americans opposed his war policies, such opposition would erode his plans to rebuild the nation's armed forces and impede his appeal to support the nation's war effort. In Wilson's April 6, 1917, address calling for a declaration of war, he warned that Germany "has filled our unsuspecting communities . . . with spies and set criminal intrigues everywhere."[3]

By 1918 many states had gone after disloyal elements based on federal laws or by passing their own statutes. Montana passed the most restrictive measure in February, which purported to protect the Constitution, servicemen, the flag and the United States "against disloyal, profane scurrilous . . . or abusive language . . . calculated to bring [them] . . . into contempt . . . or disrespect."[4] Congress followed suit several months later with its own more restrictive sedition law, which was nearly as draconian as that of Montana's. With the president's support such laws encouraged not just state and law enforcement to weed out those whom they considered disloyal; academic communities also fired or forced out some of their dissenting faculty, with the backing of the American Association of University Professors, which set guidelines on what academics could say. When professors dissented with national administration polices in the war, or even hinted at it, they were sanctioned and often fired.[5]

South Carolina fell in line with national policy and, while it did not pass its own restrictive statutes like Montana, the federal Espionage Act of 1917 was more than sufficient for state law makers and Governor Richard Manning's campaign against disloyalty. The Palmetto State's wartime governor led the charge to bring his state in line with White House goals for war preparation and participation. Assisted by David Coker, the chairman of the South Carolina Council of Defense (SCCD), Manning encouraged his constituents to consider themselves an integral part of the war effort. He and Coker used publicity to encourage patriotism, to promote the administration's efforts, and to increase participation in bond drives, conservation programs, and wartime programs. In doing so, Coker fully embraced Wilson's efforts to prepare the United States for the conflict and to reshape society in ways that would ensure success at home and abroad.

Yet in his efforts, Manning experienced strong resistance from a number of individuals, many of whom boasted a history of political opposition to him and his domestic agenda. Manning's most prominent opponent, Coleman Blease, former governor and political firebrand, had twice lost bids for reelection to Manning in 1914 and again in 1916. In spring 1917, Blease's political opposition to Manning took on specific critiques of Manning's prosecution of the war effort. Blease was joined by two newspaper editors, one from the *Scimitar* in upstate South Carolina and another from the coastal *Charleston American*. Faced with a strident and persistent counter-argument, Manning and his administration knew they had to be mindful of this opposition as they enacted policies supportive of Wilson's wartime mandates. In fact, as the war progressed, Manning,

Coker, and the state's leadership acted aggressively to ensure that citizens supported the war effort at home and abroad without question. Consequently, state officials repressed democratic principles such as freedom of the press and the right to public dissent and considered many private citizens, including the Lancaster superintendent and supposed German sympathizer Chalmers Wessinger, to be dangerous threats to their agendas.[6]

Thus, in South Carolina, Governor Manning and the SCCD promoted patriotism and built support for President Wilson through aggressive education programs and the suppression of what they perceived as dissent. In confronting such challenges, Manning conflated national and political loyalty, fearing that any opposition to his program for statewide defense might derail his efforts to align South Carolina with the demands of the American war effort. His opponents, too, combined opposition to the governor and his colleagues with opposition to the Wilson administration's prosecution of the war. As such, the debate over national defense in South Carolina provides a valuable window into the effects that campaigns for patriotism and national loyalty had on southern states negotiating their relationships with the federal government.

Since the outbreak of war in Europe in 1914, Wilson had worked to keep his country out of the conflict. However, rising tension with Germany steadily pulled the United States into the maelstrom. Beginning with the sinking of the British passenger ship *Lusitania* and deaths of 128 Americans on May 7, 1915, a growing chorus of Americans demanded that President Wilson take action against the Central Powers. Tensions rose higher over the next few months with the sinking of additional merchant ships and rumors of German sabotage plots within the United States. German-Americans attempted to defend Germany's actions, but their efforts exacerbated anti-German sentiment rising across the country. On October 11, 1915, President Wilson gave a speech to the Daughters of the American Revolution asserting that "true Americans must haze irresponsible persons who sought to use American influence for other than American aims." The president followed up his statement in mid-December during his State of the Union speech. Talking about German- and Irish-Americans, Wilson argued that many of them had "poured the poison of disloyalty into the very arteries of our national life." He then asked Congress to pass laws that would make such disloyalty illegal.[7]

Despite his criticisms of Germany and German-Americans, Wilson continued efforts to keep the United States out of the war. Nevertheless, his efforts were scuttled in early 1917. Following Germany's decision to renew the use of submarines against neutral merchant shipping and revelations that Berlin's foreign minister, Arthur Zimmermann, had secretly offered Mexico US territory in the Southwest in return for declaring war on America, many Americans demanded an aggressive response. Consequently, the president called for a declaration of war to defend American honor and "make the world safe for democracy."[8]

Although a significant majority in Congress supported Wilson's call to declare war on Germany and its allies, the administration still faced vocal opposition.[9] Republican senator George Norris of Nebraska declared that "we are about to put the dollar sign upon the American flag" while "committing a sin against humanity and against our countrymen."[10] Just a month after Congress voted for war, Wilson's own Democratic Party questioned its president and Secretary of War Newton Baker when the administration proposed a conscription law. House speaker Chancy Clark observed that "there is precious little difference between a conscript and a convict." Some congressmen feared that if a draft law were implemented there might be riots like those during the Civil War with "American cities running red with blood."[11]

While these latter predictions did not transpire, once Congress passed a conscription law, plenty of early opposition to the war and the draft emerged. Even in South Carolina, a state that prided itself as a patriotic supporter of the president's call for war, certain influential leaders spoke out against America's participation. Fred Dominick, the lone South Carolina congressman to vote against war, argued that plunging the nation into the European war had no bearing on his constituency.[12] And like certain national leaders opposed to the war, particularly Wisconsin Republican senator Robert LaFollette, Dominick challenged Wilson's call to arms because, in his opinion, the war would be fought for the "benefit of big capital."[13]

Most of Dominick's fellow South Carolinians, however, applauded Wilson's declaration of war. Even before the United States entered the conflict Governor Manning advocated the immediate introduction of military training in the state's colleges and universities. During his second inaugural address in January 1917 he noted that his native Sumter County's high school had already successfully instituted a military course. Within weeks he announced that National Guard officers in the state would no longer be permitted to resign their commissions.[14]

Manning's support for Wilson's wartime preparedness aligned with the governor's larger support for the president's political platform.[15] Manning backed Wilson's presidential campaigns in 1912 and 1916, and he supported efforts to implement Wilsonian progressive legislation in South Carolina, including such measures as new child labor laws, improved education, a comprehensive state road system, and the secret ballot. For this effort to improve state government and the conditions of its children he was applauded by most state newspapers.[16] With war coming Manning also sought the economic benefits that war mobilization could bring to his impoverished state. With his encouragement, local boosters in Greenville, Spartanburg, and Columbia successfully lobbied the army to locate training camps in their communities. In the Lowcountry, Charleston expanded its Navy Yard, which had not brought the economic bonanza that city leaders anticipated when it opened in 1901. South of Charleston, the emerging Marine Recruit Depot on Parris Island began a massive expansion that also benefited the local economy.[17]

These military and naval installations started taking shape in the summer of 1917, but they were only the beginning of South Carolina's patriotic zeal for the war. In late spring Wilson called for the creation of state-level councils of defense, to mirror the National Council of Defense. As in the national council, the state councils' main duties were to galvanize support for the war effort. The councils sought to ensure that the public backed military conscription, purchased war bonds, grew victory gardens, and conserved food, especially wheat, sugar, and fats. All of this was buttressed by a propaganda campaign through print media and public speakers, nicknamed "four-minute men." The South Carolina Council of Defense had its first meeting in early June with twenty-four appointed members who were handpicked by Manning and his new chairman, David R. Coker.[18]

Every state in the Union formed state councils for defense. North Carolina's council evolved along the same lines as its cousin to the south. Its members were appointed by the governor, often political friends and advisers that he trusted. Consequently several members of the North Carolina council were appointed who were or had been part of state government, including the secretary of state, the state geologist, and a former member of Congress. But while President Wilson encouraged membership from outside each state's current administration, as in South Carolina, North Carolina's leaders excluded their political opponents. Thus Wilson's hopes to include all sides of the political spectrum in state councils around the nation had a partisan appearance. As Secretary of War Newton Baker admitted to the president at the end of 1917, in dealing with political people in democratic states, "it is impossible to prevent partisanship on one side, or suspicion of it on the other."[19]

South Carolina's Council of Defense chairman, David Coker, was an agricultural reformer who by 1914 had started his own pedigree seeds company. He also served as a member of the Federal Reserve Board in Richmond, Virginia. The Hartsville native backed Manning in his two successful bids for the governorship, supporting his progressive agenda enthusiastically.[20] When selected by Manning to head his South Carolina Council of Defense in May, Coker and the governor aimed to fill the state council with representatives from across the state who shared their progressive ideals, ranging from comprehensive child labor laws to providing credit to cash-strapped farmers as well as supporting Wilson's national war aims. Manning and Coker determined that their state should become one of the nation's most patriotic councils. They also hoped to overcome war opposition within South Carolina by excluding individuals who disagreed with their goals. In reality such a task proved exceedingly difficult. First of all, they found it difficult to find representatives to the council from all forty-six counties that adhered to their political and national war aims. By selecting only political supporters Manning and his SCCD chairman encouraged public opposition to their plans and hindered efforts for state unity.[21]

Like Wilson, Manning viewed his progressive policies as imperative for improving the lives of South Carolina's citizens. But many of his constituents disagreed, particularly his greatest political enemies, a faction led by Coleman Blease. The former governor argued that Manning was wrong on policy and too closely associated with the corrupt elite liberals who pushed progressive reforms. To Blease such reforms only supported the middle class, which wanted to control the working man and his right to earn a living. During Blease's two terms as governor (1911–1915), the fiery politician had garnered support from the growing textile working class and other constituents who opposed progressive policies. Using his magnetic personality at stump speeches, Blease attacked the progressive agenda and its middle-class proponents. He denounced legislation such as child labor laws and maximum working hours as interfering with the rights of hardworking textile families. Politicians such as Manning who championed such legislation were often accused of being aristocrats who wanted to control and regulate the working class.[22]

Blease's attacks against progressives focused not only on policy but also on personalities. He accused Manning of being an aristocrat of the worst sort, associating him with an effete and -corrupt class who wanted to restrict the vote of workers to protect Manning and his supporters from subversion. Blease even declared that Manning was the state's worst governor in history, ranking him below the "corrupt" governors of Reconstruction. He asserted that while the leaders in Reconstruction stole people's money "at least they didn't try to steal their souls."[23]

Governor Blease attracted a large millworkers following upstate by championing their independence and integrity. With the rapid industrialization of South Carolina since the 1880s, mill workers, many from farming backgrounds, had lost control of their lives to an impersonal set of economic forces. Controlled by textile owners and their managers, these workers were disillusioned with such leaders. On stump speeches across the state, Blease declared his support of self-rule for textile workers. Consequently many workers viewed him as their champion against the elites.

Thus, when former governor Blease attacked Manning's compulsory education bill as interfering with parental rights, textile communities lauded him. When Manning called out the state militia to quell a strike in the upstate mills in the autumn of 1916, Blease called the governor a traitor who came to the aid of "Yankee mill owners to break the strike," endearing him further to textile workers.[24] While attacking Governor Manning and his progressive allies, Blease garnered powerful enemies in the political arena and among many newspaper editors, especially those of Columbia's *State* and Charleston's *News and Courier*. To many journalists in these and other newspapers Blease represented "an incoherent protest rather than a definite program" for the state.[25]

Even though Blease's two terms as governor showed little legislative reform or other accomplishment, his oratorical skills and his close association with mill communities provided him a major following amongst the textile workers and farmers long after his defeat in 1914.

Adding to Manning's concerns about Blease's opposition to the war was the former governor's support among a small but vocal group within the state that was led by two newspaper editors. Political allies before the war, these associates, often referred to as "Bleasites," were opponents of America's declaration of war in April 1917; many of them were of German descent and believed that America had nothing to gain from a war with Germany and her allies.[26]

On the coast, former Charleston mayor and newspaper editor John P. Grace regularly attacked the Manning administration in his newspaper, the *Charleston American*. In 1916 he accused Manning of attacking Charleston because it condoned (and profited from) alcohol sales and consumption. While the "loose morals" of Charleston were often at odds with the more Puritanical mores in other parts of the state, Grace also attacked Manning and his allies for supporting the Wilson administration during the growing rift with Germany. Most of Grace's opposition grew out of his Irish-American lineage and his distaste for all things connected to the British government. A strong advocate of Irish independence, Grace claimed that American munitions interests were pulling Wilson into the British camp to protect their growing investment in the Allied cause. The munitions industry, Grace claimed, feared that if America did not aid Britain, American investors would go bankrupt in the event of a German triumph.[27] As the drums of war grew louder during the winter and early spring of 1917, Grace castigated those Americans who demanded war with Germany. He wanted the nation to remain neutral and cut off economic ties to Britain. The Charleston newspaper editor saw no quarrel that should force the United States into war.[28]

As indicated previously, opposition from newspaper men also came from upstate. William P. Beard, editor of the Abbeville *Scimitar*, in northwest South Carolina, had formerly served in the Blease administration as a bodyguard. In 1914 he turned to journalism, using his political weekly to defend Blease's record and attack Richard Manning's administration.[29] He ridiculed Manning as "Savior Dick" and predicted his first term as governor would be a failure.[30] He accused the governor of corruption and suggested that he was doing all in his power to remove Blease supporters from office. He even singled out President Wilson, describing him as a man who could guide one through "the mystic maze of a church fair but a darn poor pardner [*sic*] at an Irish wake."[31] During Blease's attempt to regain his office for a third term in 1916, Beard predicted his former boss's re-election. In doing so he attacked the Manning faction for using any means at their disposal to defeat the former governor. The *Scimitar* claimed Manning's lieutenants tried to remove the third candidate, Robert Cooper, because he was the only one who could defeat Blease. But in spite of Beard's predictions, Manning bested Blease in a run-off election.[32]

Until 1917, Beard focused most of his attacks on the sitting governor, but he also defended Germany in the war with Britain and France. In late 1914, Beard described England as a "sordid mercenary" seeking to take away Germany's economic and political gains.[33] The following year he predicted that if the United States entered the war against Germany nothing but disaster would result.[34]

Beard's attacks against the sitting governor and the president gained few adherents, but to Manning and his advisers, the *Scimitar* editor posed a real threat. Fearing that such public opposition to their leadership and the nation's war policy might somehow undermine the state's war commitments, they decided to suppress Beard. They made the decision despite the fact that such opposition was relatively rare in South Carolina; most state newspapers defended Manning and generally supported his agenda. Exemplified by the Columbia newspaper *State,* Manning's policies drew widespread praise during his first administration. Likewise, as Manning followed the president's lead to prepare South Carolina for war, the *State's* editors wholeheartedly supported his war measures.[35]

As tensions increased between the United States and Germany in the winter of 1917, the German threat became real when the crew of an impounded German freighter deliberately scuttled their ship near the middle of Charleston harbor. The vessel, *Liebenfels,* and its crew sat in the port for two years before the captain, supposedly acting on the orders of German high command, carried out an act of sabotage. Late on the evening of January 31, just as Germany re-instituted unrestricted submarine warfare, the ship's crew steamed their ship into the harbor's shipping channel and sank it, trying to obstruct commerce into the southern port.[36] Although this act was poorly conceived and unsuccessful in its purpose, the crew was arrested for impeding commerce and eventually convicted of violating US neutrality. In spite of what most newspapers and South Carolina leaders viewed as an act of war, the *Scimitar* defended the German crew's actions. In Beard's view the crew was justified since Germany feared that Britain wanted to confiscate all German vessels impounded in American ports. As with his criticisms of Manning, Beard's claims gained little support.[37]

Grace's *Charleston American* appeared to have a sinister connection to the German crew's failed act of sabotage. Soon after the *Liebenfels* sank to the bottom of Charleston harbor authorities discovered that the state editor of Grace's paper, Paul Wierse, had sent a telegram to the German consulate in Atlanta congratulating them for the German crew's actions. Although Grace was not implicated, he never renounced the action and defended the German crew and Wierse against charges of sabotage and treason. Considering that the United States was not yet at war with Germany, federal authorities faced legal problems that hindered their efforts to bring such charges against the accused; however, there was a statute against scuttling a vessel in American harbors. Thus, in spite of Grace's determined defense of the German crew and his tacit support of his newspaper editor's comments, the crew was convicted along with the editor. The Germans and the editor had to pay fines and served jail terms in an Atlanta penitentiary.[38]

Although the aggressive actions of the German crew alarmed many South Carolinians, Blease seemed unconcerned. He continued to question the idea that Germany posed a threat to the nation, remaining adamant even after Congress declared war in April 1917. In July Blease addressed several hundred supporters in Newberry, many of whom were farmers and mill workers with German ancestry. He declared that Manning and his supporters viewed him as an outcast because he did not support Wilson's policies. Blease argued that his position was one of peace and stated that he would "much prefer [to] be a water boy in heaven, listening to . . . the angels, than to be the commander in chief of all the forces of hell." He then turned to religion, accusing some, both in and outside the church, of using power and money to "throttle" Christianity, and by implication, those who opposed the war. Yet Blease seemed to contradict himself when he advised the crowd that with the nation at war they must all accept their duties as Americans and do their part. He then claimed that he had offered to form a regiment for the state and lead it to Europe, but Manning had rejected it. Blease concluded his remarks by asking his audience, "If you had been a member of Congress [would you] have voted for this war?" When he asked them to raise their right hands if they agreed none went up. When asked if they would have voted against the war, the reporter wrote, "Every hand went up."[39]

Manning and SCCD chairman Coker considered Blease and his newspaper allies to be disloyal and they publicly refuted the former governor. In early August 1917 before a large audience in Columbia, Coker attacked Blease for questioning America's war aims, calling the antiwar politician's remarks treasonous. He demanded that all Americans must adopt "Loyalty to the government to the point of personal sacrifice" and he promised that such loyalty would "be preached in every hamlet . . . of the state." Blease's Newberry remarks did not go "unchecked" nor did anyone else dare to make similar treasonous comments.[40]

Such strong language in defense of South Carolina's support for the war mirrored the federal government's approach. In New York the public opposition to the war had been led by the anarchist leaders Emma Goldman and Alexander

Berkman. Centering their opposition on the plans for national conscription, both anarchists managed to attract a crowd of ten thousand to their May anti-draft rally in New York City. Even though Congress passed the draft bill soon after the rally Goldman and Berkman were arrested "for conspriacy against the draft." In spite of their defense by several prominent radicals, the anarchists were sentenced to two years in prison and fined $10,000. Many others opposed to the draft faced prosecution as well, including pacifist and social reformer Jane Addams and the socialist editor of the *Milwaukee Leader*, Oscar Ameringer, who was indicted and tried for violations of the Espionage Act. These examples are just a few of thousands of cases brought by the federal government against those opposing the war. In some sense Emma Goldman's words indicate the hysteria gripping the nation when she claimed that the new Espionage Law "turned the country into a lunatic asylum, with every State and Federal offical, as well as [many] civilians, running amuck," accusing so many Americans of disloyalty.[41]

The national hysteria across the nation during the summer and fall of 1917 appeared to influence South Carolina and its leaders. And even as Manning and Coker must have believed that Blease and his supporters posed a real threat, there were other political leaders from South Carolina who added to the South Carolina governor's apprehension about his state's full support for war. Before the Conscription Act was passed in May, Jimmy Byrnes, a rising South Carolina congressman, had publicly opposed the act, declaring in the halls of Congress that wealthy people would be able to obtain exemptions from military service while the poor "will have their sons conscripted." It is not surprising that when one of the Palmetto State's own congressional delegation made such a public pronouncement that state officials would have cause for concern.[42] Furthermore, once the draft law was implemented in early summer of 1917 it must have come to Manning and Coker's attention that the law was not universally obeyed, especially in the rural South. Although it is unknown how many South Carolinians refused to obey their call-up for military service, the fact that 28% of the nation's deserters were southerners suggested that some citizens of the Palmetto State were part of this number.[43]

While it is doubtful that former governor Coleman Blease had significant popular support, others besides Manning and Coker were concerned about the state's patriotism. Joe Sparks, secretary to the SCCD, remarked to Coker in early August that they needed to get the best speakers in the state into places such as Newberry County to convince people of the "righteousness of this war." And wherever the Newberry native Blease spoke in the future, Sparks suggested, they must carry out a "vigorous campaign of education" to offset Blease's "teaching."[44]

Others were certain that education alone would not be enough to counter Blease and his appeal. On August 10, R. J. Jaynes, chairman of the Oconee County Council of Defense, wrote to the Department of Justice accusing Blease of being one of the "most pernicious persons" in the state whom the federal government should deal with to the "fullest extent of the law." If his influence was not curbed, Jaynes predicted, those who were ignorant and illiterate could not be blamed for failing to be patriotic citizens in the crisis facing the nation.[45]

Despite such appeals to the Wilson administration Manning and his allies failed to persuade Washington to indict the fiery former governor for treason. However, while Blease escaped federal sanctions Beard did not. On April 15, just a week after Congress declared war, the *Scimitar* editor asserted that the nation would have to wallow in the blood of Americans sent to fight in the trenches in Europe. Furthermore, the United States would be burdened with "mountains of debt" to pay for the war. Beard believed that Americans did not want war and would support an effort "to keep us out of it even now." When the national draft law passed in May and the first group of conscripts began their military training, Beard insisted that there was a movement developing against the draft. He claimed that a Pickens County meeting had passed a resolution to send to Congress that would seek the law's repeal.[46]

Beard also attacked President Wilson. After calling Wilson the "Great Fizzle," Beard finally doomed his own journalistic future. The Abbeville editor had remained immune from federal authorities through the summer of 1917, but his editorial attack on Wilson incurred the wrath of US assistant attorney general Tom Thurmond. Using provisions of the Espionage Act passed by Congress in early June, Thurmond charged Beard with publishing false reports while the United States was at war and interfering with recruiting for the armed forces.[47] The Abbeville editor defended his right to free speech, but his argument was dismissed and Thurmond proceeded to bring the case to trial. The government's case was assisted by testimony from South Carolina senator Ellison D. Smith and Congressman James F. Byrnes. Easily convinced of Beard's guilt, the jury deliberated just over an hour before reaching its verdict.[48] With his paper already shut down weeks before the October trial, Beard's appeal of the conviction failed and he spent more than a year in an Atlanta federal penitentiary.[49]

As Beard faced the brunt of federal prosecutors, John Grace found himself under a similar spotlight. Through editorial pieces in the *Charleston American* during the spring and summer of 1917, Grace tried to soft-peddle some of his wrath against Wilson and his war policy. Clearly opposed to the new draft law, the Charleston editor told his readers that it was still their duty to submit since it was the law of the land. But Grace remained openly skeptical of American policy. He admitted that German militarism existed, but at the same time he averred that French and Belgian militarism was equally troubling and a threat to the world. Moreover, with the implementation of an American conscription law, "American boys must become soldiers as in Europe," fostering American militarism as well.[50] By the middle of the summer Grace argued that America had lost its democratic ideals, becoming only a mockery of a truly *democratic* nation. He suggested that in instituting conscription and suppressing opposing voices, the United States was acting in ways nearly impossible to defend.[51]

Manning and Coker sought legal action against Grace and the *Charleston American* and worked to bring the editor's pronouncements to the attention of federal authorities. Manning wrote to the Wilson administration in early summer of the Charleston paper's disloyal tone, requesting that it be investigated. Eventually, in October, the assistant postmaster general informed Grace that many of his editorials should not have been mailed under provisions of the Espionage Act. Nine specific editorials from August were declared disloyal and injurious to the United States. Grace countered that he knew the Constitution and was convinced his editorials were within the law. Although Grace may have been exercising rights guaranteed under the First Amendment, he was naïve to think that with the nation at war his strict interpretation of the law would somehow protect him from the consequences of his inflammatory opinions. When he commented in the July 12 issue of the paper that the burden of the war's fighting would fall on the American farmers while exempting those employed in "certain industries" (indirectly implying munitions), he misread the tone of the nation. Consequently, his legal arguments failed to convince the postmaster of his position and the *Charleston American's* second-class mailing privileges were revoked.[52]

Grace tried to operate without his reduced postage status by cutting his staff and the size of the paper. But his unpopular positions toward the war reduced his subscription numbers and placed his journalistic venture on the verge of bankruptcy. Thus, when postal authorities came forward with a compromise he had little choice but to sacrifice his principles. In late 1917, in a deal that would allow the paper to regain its second-class postage status, Grace reluctantly resigned as editor, though he was allowed to keep his stock and remain chairman of the board.[53] The *American* continued publishing, but adopted a favorable editorial position on America's role in the war.

With the state's two most critical newspapers suppressed, Manning and his Council of Defense effectively removed the most public threats to South Carolina's prowar position. Yet somehow, Coleman Blease escaped prosecution, for reasons that remain unclear. However, by the end of summer 1917, Blease must have realized that he could not muster the large constituency that he claimed supported his antiwar position, and his oppositional rhetoric ceased appearing in the newspaper. In doing so, he hoped that attempts to indict him would cease, which they did. Moreover, Blease planned to run for a US Senate seat the following year, and he must have known that to have any chance of success he would have to support the war effort.[54]

But serious concerns remained for Manning and Coker. In their opinion, many South Carolinians still did not support the war sufficiently. Coker and the executive committee of the Defense Council worked hard to distribute leaflets around the state explaining why the nation was at war. The council encouraged every county to hold public meetings with the four-minute men to build local support for the draft, food conservation, and the purchase of liberty bonds. By August, the SCCD secretary boasted to his Washington counterpart that the state had recruited all motion-picture houses to permit speakers to discuss the nation's war aims and convince their audiences to support the war. The four-minute speakers also held programs in school auditoriums and other public places. Coker's executive secretary claimed that in this way, the state council could reach forty thousand people a day.[55]

Yet because the state was so rural, the message to the public did not seem to reach enough people, at least in the opinion of the council's leaders. Nearly a year into the war, Hugh Murchison, field secretary for the council, observed that in his travels around the state he found "apathy and indifference . . . [for those] not actually engaged in some form of Government service."[56]

The limits to the council's appeals were apparent in an October 1917 speech given by Coker to the State Executive Committee for Liberty Loans. In his address, held at Columbia's Jefferson Hotel, Coker explained how important it was for people to understand why they needed to buy war bonds. While the first loan drive failed to meet the designated quota, largely due to poor organization, he called for better management and an effort to reach out to the farmers and tenants in rural areas. Since wartime demand for agricultural products caused many farmers and their tenants to boast more wealth than ever before, the council hoped "to stir up to a higher pitch the patriotism of the people." Coker believed that to reach the farmers, loan representatives needed to meet with them when they came into market towns each week to sell their products and purchase supplies. He predicted that this would not be difficult because the government was offering a better interest rate than savings banks.[57] The approach apparently worked, and the state exceeded its quota in the second liberty bond drive late that year.

A similar campaign to conserve foodstuffs began in the late spring of 1917. In May, Wilson appointed Herbert Hoover as the national food administrator. One of Hoover's first goals in his new office was to urge every state to comply with his national campaign for strict food conservation in each household.[58] Heeding his directive for South Carolina, Coker, who was also appointed a federal food administrator, worked with the South Carolina Women's Committee to head a pledge card campaign to register women in the state to reduce food waste and conserve important staples, particularly wheat, fat, and sugar. By December 1917 the results of the liberty loan and the food pledge card subscriptions pleased state and federal administrators. Almost $19 million were subscribed for the second liberty loan campaign and one hundred thousand homes had signed the food pledge cards. Whether this campaign actually was as effective as leaders boasted, it certainly created more awareness of the nation's role in the war while providing more individuals with the sense that they were contributing to the national defense effort.[59]

Despite widespread support for the food conservation campaign there were those who resisted. Writing on behalf of his wife, attorney H. Kluge Purdy of Ridgeland explained that despite Mrs. Purdy's tireless efforts to get county support for food conservation, she had "failed hopelessly" because her efforts were very unpopular in the county.[60] In Union another local pledge recruiter reported mixed results in the food pledge card campaign. One woman who operated a boardinghouse signed the card but would not exhibit it. Another who signed also refused to exhibit it because it was "too conspicuous." Several other women refused to sign it at all because they already were "saving all they could." The local recruiter reported that these mixed results demonstrated that her community "failed to catch the right vision and could not understand that signing was a pledge of loyalty."[61]

Although it is uncertain how much resistance there was in other counties, it concerned the state's leaders that significant apathy to the war still remained in South Carolina. In an effort to reduce such apathy, Coker decided to publish stories of enemy atrocities. The chairman asked his brother in Washington to send the state council as many authenticated stories of German atrocities ashe could. He planned to distribute these for publication in "state dailies and weeklies and brochures." As a follow-up to Coker's request to his brother, the secretary of the South Carolina Council of Defense appealed to the Committee on Public Information in Washington for a large supply of pamphlets entitled "How the War Came to America" because the state needed to inspire indifferent residents "to wake up."[62]

While state officials attributed the people's indifference to their lack of knowledge, Manning and Coker believed that pro-German sentiment remained a problem even with Blease and his allies effectively silenced. As late as June 1918 Coker was contacted by the head of the American Defense Society headquartered in New York seeking information on what the SCCD was doing to stamp out German propaganda. Furthermore, the New York society wanted to know what had been done to end the teaching of German in South Carolina schools and to suppress German-language newspapers.[63]

It is difficult to determine how legitimate the existence of disloyalty was in the nation. Nevertheless, throughout the war, the Wilson administration through its National Council of Defense sent out bulletins and directives on how to maintain loyalty and support for the war's prosecution. In December 1917, a document entitled "War Americanization" mailed to the South Carolina Council of Defense detailed how various states were teaching aliens working in industrial plants about American citizenship. Near the end of the war the Council of National Defense was still distributing instructions on Americanization. In a pamphlet entitled "Americanization: Organization of Local Committees," the council advised the states to coordinate their work with foreign-born individuals in communities. One of the key duties of these Americanization committees was to keep count of non-natives in their communities and to know who their leaders were, the location of their churches, and where their pastors resided. On the surface this appeared relatively innocent, a sound way to assist integrating foreigners into the fabric of American society, but such tactics tended to serve a sinister aspect, rooting out German spies and disloyal individuals that many feared lurked in communities around the nation.[64]

In addition to outlining methods of detecting disloyalty, Wilson also set a precedent for dealing with individuals accused of unpatriotic activity, no matter how slim the evidence. While he had professed to support dissent in 1917, in practice he tacitly permitted his administration to suppress opposition. He ignored pleas to defend German-Americans under attack and even rumors of dissent or negative comments were pursued. When an anonymous individual threatened Secretary of War Baker, Wilson was outraged. He declared in a cabinet meeting that the unidentified person should be punished for sedition and "exposed" to the public so he "would be forever damned by the people."[65]

The campaign against suspicious individuals, no matter how ultimately inconsequential, permeated the work of the South Carolina Council of Defense and the governor's office. Efforts to crack down on disloyalty in the state peaked during the spring and early summer of 1918.[66] These actions were aided by new acts, called the Sedition Amendments to the Espionage Act, passed in May 1918. The legislation gave local federal attorneys wide discretionary authority about whom they could prosecute. As David Kennedy has observed, this new set of acts encouraged a "wildly arbitrary application of justice" through the rest of the war.[67] South Carolina codified this zealous response to disloyalty in the *South Carolina Hand Book on the War* that the state's Council of Defense published in late 1917. In the preamble, its authors proclaimed that "Those not for us are against us."[68]

Manning and the Council of Defense received many reports of disloyal activity that needed investigation. However, those who came under suspicion were more often than not political enemies rather than spies or disloyal citizens. In McCormick County the local doctor, D. A. J. Bell, claimed that John R. Blackwell, "a law breaker all his life," was preventing local African Americans from registering for the draft by forcing black residents to swear before the local draft board that they were either too young or too old for military service. What made the disloyalty claim against Blackwell suspicious turned on his political affiliation. Bell claimed Blease appointed Blackwell as a local magistrate even though he was defeated "two to 1."[69] Although Bell claimed that he had two local witnesses that would validate his claim, he did not want his name publicized.

In 1918 local opposition to conscription came to the Council of Defense's attention. In June Horry County secretary manager Haskell Todd informed

Governor Manning that a group of people in his locality were trying to block the "Draft Law." Todd claimed that earlier that spring he was "waylaid" by a local rival, James Adams, who then shot him a few days later. While alarming in itself, once Manning received details of the assault he discovered there was more local rivalry behind it than disloyal sentiments. The county sheriff informed the governor that Todd and Adams had been feuding a long time. According to the sheriff, Adams believed Todd, a local draft board registrar, was singling out his small community and "imposing upon" them. Although it was not clear what this actually meant, the sheriff implied that Todd was using his position to change the "class" of some of those eligible for conscription, which Adams feared would hurt his group. The outcome of this episode is unknown, but the sheriff's report suggested that the draft law was just a pretext for a much bigger argument connected to local politics and personalities.[70]

Manning and his Council of Defense dealt with many other conflicting, nebulous stories of opposition and disloyalty from localities statewide which they found baffling and impossible to resolve. However, there were two individuals in 1918 whom the governor and Coker had no doubts were disloyal. Chalmers Wessinger had served as superintendent of Lancaster County Schools since 1913. A native of Lexington County, on the outskirts of the state capital, Wessinger earned two degrees at South Carolina College and was a noted football player while at the Columbia campus. After beginning a teaching career in Georgia, he built his reputation with positions teaching in Greenwood and Inman, South Carolina, before his tenure as Lancaster schools superintendent.[71] In spite of his impressive credentials, by 1918 rumors had begun to circulate that Wessinger showed little patriotic zeal for America's war aims. One rumor suggested that he had gone to some lengths to prevent his brother from getting a medical operation so he could then be allowed to serve in the military. The Lancaster educator was also rumored to have told some friends that Germany had every right to declare unrestricted submarine warfare to defend itself against the Allies.[72]

Despite these allegations, Wessinger had demonstrated patriotism during the winter and spring of 1918. In February the local paper ran a story that the superintendent and several of his teachers had compiled a list of those residents of the county eligible for the draft. This tedious work was commended by the writer. Then in April, Wessinger gave a speech to a local school to promote the funding of the Junior Red Cross but it proved too little and too late for Coker and his close advisers.[73]

Wessinger protested his innocence and claimed his complete support for the nation's war effort; his teaching staff publicly maintained that he was a good teacher and a loyal citizen.[74] Perhaps just as importantly, Lancaster mill owner and wealthiest citizen, Leroy Springs, ardently defended his school superintendent. As chairman of the Lancaster school district, Springs had appointed Wessinger five years before. There is no doubt where Springs's loyalty lay. His only son, Elliot White Springs, was a pilot about to begin his combat duties on the Western Front. In a series of letters between Springs and Coker, the mill owner defended Wessinger as patriotic and he invited Coker to visit him in Lancaster where he would convince the Council of Defense chairman completely "of the injustice of the rumors" against Wessinger. Along with his wife, Springs was the public face of the local war effort, and so his vigorous defense of the superintendent undoubtedly carried some weight.[75]

Nonetheless, even Springs's good offices and determined defense could not influence Coker to change his opinion on Wessinger's patriotism. Hugh Murchison, the Council of Defense's field secretary, supported the chairman's position. During his May visit to Lancaster he corroborated all the rumors after interviewing "some parties." He also advised Coker not to visit Lancaster but rather to hold an executive board meeting at which an answer could be formulated to respond to Springs's "disappointing" position in the Wessinger case.[76]

As far as can be determined Coker took his field secretary's advice and never visited Lancaster or interviewed Springs. Backed by his executive committee and US District Attorney Francis Weston, Coker set a hearing to review the evidence and decide on Wessinger's fate. Although the Council of Defense did not have the legal power to prosecute cases, any recommendations they made to federal prosecutors had a significant effect on the direction of the case. Unfortunately for Wessinger, the pressure of the situation was too much and he resigned as superintendent before the school year ended. Even after his resignation his colleagues on the teaching staff held him in high regard. In a resolution of support, fifteen Lancaster teachers insisted that Wessinger was "absolutely loyal to the American soldier, the American flag, and the American Government."[77]

Evidence gathered by Murchison and other officials was vague. In spite of witness testimony claiming Wessinger had made disloyal sentiments, the field secretary admitted to Coker that the Lancaster educator "is not seriously disloyal" even though his "awkward statements after our entrance into the war laid him open to suspicion and criticism."[78] Although many "serious minded and just persons" did not consider Wessinger as loyal as he "should be," he still showed that "he stands for his country." In the end Murchsion admitted that it was embarrassing for someone like Wessinger to be forced to defend his loyalty to his country. Once under suspicion, regardless of the true nature of his patriotism "his usefulness is at an end in that community." Consequently Wessinger resigned, Murchison apparently believed, because his reputation was compromised simply by suspicion and innuendo.[79]

Wessinger was not the only public official in South Carolina to face such scrutiny at the hands of the South Carolina Council of Defense. In March 1917, Friedrich Johannes H. von Engelken was appointed president to Columbia's new regional Federal Farm Land Bank.[80] Although a native of Germany, he had immigrated to Florida many years before.[81] Over time he became an authority in economics and finance. By 1906 his reputation had grown to the point that he was sent to Europe to study rural credits. Ten years later the Wilson administration selected him as president of the US Mint, and a year later von Engelken assumed the new position at the Federal Land Bank for District 3. Not long after the United States entered the war von Engelken came under suspicion for unpatriotic sentiments. According to affidavits taken in the spring of 1918 von Engelken had not supported the first liberty loan drive in May 1917. The deponent, William Banks, editor of the *Columbia Record,* claimed that the Land Bank president had declined to subscribe while showing "great discourtesy to the committee." He had also declined to support the American Red Cross and other campaigns for the war effort.[82]

Another deponent claimed that von Engelken assumed no one would subscribe to the first liberty loan. The individual also stated that the Land Bank president belittled the nation's war preparations and denied the accusation in the press of German war atrocities; and in one final exclamation stated that von Engelken did not think Germany "would be licked."[83]

By contrast the same deponent admitted that von Engelken continued to "protest his loyalty to the United States." And when William Banks published a warning in the *Columbia Record* against disloyalty in summer 1917 von Engelken sent a letter through Mr. R. H. Welch, general counsel to the Columbia Land Bank, addressed to Banks assuring him that he, von Engelken, was a loyal, patriotic American citizen. He admitted that he had not subscribed to the local patriotic causes but had actually sent his contributions to the liberty loan drive directly to Washington. Not long after Welch met with Banks, von Engelken met with the editor to prove his loyalty more clearly by producing letters from officials of the Land Bank supporting his claims of patriotic support for the nation. Then at the end of the same affidavit Banks claimed that von Engelken admitted his German parentage and that he had relatives in the German army. Most curiously of all, Banks continued, the Land Bank president stated he had been offered a commission in the German army but had declined on the "ground that he could serve Germany better in America."[84]

This contradictory evidence against von Engelken still suggested to people in the local community that he was "disloyal." The evidence certainly convinced Manning, Coker, and Christie Benet, lawyer and vice-chairman of the state council. When the *Record* reported in April that the Land Bank president was to speak at a public forum in support of the war Manning and his advisers protested to Washington and the Treasury Department. They demanded that von Engelken must not speak to an audience because of his questionable loyalty. Even though the Treasury Department had publicly defended the Land Bank president against local rumors of disloyalty, his accusers continued their attacks long after he had left Columbia. It is likely because of these persistent attacks that Washington officials decided to transfer von Engelken from Columbia to New York at the end of April. His place was assumed by one of his staff, David A. Houston, the former treasurer of the Land Bank.[85]

Governor Manning and Christie Benet continued to insist that von Engelken was disloyal after the Armistice. In February 1919, to vindicate their position, they presented their evidence to the Senate Subcommittee on German and Bolshevik Propaganda. However, the committee members seemed unimpressed, especially after they read a letter from US Treasury Secretary William McAdoo to President Wilson that called the charges against von Engelken groundless. In any event, von Engelken continued in government service, serving on a commission to investigate postwar Europe's economic conditions.[86]

The cases that Manning and Coker brought against two seemingly distinguished public servants are difficult to evaluate in light of contradictory evidence. Both men showed ability in their respective duties, one as an educator and the other as an economist and administrator. Both Wessinger and von Engelken had the support of their staff and superiors. Perhaps in their positions they posed an undefined political threat to local people that had the ears of Manning and Coker. Wessinger and Springs claimed that a small group of parents in the Lancaster schools had children who had been disciplined by the superintendent, leading to rumors that Wessinger was disloyal so he would be forced out. Likewise von Engelken had assumed a huge responsibility for the new Land Bank. With little guidance other than the law passed by Congress, he had organized a staff, accepted innumerable applications from farmers in four states, and determined who should receive low-interest loans. Nonetheless, in one year he succeeded in growing a staff of six into one of seventy-five while providing $9 million in loans. From all appearances, both from local papers and Washington leaders, von Engelken was a great success. However, South Carolina's governor and his chairman of the State Council of Defense found enough proof, at least in their own minds, that the Land Bank president did not demonstrate adequate loyalty to remain at his post.

The South Carolina Council of Defense had been organized to educate the state's citizens about why they should support the war. The Palmetto State's leaders believed in the nation's call to arms and wanted the state to demonstrate its patriotic support. However, the council faced what it perceived as significant opposition in its efforts, opposition it worked to confront and suppress. Once they succeeded in stopping political leaders and newspapers from publicly opposing the war, fears of disloyalty continued to fester in the minds of the state's leaders. To stem this apparent threat to national security the Council of Defense, following the lead of the National Council of Defense and President Wilson, continued to publicize patriotic messages in every community throughout the state, seeking to overcome disloyal tendencies and a more generalized indifference to the war effort. In doing so, the SCCD worked closely with and within the bounds of the Wilson administration's guidelines for loyal, patriotic participation in the national war effort. To demonstrate its patriotic support while trying to enforce loyalty among all its citizens Governor Manning, David Coker, and others went after suspected individuals aggressively and, perhaps in most cases, unjustly. In doing so, leaders like Richard Manning and David Coker demonstrated to the president and his cabinet their commitment to the national policies during a crisis which some people did not support with the zeal demanded. Their actions suggest that at least in South Carolina, the war effort provided an opportunity for southern leaders to align themselves with national policy and, in the process, quiet dissent and shape state and local politics in lasting ways.

NOTES

1. For details on the Wessinger case, see Leroy Springs to David R. Coker, May 25, 1918, David R. Coker Papers, Box 2, South Caroliniana Library, University of South Carolina, Columbia (hereafter Coker Papers, SCL). For examples of testimony against Wessinger, see DRC to Hugh Murchison, April 27, 1918, Military Dept., Council of Defense, Correspondence files, 1917–19, Series 192069, Box 2, SC Department of Archives and History, Columbia, SC (hereafter cited as SC Council of Defense Papers, SCDAH).

2. Terry Helsley, "Voices of Dissent: The Anti-War Movement and the South Carolina State Council of Defense, 1916–1918" (M.A. thesis, University of South Carolina, 1974), 128.

3. For quote see Geoffrey R. Stone, *Perilous Times: Free Speech in Wartime, from the Sedition Act of 1798 to the War on Terror* (New York: W. W. Norton, 2004), 137–38. For a perspective on Wilson's concern about American support and loyalty, see David M. Kennedy, *Over Here: The First World War and American Society,* paperback edition (New York: Oxford University Press, 2004), 88–89.

4. Quote from Page Smith, *America Enters the World: A People's History of the Progressive Era and World War I* (New York: Penguin Books, 1991), 550–51.

5. Ibid.

6. On the Blease faction and its supporters, see David Carlton, *Mill and Town in South Carolina: 1880–1920* (Baton Rouge: Louisiana University Press, 1982), 220–23; for the close 1916 election, see Robert M. Burts, *Richard Irvine Manning And the Progressive Movement in South Carolina* (Columbia: University of South Carolina Press, 1974), 126, 129–31; Helsley, "Voices of Dissent," 121–22, 128.

7. *New York Times*, October 12, 1915, 1; Woodrow Wilson, "An Annual Address on the State of the Union," December 7, 1915, in *The Papers of Woodrow Wilson*, ed. Arthur Link (Princeton, NJ: Princeton University Press), 35:293–310; A. Scott Berg, *Wilson,* (New York: G. P. Putnam's Sons, 2013), 378, 384.

8. Kennedy, *Over Here*, 5, 10; Sixty-Fifth Congress, 1 Session, Senate Document No. 5, 3–8.

9. Although only six senators and fifty representatives voted against Wilson's war resolution, some observers believed that this number understated the true extent of Congress's opposition to the war; see Kennedy, *Over Here*, 23.

10. Stone, *Perilous Times*, 137; Kennedy, *Over Here*, 21–22.

11. Stone, *Perilous Times*, 137. See Kennedy, *Over Here*, 148, for details on the opposition to the draft and the factors that finally led to the passage of the law despite strong opposition from western and southern delegations.

12. Janet Hudson, *Entangled White Supremacy: Reform in World War I–era South Carolina* (Lexington: University Press of Kentucky, 2009), 88.

13. On LaFollette's major reasons opposing the war see Kennedy, *Over Here*, 22.

14. *The Watchman and Southron* (Sumter, SC), January 20, February 10, 1917.

15. For details on Manning's support for Wilson before 1917 and his second inaugural, see *The Watchman and Southron* (Sumter, SC), January 20, February 10, March 3, 1917.

16. George B. Tindall, *The Emergence of the New South, 1913–1945* (Baton Rouge: Louisiana State University Press, 1967), 21–22; Walter B. Edgar, *South Carolina: A History* (Columbia: University of South Carolina Press, 1998), 475.

17. Burts, *R. Manning*, 158–60. For more details on the developments of these various installations for training and their economic impact for neighboring communities, see John H. Moore, *Columbia and Richland County: A South Carolina Community, 1740–1990* (Columbia: University of South Carolina Press, 1993), 318–20; A. V. Huff, *Greenville: The History of City and County in the South Carolina Piedmont* (Columbia: University of South Carolina Press, 1995), 253–60; Fritz Hamer, *Charleston Reborn: A Southern City, Its Navy Yard and World War II* (Charleston: History Press, 2005), 16, 20–21; John H. Moore, "Charleston in World War I: Seeds of Change," *SC Historical Magazine* 86 (January 1985): 1–31; Eugene Alverez, *Parris Island: Once a Recruit, Always a Marine* (Charleston: History Press, 2007), 3–16.

18. For details on the origins of the National Council of Defense, see Berg, *Wilson*, 444–46; and for the origins of state Councils of Defense, see William J. Breen, "The North Carolina Council of Defense during World War I, 1917–1918," *North Carolina Historical Review* 50, no. 1 (1973): 1–3. For Manning's reasons for the SC Council of Defense, see RM to Sir (?), June 9, 1917, Box 2, SC Council of Defense Papers, SCDAH; Burts, *R. Manning*, 165.

19. Breen, "North Carolina Council of Defense," 3, 9. Alabama's Council of Defense also saw its governor appoint people to his council who were business associates or political friends from the past: see Dowe Littleton, "The Alabama Council of Defense, 1917–1918," in Martin T. Olliff, ed., *The Great War in the Heart of Dixie: Alabama during World War I* (University of Alabama Press, 2008), 153.

20. Peter Coclanis, "Seeds of Reform: David R. Coker," *South Carolina Historical Magazine* 102 (July 2001): 202–18; Ernest M. Lander, Jr., *A History of South Carolina, 1865–1960* (Columbia: University of South Carolina Press, 1970), 57, 118–19; for a detailed account of Coker's political support for Manning and the war, see James R. Rogers and Larry E. Nelson, *Mr. D.R.: A Biography of David R. Coker* (Hartsville: Coker College Press, 1994), 66–96.

21. Burts states that Manning recruited a balanced representation from the state's professional classes, from business, industry and agriculture but failed to see that all of the state's forty-six counties were represented. Burts, *R. Manning*, 165–66.

22. Bryant Simon, "The Appeal of Cole Blease of South Carolina: Race, Class and Sex in the New South," *Journal of Southern History* 62 (February 1996): 80.

23. Anthony B. Miller, "Coleman L. Blease: South Carolina Politician" (M.A. thesis, University of North Carolina-Greensboro, 1971), 122.

24. *The Scimitar* (Abbeville), December 1, 1916; for further details on Blease's appeal to textile workers, see Carlton, *Mill and Town*, 10–11, 214; and Stephan Kantrowitz, *Ben Tillman and the Reconstruction of White Supremacy* (Chapel Hill: University of North Carolina Press, 2000), 296–97.

25. Lewis P. Jones, *South Carolina: A Synoptic History for Laymen* (Lexington: Sandlapper Store, Inc., 1978), 238–39; for a somewhat different view of Blease in South Carolina politics, see Carlton, *Mill and Town*, 221–23.

26. For the long-standing ethnic ties in these counties, see Edgar, *South Carolina*, 187, 290; for a good overview of German communities in South Carolina, see Michael Bell, "Germans," *South*

Carolina Encyclopedia, ed. Walther Edgar (Columbia: University of South Carolina Press, 2006), 370–71. Up until the fall of 1917, Charleston had its own German-language newspaper.

27. *Charleston American*, August 30, 1916; June 2, 1917.

28. *Charleston American*, August 25, 27, 28, 1916; Doyle W. Boggs, "John Patrick Grace and the Politics of Reform in South Carolina, 1900–1931," (PhD diss., University of South Carolina, 1977), 107–8.

29. Lowry Ware, *Chapters in the History of Abbeville County, The "Banner County" of South Carolina* (SCMAR: Columbia, SC, 2012), 201–2. "Beard Obituary," *State*, July 8, 1940.

30. The *Scimitar*, February 1, 1915.

31. Ibid.

32. Ibid., September 15, 1915; July 1, 1916. Burts, *R. Manning*, 126–32.

33. The *Scimitar*, October 3, 1914.

34. Ibid., May 15, 1915.

35. Edgar, *South Carolina*, 475; other newspapers that defended Manning early in the war against Blease's attacks included the *Edgefield Advertiser* and *Charleston News and Courier*; see Burts, *R. Manning*, 174.

36. *State*, February 2, 1917; in this article the claim is made that the vessel was sunk on the morning of February 1, but it was actually late the previous evening.

37. For background to the bizarre actions in Charleston harbor, see Moore, "Seeds of Change," 2–4.; for other reactions to the *Leibenfels* episode see *State*, January 31, 1917; for Beard's editorial against the Wilson administration and defense of the German crew's actions, see *Scimitar*, February 1, 1917.

38. Moore, "Seeds of Change," 3–4. In the case of Paul Wierse: he was convicted of conspiracy and sentenced to two years in prison and a $1,000 fine in October 1917. After more than a year of appeals he was taken into custody to serve his sentence in December 1918; for details see *State*, June 8, October 13, 1917, and December 22, 1918.

39. August 4, 1917, *State*, copy of article, "Blease Speech Show Position," in Coker Papers, Box 1, SCL.

40. The *County Record* (Kingstree, SC), August 2, 1917.

41. For quote by Goldman, see Smith, *America Enters the World*, 545–46; for other people and organizations accused of disloyalty, see ibid., 543–57.

42. For Byrnes's remarks, see Jeanette Keith, *Rich Man's War, Poor Man's Fight: Race, Class, and Power in the Rural South during the First World War* (University of North Carolina Press, 2004), 53.

43. Ibid., 2.

44. Joe Sparks to David R. Coker, August 3, 1917, Coker Papers, Box 1, SCL.

45. R. J. Jaynes to Department of Justice, August 10, 1917, Coker Papers, Box 2, SCL.

46. *Scimitar*, April 15, September 1, 1917.

47. For details of the charges against Beard, see *State*, October 12, 1917.

48. Boggs, "Grace and Politics," 120–21.

49. The *State* newspaper reported October 12, 1917, that the US Post Office had curtailed Beard's mailing privileges "some weeks ago" based on the Espionage Act, which made it illegal to send seditious materials through the mail.

50. *Charleston American*, June 5, 1917.

51. Ibid., July 12, 1917.

52. Ibid., July 12, 1917; for further details on Grace's argument and the decision of the postmaster see Boggs, "Grace and Politics," 122–24.

53. Boggs, "Grace and Politics," 122–23.

54. For his race in the 1918 primaries, where he argued for supporting the national war measures, see David D. Wallace, *History of South Carolina* (Columbia: University of South Carolina Press, 1984), 670. At least one of his stalwart antiwar supporters condemned him for abandoning his principles, notably William Beard. See his published comments about how he claimed Blease deserted him in his hour of need in the 1917 trial, *State*, July 2, August 11, 1918.

55. Executive Secretary, SC Council of Defense, to George Warner, President, National Council of Defense, August 23, 1917, South Carolina Council of Defense Papers, Box 2, SCDAH.

56. Murchison to Coker, March 22, 1918, Coker Papers, Box 2, SCL.

57. DRC speech to State Executive Committee of Liberty Loans, October 8, 1917, Coker Papers, Box 1, SCL.

58. Kennedy, *Over Here*, 1981, 117; for details about this in greater depth, see William Mullendere, *History of the U.S. Food Administration, 1917–1919* (Stanford, CA: Stanford University Press, 1941).

59. On the food campaign in South Carolina, see "Report SC State Council of Defense," July 30, 1917, Gov. Richard R. Manning Papers, Series 534005, Box 45, SCDAH, hereafter cited as Manning Papers; DRC to Miss Katie Lee, July 28, 1917, ibid. For the results of the two campaigns see "Report of Reed Smith, U.S. Food Administration, Food Administrator for South Carolina," December 6, 1917, SC Council of Defense Papers, Box 2, SCDAH. For details on the nation's liberty loan drives see Sung Won Kang and Hugh Rockoff, "Capitalizing Patriotism: The Liberty Loans of World War I," *Financial History Review* 22, no. 1 (2006): 45–78, accessed January 27, 2017, at http://www.nber.org/papers/w11919.

60. H. Kluge Purdy to Mrs. F. L. Mayes, September 18, 1917, Manning Papers, Box 45, SCDAH. On Washington's claim that the national success in recruiting women for agricultural work in 1917, see *Woman's Land Army of America* (brochure), March 1918, second edition, Manning Papers, Box 45, SCDAH.

61. Mrs. J. W. Mixson, Workers Daily Reporting Sheet, U.S. Food Administration Campaign, no date, State of South Carolina, Manning Papers, Box 45, SCDAH.

62. Secretary, SCCD to George Creel, August 4, 1917, SC Council of Defense Papers, Box 2, SCDAH; *County Record* (Kingstree, SC), August 2, 1917.

63. Dr. Perry Dickie, American Defense Society, to DRC, June 15, 1918, Coker Papers, Box 2, SCL.

64. For examples of these loyalty publications, see Bulletin No. 99, *Loyalty and Sedition*, June 11, 1918; Bulletin No. 16, *War Americanization*, Immigration Committee, December 1, 1917; *Americanization: Organization of Local Committees*, Council of National Defense, September 26, 1918, all in Coker Papers, Box 2, SCL.

65. Kennedy, *Over Here*, 87–88.

66. Helsley, "Voices of Dissent," 135. Helsley states that during the period from April to June, 1918, the South Carolina Council had the greatest number of pro-German accusations to review.

67. Kennedy, *Over Here,* 82–83.

68. Quoted from Edgar, *South Carolina History,* 477. Coker and his council demonstrated their increased zeal against German infiltration when the chairman gained the unanimous support of the South Carolina Council of Defense in proposing to send a resolution in March 1918 to the War Department in Washington "to take more stringent measures against German spies and incendiaries"; see Council Minutes for March 8, 1918, Coker Papers, Box 2, SCL.

69. DAJ Bell, M.D., to DRC, June 22, 1918, Coker Papers, Box 2, SCL.

70. B. Haskell Todd to RM, June 1, 1918, Manning Papers, Box 13, SCDAH; Sheriff Lewis to RM, June 6, 1918, Manning Papers, Box 13, SCDAH.

71. For a brief outline of Wessinger's teaching career and more, see his obituary in *State,* November 22, 1948; and for the date when he began his tenure at Lancaster, see Leroy Springs to DRC, May 25, 1918, Coker Papers, Box 2, SCL.

72. Sworn Statements of Prof. Grady Bowman, May 23, 1918, and Mrs. M. R. McCardle, May 23, 1918, SC Council of Defense Papers, Box 1, SCDAH.

73. *Lancaster Daily News,* February 26, 1918.

74. C. Wessinger to DRC, telegram, May 15, 1918, Coker Papers, Box 2, SCL.

75. Spring to Coker, April 24, 1918; Coker to Springs, April 27, 1918; Springs to Coker, May 14, 1918, all in SC Council of Defense Papers, Box 1, SCDAH. On Elliott W. Spring's service on the Western Front as a fighter pilot, see David K. Vaughan, ed., *Letters from a War Bird: The World War I Correspondence of Elliott White Springs* (Columbia: University of South Carolina Press, 2012), xiii–xxiii.

76. Hugh Murchison to DRC, May 18. 1918, SC Council of Defense Papers, Box 1, SCDAH.

77. Resolution of fifteen teachers of the Lancaster Graded Schools read at the graduating exercises by Col. Leroy Springs, attached to Springs to Coker, May 25, 1918, Coker Papers, Box 2, SCL.

78. Murchison to Coker, April 29, 1918, SC Council of Defense Papers, Box 1, SCDAH.

79. Ibid. Wessinger returned to his native Lexington after his resignation. He sold cotton for a few years before finding employment in the school system in Raleigh, NC, where he continued to receive high marks for his teaching. While there, he earned a law degree and in the late thirties returned to Lexington, where he served a term in the South Carolina House of Representatives. See *SC Legislative Manuel,* 1939 and 1940; "Wessinger Obituary," *State,* November 22, 1948.

80. On brief early history of the Federal Land Bank, see *State,* May 8, 1927.

81. There is confusion regarding where von Engelken actually came from. Several sources in South Carolina identify him as a native of Germany while another source claims he was a Danish native; for the former see Christie Benet affidavit on loyalty of von Engelken, May 25, 1918, Coker Papers, Box 2, SCL; for claim that he was from Denmark, see William E. Connelly and Ellis M. Coulter, *History of Kentucky,* vol. 4 (American Historical Society, 1922), 377.

82. William Black Affidavit on von Engelken, May 22, 1918, Coker Papers, Box 2, SCL; *Watchman and Southron* (Sumter, SC) February 15, 1919; *State,* February 19, 1917.

83. Affidavit of Moffatt G. McDonald, May 24, 1918, Coker Papers, Box 2, SCL.

84. Affidavit of William Banks, May 22, 1918, Coker Papers, Box 2, SCL.

85. *Bamberg Herald* (SC), March 22, 1919; Daniel Roper to DRC, April 26, 1918, Coker Papers, Box 2, SCL.

86. For overview of the subcommittee hearing and its results regarding von Engelken, see *Watchman and Southron* (Sumter, SC), February 15, 1919; *Bamberg Herald,* March 27, 1919. In Coker's biography the authors explain that DRC was caught up "in patriotic ardor" that overrode "cautious judgement"; see Rogers and Nelson, *Mr. D.R.*, 84–85.

4

Food Soldiers

Rural Southerners and Food Regulation during World War I

ANGELA JILL COOLEY

n January 1918, The United States' president, Woodrow Wilson, issued a proclamation calling on "every loyal American" to follow new regulations issued
by the US Food Administration, a temporary federal agency established to
manage the nation's food resources during World War I. The agency's goal for
1918 was to reduce the nation's wheat consumption to 70% of that used in the
previous year. Neither Herbert Hoover, the head of the agency, nor Wilson
wanted to employ food rationing, which the European nations, at war for more
than three years, had implemented. Instead, they called for conservation in the
form of a patriotic appeal while downplaying the more coercive aspects of regulation. Wilson's proclamation and the Food Administration's rules imagined
a nation of strong, loyal citizens willing to substitute cornmeal for wheat flour
and beans for meat, among other culinary sacrifices, as their contribution to the
war effort. Wilson's plans, as well as those of Hoover, assumed the men, women,
and children in homes across the nation would, in the words of Illinois state
administrator Harry Wheeler, become "food soldiers" during the war.[1]

The Food Administration's messages of thrift, economy, and patriotism spoke
directly to the nation's emerging middle class. These men and women, who participated in the buying and selling of foodstuffs, largely supported conservation.
The Food Administration assumed all Americans would embrace its regulations
as part of their contribution to the war effort, but the nation's merchants, bankers, educators, and businessmen, and their wives and families, more fully embraced the agency's dictates. This was also the case in the American South. The
region, however, remained predominately rural and agricultural, and the Food
Administration failed to effectively account for the differing culture, business

practices, and labor systems of rural people. Farmers across the nation had little say in the wartime agency's decision making.

Although southern states identified food production as a goal at the start of the war, the resulting regulations focused largely on issues of marketing and consumption. The concerns of farmers, especially as consumers, seemed to be an afterthought. Scholars have suggested that this oversight may have been the result of a regulatory system focused on food production, a system in which regulators emphasized implementing and expanding progressive reform in industrial agriculture and consumer culture.[2] As a result, wartime food regulations often conflicted with the ways farmers lived their lives and conducted their businesses. Although food conservation and production should have put farmers at the center of the nation's food focus—not on the periphery—the nation's more powerful commercial interests, such as grocers, banks, processors, and other players in agribusiness, controlled the regulatory process.

The distinctive features of southern agriculture exacerbated this disconnect between farmers and regulators. By the start of the twentieth century, as farmers elsewhere mechanized, southern agriculture remained labor-intensive and race-based. In 1917, at the start of the nation's participation in World War I, most African Americans lived and worked in the South, generally in sharecropping or tenancy arrangements on plantations owned by white landowners. Moreover, the region remained committed to cash crops, especially cotton. Although some southern farmers grew corn for their own use, the region largely neglected food crops.[3] Importantly, the region did not cultivate wheat, primarily because the hot and humid climate did not favor the hard red varieties that dominated the nation's wheat crop by World War I.[4] These regional differences in production influenced the business practices of farmers and the marketing and eating habits of their families. Accordingly, World War I–era food regulation affected southern farmers in ways that differed not only from townspeople living in the South but also from farmers in other regions.

For many reasons, southern farmers should have been well situated to follow the new rules. Food control emphasized conservation, such as baking Victory bread made from a flour with 20% nonwheat grains and buying equal amounts of a wheat substitute with every purchase of flour. Corn was both a popular wheat alternative and a mainstay of southern agrarian diets. But substitution rules assumed that all Americans purchased grain in the marketplace, and antihoarding laws assumed greater and more frequent access to markets than southern farmers often experienced. Real and perceived labor shortages threatened southern agriculture and exacerbated racial tensions in the region even as food conservation gave African Americans a way to prove their loyalty. For the most part, rural southerners, black and white, responded positively to the Food Administration's appeal for compliance as a patriotic duty. But noncompliance and ambivalence co-existed with calls for loyalty in the southern countryside. Moreover, compliance with food conservation rules remained difficult in the rural South. Farmers generally lacked formal access to the regulatory process and instead relied on local, often personal, negotiations with federal and state officials as well as agrarian organizing to advance their interests.[5]

In August 1917, Congress authorized the formation of a federal agency to control the nation's food supply and to conserve food for export to soldiers and allies abroad. President Wilson exercised that authority by creating the US Food Administration. The food control law did not pass easily, however. South Carolina congressman Asbury Francis Lever introduced the legislation that would bear his name during the first week of May 1917. At the same time, the Federal Trade Commission and the Department of Agriculture sponsored a hearing to investigate the nation's food supply. Officials at the hearing questioned the existence of actual scarcity; rather, they identified hoarding by housewives as the cause of any perceived shortages. Several state officials who attended the hearing pointed to inequitable marketing practices as another problem. One example was the fact that farmers who grew the produce made little profit compared to the processors and retailers who manufactured and sold the food.[6] Even before the United States declared war, urban newspapers reported on a few food riots in some cities. According to the historian James H. Smith, one Brooklyn housewife who had documented rising food prices noted that vegetables cost five times as much in February 1917 than they had just eight months earlier.[7] The Lever bill had provisions to control these aspects of the nation's food system, thereby limiting unrest.

Congress continued to debate food control throughout the summer as the nation mobilized for war. The resulting act gave the president extensive authority to regulate the nation's food system including the ability to create and appoint an administrator for a new agency, eventually called the Food Administration. Despite its broad legislative authority, the agency shunned the formal rationing that many European nations had implemented and instead relied more on cooperation and incentive. Nevertheless, the law gave the agency power to license businesses that manufactured, stored, and distributed necessities and to punish those who hoarded, conspired to control, or destroyed food supplies in an effort to artificially inflate the price of food commodities.[8]

As Congress debated the law, one of the more controversial aspects of food regulation proved to be the notion of a food administrator. Although this was not in the original bill, Congress began to consider the position when Hoover, who had been in Europe helping with Belgian food relief, returned to the United States to report on the food situation overseas. The president thought a centralized office that controlled buying and selling food commodities would do away with the need for formal price fixing in the agricultural sector. In mid-May 1917, even before Congress passed the food control law, Wilson appointed Hoover to head the soon-to-be-created agency. He justified such unprecedented control over the nation's food supply as a temporary wartime measure that would act on a volunteer basis independent of the normal operations of government.[9]

Many southern legislators, like Lever, supported Hoover's temporary and voluntary role to control the nation's food system. But some, especially in the Southwest, considered it to be an autocratic position that had no place in democratic processes. Both Congressman Atkins Jefferson McLemore of Texas and Senator James Alexander Reed of Missouri called Hoover a "food dictator." McLemore not only disapproved of the concept of a food administrator, but he specifically targeted Hoover's appointment. With regard to the position more generally, McLemore considered it ironic that "in our effort to destroy autocracy and establish democracy in the nations of the Old World, that we should completely un-Americanize ourselves" and establish "a 'food dictator' who is invested with autocratic powers greater than those ever conferred upon any Old World ruler." McLemore also doubted the loyalty of the longtime expatriate and questioned Hoover's experience. The congressman described the future president as someone "who knows absolutely nothing of farming and of cattle raising, yet who has been brought over here to assume a dictatorship over our producers." Although much of his exposition may have been political hyperbole, McLemore's denunciation of Hoover's credentials suggested a number of ways that Hoover's food policies might affect southern farmers.[10]

Despite the congressman's personal criticism of Hoover as food administrator, most Americans came to revere him in this role. In highlighting Hoover's lack of practical experience for the position, however, McLemore had a point, at least when it came to southern agriculture. Hoover had grown up in and around agriculture—he spent his childhood in Iowa and his adolescence in Oregon, where he labored as a clerk for his uncle's fruit orchards. But from the time he entered Stanford University at age seventeen, his life revolved around geology and mining engineering. Nevertheless, Hoover did have some experience in food policy. For three years, from the time Germany invaded Belgium to the US declaration of war against Germany, Hoover, working from London, organized and operated the Commission for Relief in Belgium to feed 9 million near-starving Belgians who lacked access to their normal supply of food imports. His conservation efforts abroad impressed world leaders, including Wilson.[11] Hoover's feat certainly demonstrated a gift for organization and leadership, but he had no personal experience with the lifestyle, culture, or business practices of the southern farmer.

Moreover, the administration Hoover created in Washington and in each of the states tended to include prominent townspeople, including merchants, grocers, bankers, newspaper editors, and university professors. The nature of the administration's work meant its leaders, like Hoover, needed to have some amount of wealth, prestige, and flexibility. Leadership positions were full-time volunteer spots, which excluded most farmers, whose day-to-day labor did not leave time for such a commitment. Hoover appointed an administrator in each state, generally someone with political connections, to implement the federal regulations. Many southern administrators represented commercial interests. In Alabama, state administrator Richard M. Hobbie operated a wholesale grocery business. Henry A. Page, state legislator, railroad president, and son of a prominent North Carolina family, operated that state's administration. In Mississippi, bank president Phillip M. Harding served as state administrator. South Carolina's administrator, William Elliott, was a lawyer. Elliott placed newspaper editor August Kohn in charge of conservation and production. There was no evidence Kohn had experience in farming, but he was a trustee of the University of South Carolina and, according to Elliott, "a prominent and respected citizen." Even state administrators who had agricultural positions tended to be educators instead of farmers, such as Georgia's Andrew M. Soule and Tennessee's Harcourt Morgan, both of whom served as president of their state's agricultural college.[12] After the war, farmers complained that the voluntary leadership of the Food Administration had been composed largely of millers and processors who curried favor with Hoover and failed to represent their voices.[13]

Each state administrator established an organization to implement the federal regulations within his jurisdiction with officials in charge of publicity, conservation, compliance, and other aspects of the law. At the county level, prominent local professionals helped to implement food control laws.[14] Nathaniel L. Willet, the rather controversial county food administrator in Richmond County, Georgia, owned a seed company. Although federal rules were supposed to be interpreted in a similar manner nationwide, he often angered other officials by construing agency dictates in ways that conflicted with official statements. In one example, Willet allowed Irish potatoes to serve as a wheat substitute although the federal agency prohibited this substitution. Residents of neighboring counties in South Carolina, who were not allowed the same substitution, complained.[15] The county food administrator was an unpaid volunteer position often nominated by the most influential professionals in the community and appointed by the state administrator.[16] Each state administrator presumably had the discretion to dismiss county officials, but there is no evidence Soule took this action with regard to Willet. Although Willet is an extraordinary example, his ability to disregard central commands without facing any apparent consequences supports the notion that his prominence in the community likely preserved his position. The most ubiquitous county workers were the home demonstration agents, who traversed the countryside establishing canning clubs and educating housewives on substitutes. They were mostly educated women whose expertise in home economics was considered to be essential to conservation.[17] Across the Food Administration, federal, state, and local leadership disproportionately included urban merchants, progressive educators, and other townspeople, even in the predominately agricultural South.

Because of its agricultural productivity, scholars often wonder at the South's apparent inability to feed itself. Although the region's food deficit dates back to the antebellum period, Sam Bowers Hilliard and Marcie Cohen Ferris, both of whom have written about food access in the South, agree that changes wrought by the Civil War exacerbated the problem for many southern farmers. Planters focused primarily on cotton cultivation and often neglected food crops. Sharecropping and tenancy replaced slavery as the region's main labor system. Landless farmers—black and white—had little say in their food choices. An expanding industrial food system made food cheaper to buy than to cultivate. By the early twentieth century, these factors collaborated to make the region more dependent for its food.[18]

Early in the war, southern states were acutely aware and concerned about this fact. Even before the federal government formed the Food Administration, prominent Alabamians gathered to discuss the state's lack of self-sufficiency. They estimated that Alabama had a $106 million food deficit. Governor Charles Henderson called on farmers to plant additional food crops, and Ida Elizabeth Mathis, a popular farm lecturer and proponent of diversification, led the publicity campaign to increase food production. Mathis claimed the food situation in the state was more perilous than it had been during the Civil War. For many Alabama farmers, diversification meant growing more corn. The *Birmingham Age-Herald* seconded Mathis's efforts. "Less cotton, more corn," the newspaper advocated. "Less buying abroad and more raising the things we need at home."[19] Corn was already a popular crop in the region, but many Alabamians and other southerners relied on western imports to the state.

South Carolina also recognized its inability to feed itself. The state's first food administrator, David R. Coker, admitted in his correspondence to Hoover that South Carolina "is not primarily a food producing state" and identified a $70 to $100 million annual food deficit—the result of a reliance on industrial foods including roughly $21 million in meat, $16 million in western corn, $13 million in canned goods, and $11 million in processed wheat flour. He wanted to increase food production by 20% to make South Carolina more self-sufficient, encourage food exports to other states, and free up national transportation networks for war purposes.[20] This common call for self-sufficiency among southern states allowed elite southerners to claim their loyalty to the United States while still upholding the central importance of the state. But systemic and cultural barriers existed to southern self-sufficiency in food production.

Among the issues that southern farmers needed to address to produce more food was the question of labor. The war contributed to real and perceived labor shortages in fields across the nation as landowners worried about how ordinary migration and wartime conscription would affect farm labor. During a Senate hearing, John E. Milholland, owner of "Meadowmount" in Essex County, New York, expressed this concern on behalf of eastern farmers. "We lost 16 per cent of our farm hands last year in a time of peace," Milholland stated, quoting another New York farmer ascribing the loss to factory work. "Now we have war, and you are going to fill up the Army and Navy and National Guard by conscription."[21] White southern planters, administrators, and politicians worried about these same issues, but they saw the southern labor situation as particularly acute because of the region's greater reliance on field labor and on black sharecroppers and tenants in particular. In 1910, for example, African Americans made up almost 30% of farmers in the South, but more than 75% of black farmers did not own their own land. By contrast, less than 40% of white farmers lacked land.[22] In short, despite any emotional and occupational ties black farmers had to the land, they had little ownership interest. Moreover, southern farming continued to be a labor-intensive industry through the 1920s.[23] Although white landowners often belittled black work habits and aptitude, they nevertheless depended on black tenants and sharecroppers to bring in the crops. For their part, African Americans worked hard and possessed valuable agricultural skills but had little incentive to stay on the land.

The war, and corresponding decrease in European immigration, provided opportunities for black farm laborers to pursue factory jobs in the North—the start of a long-term pattern known as the Great Migration.[24] During the war, white planters and southern officials criticized labor recruiters who came to the South promising African Americans better opportunities elsewhere. They considered the practice to be a threat to the nation's food supply and requested federal help to halt it. In April 1917, less than two weeks after the nation declared war against Germany but before Congress passed the Lever Act, G. W. Koiner, Virginia's commissioner of agriculture, declared the labor situation to be "perilous" and identified its shortage as a significant threat to agriculture in the state. He claimed the cost of day laborers, as well as seed and other supplies, had increased significantly. As Congress debated food control, Koiner asked the government to focus on reducing the price of doing business for farmers, especially the cost of labor, instead of doling out unnecessary advice.[25]

Secretary of Agriculture David F. Houston did not see the issue as urgent. At a Senate hearing, Houston admitted farm labor was scarcer in areas closer to industrial cities, which generally excluded much of the South, and characterized the South's labor situation as "normal, or only slightly below normal." When asked specifically about the migration of African American farmers, Houston responded that "some migration [to the Northeast and Midwest] has been reported in Alabama and Georgia." But on the whole, he considered talk of a black exodus to be "an exaggeration." White southerners, however, did not minimize the risk of African Americans migrating from southern farms to northern factories. In a letter to US senator John H. Bankhead, Alabama state senator John R. McCain considered the issue to be urgent. Northern factories, public works projects, and southern sawmills pulled African Americans from agricultural work, according to McCain, making "negro labor on the farms, in many places . . . almost a thing of the past." He asked Bankhead to take action to make sure that labor stayed on the farm lest food production suffer.[26]

Federal policy also affected how black farmers conducted their work. The Food Administration asked Alabama administrator Richard M. Hobbie to pressure black laborers to increase their work in the fields. According to this correspondence, African Americans had become accustomed to a five-day work week—with Saturdays and Sundays off. "It is estimated that a negro and mule working an additional day per week," wrote H. Alexander Smith of the federal Food Administration, "could take care of at least three additional acres during the crop season."[27] Such appeals show that white southerners did not eschew government intervention if it furthered their own racial and economic interests. In fact, white southerners likely embraced Smith's suggestion for regulations that forced black farmers to work harder. Despite a racial hierarchy that kept African Americans in the lowly occupations of cultivating, harvesting, preparing, cooking, and serving food, or perhaps because of it, white southerners generally assumed black laborers would be inefficient and disloyal unless evidence existed to the contrary. They blamed wasteful extravagance in the countryside on black consumers. "Negroes have a world of money," Nathaniel Willet wrote, "and are buying all the sugar and flour at a time they want." Willet accused African Americans in Waynesboro, Georgia, of "carrying out supplies by the wagon lots."[28] White men like Willet considered wastefulness to be a racial trait and openly worried African Americans would hinder food conservation efforts. The Food Administration actively worked with black communities to encourage production and conservation. But in keeping with the segregated nature of southern society, the agency treated black southerners as a separate population with lectures targeted directly toward black audiences and black home demonstration agents who worked solely with black farm families.[29]

For their part, African Americans identified wartime food production as a way to demonstrate their loyalty and advocate for better treatment by white southerners. Black churches held meetings to advocate patriotism; black communities issued resolutions vowing to be loyal to the American war effort; and black citizens wrote letters about their patriotic efforts. In the process of expressing their loyalty, they also engaged in a public conversation about citizenship and human rights. A loyalty resolution adopted by the A.M.E. Methodist Alliance in Birmingham emphasized the patriotism demonstrated by African

Americans in previous wars and their willingness to continue doing so "notwithstanding the disfranchisements, proscriptions and other injustices." A letter to the editor of the *Birmingham Age-Herald* from C. B. Moseley, a black pastor, claimed that most African Americans wanted to stay in the South, but they also expected "equality in the courts of justice and the right to live in peace and quietness with equal educational facilities for our children." Moseley made sure to state that African Americans did not want "social equality" and were content as servants so long as they were treated well and paid fairly. In Montgomery, Alabama, African Americans organized to plant gardens, raise chickens and pigs, and conserve food.[30] In general, black southerners balanced a genuine desire to contribute to war work with their understanding that white southerners continued to devalue their lives and the contributions of their communities.[31]

Through constant repetition and saturation of the media, especially newspapers and posters, the Food Administration promoted the values of conservation and economy and discouraged the practices of speculation and waste. To encourage conservation, the agency organized a rather complicated system of meatless and wheatless days and meals. The president's January 1918 proclamation, and the Food Administration's accompanying guidelines, declared Mondays and Wednesdays to be wheatless days. Americans were supposed to avoid wheat-based products all day and use substitute grains instead. Wilson designated Tuesday as a meatless day during which Americans consumed no meat, seeming to include any animal flesh, and Saturdays as porkless days when Americans consumed no pork. Additionally, Wilson asked each American to observe one wheatless and one meatless meal each day. These were patriotic appeals without the force of law.[32]

To encourage conservation, and to discourage speculation and waste, the Food Administration also prohibited hoarding, which constituted a practice that hard-working and conscientious farmers habitually performed. In January 1918, D. F. McClatchey, executive secretary of the Georgia Food Administration, announced Washington's new rules against the practice. The Food Administration defined hoarding as having more than a thirty-day supply of a licensed commodity, such as wheat flour. Although the Food Administration upheld antihoarding as a patriotic endeavor, unlike many of their guidelines this rule also had the force of law. Violators faced a $5,000 fine and/or a three-year prison sentence. Those who suspected upcoming shortages might have been tempted to stockpile supplies, especially of nonperishable foods, but the Food Administration forbade the practice because such accumulations could lead to waste and scarcity. Early in the war, federal officials had identified speculation and hoarding as dangers, and they continually tried to combat these practices.[33]

In addition to limiting the amount of food supplies Americans kept on hand, the Food Administration tried to limit the amount of flour Americans purchased by requiring consumers to buy an equal amount of a wheat substitute. This rule was also part of the food control regulations issued in January 1918 when the Food Administration decided the wheat situation in Europe was particularly dire and, as a consequence, Wilson expected the nation to reduce its wheat consumption by 30% from the previous year. Under the new regulation, called the "fifty-fifty plan," every flour purchase had to include 50% of an alternative grain. About forty or fifty substitute grains satisfied the rule, including corn, oats, rye, rice, barley, potato flour, and similar alternatives. The Food Administration advertised the fifty-fifty plan through a variety of media and expected merchants to understand and enforce the rule.[34]

This intricate system of regulation—including food calendars, antihoarding laws, and purchasing rules—fit well with a middle-class lifestyle. Middle-class women had the time, responsibility, and financial resources to make frequent trips to the market and to plan their families' meals carefully. They also valued thrift and economy.[35] But the regulatory structure did not correspond well with the customs or values of most southern farmers. First of all, in the ordinary course of business, farmers hoard. They store food, supplies, and crops as part of their day-to-day activities. They hold onto crops awaiting better market prices. For farmers who grew their own food for subsistence, it was common and necessary to cultivate, harvest, and preserve foodstuffs to feed their families throughout the year. For foods they did not or could not cultivate, farm families made large purchases to hold them over until they could return to town. White landowners purchased large supplies of food to distribute to tenants and sharecroppers. Hoarding was not considered immoral in the countryside; to the contrary, it was a responsible business practice that enabled farm families to persevere through winters, droughts, and other times when cultivation or marketing was not possible.

Yet, the Food Administration designated the act of stockpiling large amounts of food as unpatriotic. This caused special consternation for farmers who had purchased supplies prior to the new regulations and now found their ordinary preparation to be illegal. In Wilkes County, Georgia, local food administrator W. T. Johnson wrote to the state asking how he should apply the antihoarding laws to farmers who had stocked up for the winter. He noted that many farmers in his county had more money on hand that fall and that they had purchased large quantities of supplies including flour. Farmers like those in Wilkes County would have had more money in the fall in any case because of the seasonal nature of agriculture. In 1918, they likely had more money than usual because of higher wartime crop prices. This is likely the factual situation Johnson described. He asked whether the farmers needed to sell their excess flour. In this case, the state replied that farmers who maintained the spirit of the antihoarding laws and did not speculate in foodstuffs did not have to divest themselves of their flour stocks.[36]

Georgia's response in this case depended on a subjective interpretation of the facts and differed from the response in similar situations. In another case, a merchant wrote to the Georgia food administrator to explain the situation of customers who lived far from town. "We have farmers who live from 40 to 50 miles from Augusta that do business with us," the merchant wrote, "and they have always been in the habit of buying enough when they come to last them from the time until they come back [to town]." The merchant dealt with large and small farmers, so some of them had greater resources than others, but many traveled to town only two or three times each year. Although the Food Administration was willing to give rural farmers greater leeway on provisioning than city dwellers, the state Food Administration replied that farmers were not exempt from the antihoarding laws, writing, "Under no circumstances are you permitted to sell to any one more than a sixty days supply of any food commodities."[37] The two-month limit on provisions changed the way some farmers accessed and maintained food supplies and certainly required many to make more frequent trips into town.

In addition to saving food for their own households, many southern landowners provided for sharecropper and tenant families who lived on and worked their lands. Planters often provided for tenants from commissaries. The commissary sometimes took the form of a country store where sharecroppers and tenants purchased supplies on account. More often, the commissary was a simple distribution point—a barn perhaps—where the landowner distributed rations generally in the form of cornmeal or flour to the families who labored for him.[38] In any case, it meant that southern landowners made large purchases from wholesalers or merchants to supply the needs of multiple families. Although the

Food Administration generally allowed planters to purchase supplies for their tenants, antihoarding laws nevertheless demonstrate one way in which farming lifestyles were not taken into consideration in the process of regulation.[39]

Second, just as with antihoarding rules, rural consumption patterns did not easily incorporate the fifty-fifty plan. Most southerners used cornmeal and hominy grits as diet staples, making corn a popular substitute for wheat. Many southern farmers cultivated and ground their own corn or had it ground in local mills. Most southerners knew how to prepare cornmeal to make corn bread as a common regional alternative to wheat bread or biscuits. This reality should have made substitution an easy choice for southern farm families. The fifty-fifty plan, however, caused much frustration for farmers, rural merchants, and state and local officials. Southern farmers needed to purchase flour because they neither grew wheat nor processed the grain. But they did not understand why they should purchase another substitute when they had plenty of corn on hand. The notion that some southern farm families grew enough corn for their own use simultaneously complemented the states' goals toward self-sufficiency and frustrated federal regulations.

The Food Administration soon found out that this was a problem throughout the South. In February 1918, a group of merchants in the town of Senoia, southwest of Atlanta, wrote to the Georgia Food Administration to explain that most farmers in the area had at least five pounds of cornmeal to one pound of flour and already consumed more corn than wheat. Their spokesman, B. P. Daniel, had initially written to their congressman, William Carter Wright, to seek relief. Wright responded that Hoover's office assured him the state administrator had discretion to issue waivers in rural areas. But the merchants and farmers who criticized the new regulations received mixed messages from various official responses. Initially, the national Food Administration refused to provide a general exception to farmers who cultivated their own corn. A federal official replied to the Senoia merchants, "The flour situation is so critical that we do not feel that we are in a position here to make any general exceptions to the ruling that flour will be sold only in conjunction with an equal weight of other cereals."[40] The Food Administration was more focused on the global and national food situation than on the particular needs of individual farmers or rural merchants.

Although the United States never experienced any real food shortages during World War I, the wheat situation in January 1918 did seem dire. Shortages existed among allies in Europe, and they appealed directly to the United States for assistance. The previous fall, the French foreign minister and British food regulators contacted American officials to describe their nations' desperate wheat situations. France reported that no wheat was available and, as a result, the French people and army were on the verge of starvation. Great Britain reported a less dire situation but nevertheless requested greater wheat imports. A January 1918 telegram read, "It now lies with America to decide whether or not the Allies in Europe shall have enough bread to hold out until the United States is able to throw its force into the field." In the United States, appeals to pure patriotism after war broke out in April 1917 had failed to encourage the conservation of sufficient quantities of wheat to meet the nation's needs and export supplies to European allies. In fact, for many reasons related to production and consumption, the most recent harvest had resulted in only about half the supply of wheat that had been available the previous year.[41]

These global and national circumstances gave the government cause to release the new regulations that included the fifty-fifty plan at the start of 1918. They also encouraged the Food Administration to pursue strict enforcement to the aggravation of many productive and thrifty southern farmers. Although there was some suggestion from federal officials and the regulations themselves that state food administrators could make exceptions to the fifty-fifty plan, Georgia officials seemed initially hesitant to do so. E. D. Emigh, of Augusta, Georgia, wrote to Andrew Soule that he had a sufficient amount of corn raised at home to feed his wife and five children but needed some flour. The state replied they could not make any exceptions to the fifty-fifty plan. Executive Secretary D. F. McClatchey advised Emigh to sell his corn in the marketplace because "there is a demand for these products . . . at the present time." He could then purchase appropriate substitute grains necessary to acquire flour. Although the fifty-fifty plan had the force of law, McClatchey encouraged Emigh to comply as a statement of his loyalty to the war effort. "This is to be the real test of our patriotism and will prove what we, as American people, are willing to sacrifice in order that we may send more wheat flour to our fighters in France," he wrote. "Each pound so saved is a step towards victory."[42]

For roughly two weeks after the Food Administration released these new regulations, McClatchey gave the same advice to other Georgia farmers. He also commonly reminded farmers, and the merchants who sold to them, that if they didn't need cornmeal, there were many other substitute grains that satisfied the fifty-fifty plan. McClatchey informed B. C. Wall, a rural merchant near Augusta who did most of his business with farmers and who could no longer sell flour after implementation of the fifty-fifty plan, that there were no exceptions to the rule. "This does not mean," he wrote, "that the farmer must always buy an amount of cornmeal equivalent to each purchase of wheat flour but offers a variety of substitutes which he may buy in combination to equal the amount of wheat flour purchased."[43] There is no response from Wall to suggest that forcing farmers to purchase grains they neither needed nor wanted failed to further the goal of food economy. E. D. Emigh, however, made this point in his letter to the state when he questioned whether purchasing unneeded corn in order to acquire needed flour "would in fact mitigate against the policy of conservation, and not for it." This reaction may have involved a little stubbornness on the part of the southern farmer; nevertheless, for those who grew corn for subsistence, although not for market, the federal regulations made little sense.[44]

The paradoxical policy of purchasing unnecessary foodstuffs in the interest of food economy was not the only inconsistency southern farmers identified in the fifty-fifty plan. Another problem with a policy requiring farmers to purchase a substitute grain was that southerners in general, and southern farmers in particular, already used more corn products than they did wheat. Emigh wrote that his family used "a limited amount of wheat flour, of which we use about 1/3 as much [as they use of] home ground cornmeal and grits." In this way, Emigh resembled other southerners who consumed a diet composed largely of corn by necessity, convenience, and choice.[45] As a result, although southerners commonly knew how to prepare corn breads, hominy, and grits, they had less knowledge and skill in using other substitute grains such as oats and rye. J. L. Betto, a merchant in Woodbury, Georgia, noted that southern farmers rarely purchased grains other than corn or wheat and that they greatly preferred the taste of their home-grown cornmeal to the mass-produced meal made from western corn.[46]

There was also a problem for farmers who wanted to sell their corn, as Secretary McClatchey had suggested, to purchase flour along with equal amounts of a substitute. Although McClatchey was correct that there was a national demand for corn products, the real possibility existed that the fifty-fifty plan might put the rural gristmills where local southern farmers generally processed and sold their corn out of business. H. M. Franklin owned a small mill near Tennille, Georgia, that ground three hundred to four hundred bushels of corn per week for local farmers. Some of that corn went back to the farmers for their personal use, but Franklin sold the rest of it to local merchants. As a result of the new regulations, the merchants who purchased from Franklin told him they could no longer buy his cornmeal because of the fifty-fifty plan. The local merchants had to buy their substitute from the national wholesalers who sold flour. Whether or not it was the intention of the federal regulators who established the rule, this new law had the potential to hurt small southern gristmills that sold only corn products, and the local farmers who grew the corn, and to benefit the large manufacturers and wholesalers who sold a wide variety of products.[47]

The complaints by rural southerners over the Food Administration's strict adherence to the fifty-fifty plan encouraged the agency to create a general exception to the policy for farmers, despite its original unwillingness to do so. This exception may have been formulated at a meeting of the South Carolina Food Administration. On February 4, 1918, the county food administrators met with William Elliott, the new state food administrator, to discuss application of the fifty-fifty plan as it related to farmers who grew their own corn. They decided such farmers should be able to present a miller's certificate to a merchant to demonstrate they had sufficient quantities of cornmeal to purchase flour without a corresponding substitute. Elliott forwarded the new plan to Washington where federal officials approved it. Other southern states began using a certificate or permit system as well. To get a permit to purchase flour without buying a substitute, the farmer contacted the county food administrator and gave a statement about the type and amount of substitutes his family had on hand. The local official issued the permit, and the farmer gave the permit to the merchant, who maintained it to document compliance. The farmer could not use the same cornmeal to offset multiple purchases of flour.[48] Although the Food Administration proved flexible in this case, southern farmers and merchants drove this exception, not the agency.

Moreover, there were several problems with the permit system itself. First, it was a time-consuming process, and one county administrator complained that he could spend all his time taking statements and issuing permits.[49] Second, it was limited in scope. Only active farmers could use a flour permit (or miller's certificate in South Carolina). So farm owners who lived and worked in town but took produce from their plantation in the countryside could not make use of the permits.[50] Finally, and perhaps most importantly, it was incredibly bureaucratic, and southern farmers in 1918 were not yet entirely familiar with negotiating a large federal bureaucracy. But the new exception—the result of numerous individual complaints and negotiations on the part of farmers and rural merchants—allowed farmers to purchase flour without buying additional corn they did not need or another grain they did not know how to use.

Aside from the problems farmers had in conforming their consumption habits to federal regulations, the Food Administration ignored southern families whose health and vigor was threatened by the lack of food. After all, meatless meals meant very little to a family that could not afford to purchase meat. Studies of southern farm families in the early twentieth century confirm that many went without sufficient amounts of food. Such studies reached this conclusion based on the emerging field of home economics, which found favor with Hoover's Food Administration. Early twentieth-century home economists identified the amounts of protein, fats, carbohydrates, and other nutritional requirements a body needed to maintain health as well as the types of foods that fulfilled each specific need. Starting in 1914, the federal government funded specialists, called home demonstration agents, to teach rural women how to satisfy a family's nutritional needs. Home agents also conducted studies of the nutritional status of farm families.[51] In the decade that followed World War I, Dorothy Dickins, Mississippi's state home demonstration agent, found that, although the nutritional value of Mississippi farm diets differed depending on race, class, and geography, overall rural Mississippi diets were deficient in essential nutrients, especially iron and Vitamin C, based on nutritional standards of the day. African Americans suffered greater deficiencies, with over half the black farm families in the Mississippi Delta at least 10% below nutritional standards in protein, calcium, and iron. Dickins describes largely monotonous diets of corn meal, salt pork, and, in the case of white farmers, milk.[52] Although Dickins conducted these studies a decade after World War I, there is no reason to believe farm diets had necessarily deteriorated after the end of the war.[53]

As these home demonstration studies reveal, the demands of cotton cultivation and realities of tenant life meant that many southern rural families did not have the luxury of meal planning. According to the food studies scholar Marcie Cohen Ferris, most rural southerners—rich and poor—ate a diet similar to that Dickins found in the Delta, a diet consisting of the "three m's—meal, meat, and molasses." Meal referred to cornmeal or hominy grits; meat generally took the form of pork fat; and molasses served as a rare source of nutrition. Tenants and sharecroppers had less access to these staples and generally had poorer diets than landowning families.[54] Because flour and meat were inaccessible to poor farmers, the meal calendar publicized by the Food Administration would have held little meaning for many rural southerners. Certainly, food regulations provided little grief for most of these low-income farmers. They consumed and wasted too little food to worry about conservation.

Wilson and Hoover established their voluntary system so Americans would not have to sacrifice when it came to food. They assumed Americans would continue to get the nutritional value they needed to remain healthy and would do so using substitutions suggested by home economists—eating corn instead of wheat, beans instead of beef. As they called on Americans to do their part by following Food Administration guidelines, Wilson and Hoover continued to emphasize the strength and vigor of the American population.[55] Yet, this depiction did not necessarily represent reality in the rural South. The United States Selective Service considered a relatively large number of World War I draftees ineligible for military service because of their lack of physical fitness, which included nutritional deficiencies.[56] Southerners in particular experienced a high rate of pellagra, later identified to be the result of a niacin deficiency produced by a diet consisting predominately of corn.[57] This knowledge was not available during World War I and so food administrators had no reason to understand that substitution regulation could contribute to, and perhaps even exacerbate, the broader problem of nutritional deficiencies in the rural South. Nevertheless, the reality of want in the southern countryside demonstrates the disconnect the Food Administration had with the already marginalized population of tenant and sharecropper families, who often failed to maintain a basic level of sustenance.

Many rural southerners who had the means to concern themselves with food conservation outwardly supported the Food Administration and its patriotic objectives. Nevertheless, recurrent examples of noncompliance existed as well. The opportunity for ambivalence toward food regulation started with the pledge card campaigns. There were two such efforts in 1917. In July, the Women's Committees of the Council of National Defense conducted the first campaign. In his history of the Food Administration, William Clinton Mullendore recalls that the summer campaign failed to reach many households. In the fall, the Food Administration led the second campaign that, according to Mullendore, used more canvassers and covered a larger area. Volunteers went from house to house and asked housewives to sign the pledge. When housewives did, they joined the Food Administration, committed to follow its dictates, and received a window card to demonstrate their loyalty. Mullendore recounts that 500,000 volunteers across the nation participated in this second campaign.[58]

Despite this nationwide response, there is evidence of ambivalence among some local administrators in the South. South Carolina, in particular, found it difficult to solicit signed pledges. During the campaign, David R. Coker, the state's initial food administrator, reported only 12,000 of 350,000 households had signed the pledge. He asked the county chairmen and other local officials, "Is South Carolina to fail in this test?" In fact, many reasons contributed to the state's apparent failure, starting with administrative problems. Coker fell ill and had to resign in January, which delayed putting a state bureaucracy into place.[59] But there is also evidence that local officials did not necessarily consider the campaign to be a priority. R. T. Jaynes, of Walhalla, South Carolina, refused to canvas his rural district, writing, "I fail to see very much practical benefit to be derived from procuring the signatures to such cards." Farmers were harvesting their crops, according to Jaynes, and would preserve their harvest whether they signed a pledge to do so or not. In this way, Jaynes seemed to marginalize the housewives who were the target of this campaign and thought his time was better served with other war work.[60] Across the South, as in South Carolina, inconsistent leadership, poor roads, and isolated homesteads hampered efforts to contact rural folk, obtain signed pledges, and educate farm families about the new rules.[61]

In addition to geographical problems, many southerners simply refused to comply. In letters to the Food Administration, rural southerners called out their neighbors for disloyalty.[62] In Pierce County, Georgia, the local administrator reported that most citizens complied: "I find the public are very loyal and willing to abide by all rules." But he identified one individual who considered the regulations to be "arbitrary." Nathaniel Willet, the rather difficult county food administrator in Augusta, who would later accuse African Americans of violating the laws, at first blamed food waste on rural people in general. In a letter to the Georgia Food Administration, he accused, "Country folks hoard ten times as much as city dwellers." In some cases, merchants accused their competition of gaining an unfair advantage by violating the rules. A small grocer in Naylor, Georgia, complained that merchants in the larger town of Valdosta sold flour without any substitutes. When contacted, the Valdosta food administrator indicated he had not seen any of the new regulations.[63]

Although the occasional xenophobic hyperbole blamed "pro-German" sabo-teurs for turning farmers against food efforts in the rural South, in most cases, the Food Administration explained violations as a matter of ignorance. In his response to Willet, Executive Secretary D. F. McClatchey expressed his confi-dence in "universal" compliance as soon as everyone understood the rules and the "seriousness of the situation." Illiteracy could be high in the countryside, and it was difficult for unfamiliar laws to reach everyone. Violators often settled the matter with donations to the Red Cross rather than with criminal penalties.[64] More often than not, rural southerners resolved misunderstandings and dis-agreements with the Food Administration through personal negotiations with state and local officials, providing greater leeway to those with access.

In addition to personal negotiations, southern farmers organized with farm-ers from other regions to give voice to their common concerns. The Federal Board of Farm Organizations formed to advocate on behalf of farmers from various groups across the nation. A. C. Davis of Gravette, Arkansas, in his role as spokesman for the organization, delivered a petition to the White House out-lining their common grievances. The gist of their concerns was the failure of the federal government to include farmers in the decision-making process despite including experts in other industries. Specifically, they were concerned about the increasing scarcity of farm labor and the higher costs of seed, farm tools, and transportation. They requested appointment of a commission composed of farmers and based in the capital, to advise the president on matters involving agriculture for the duration of the war. They advocated for such a commission because they saw no consistent voice for farmers in Washington. According to Arthur S. Link, who edited Wilson's papers, it is likely that Wilson never saw this petition so it had no real effect on the president's actions.[65] Nevertheless, this type of formal organizing, although less common, gave southern farmers a voice to express their collective concerns to the Food Administration and other federal officials.

Food conservation during World War I represented a national effort. But the distinctive features of the South—a primarily rural and agricultural region with a focus on cash crops that limited its ability to feed its people—meant that pro-duction and conservation efforts worked differently in the region. Acutely aware of their lack of self-sufficiency, southerners wanted to increase food production. As a national agency, however, the Food Administration was less focused on the self-sufficiency of individual states and more attentive to national supply and global demand. As such, the federal Food Administration emphasized conservation—consuming substitutes, avoiding waste, and combating hoarding.

The regulatory structure developed to further these objectives was based on the values and consumption patterns of urban and small-town Americans as well as the growing demands of agribusiness. For southern farmers, this meant acceding to rules and regulations that often did not reflect their normal food habits or business practices. This is not to say that all southern farmers suffered during World War I. To the contrary, global demand led to higher crop prices encouraging farmers across the nation to expand acreage. Moreover, the Food Administration was not responsible for suffering that already existed in the countryside. Southern hunger was a pervasive problem in the region with or without the agency. But, during the war, rural southerners often had trouble complying with the regulatory demands of food control. Many responded with ambivalence toward the national project while others relied on personal appeals and national organizing to further their own interests. In the end, the war complicated the relationship between southerners and the federal government, providing a space in which farm families carefully negotiated legislative restrictions, regulatory demands, patriotic appeals, and their regional foodscape.

NOTES

1. William Clinton Mullendore, *History of the United States Food Administration, 1917–1919* (Stanford: Stanford University Press, 1941), 104; "President's Proclamation Calling on Citizens for Meatless, Porkless and Wheatless Periods," *New York Times,* January 27, 1918; "Hoover Decrees 'Victory Bread' and Cut Rations," *New York Times,* January 27, 1918. The phrase "food soldiers" comes from a statement by Wheeler originally published in a Chicago newspaper and repeated in Oscar B. McGlasson, "The Elimination of Premiums as a Conservation Measure," *Bulletin of the National Wholesale Grocers' Association of the United States* 3, no. 4 (February 1918): 33.

2. See, e.g., James H. Smith, "Cultivating Intelligent Consumption: The United States Food Administration and Food Control during World War I" (PhD diss., West Virginia University, 2015); Helen Veit, *Modern Food, Moral Food: Self-Control, Science, and the Rise of Modern American Eating in the Early Twentieth Century* (Chapel Hill: University of North Carolina Press, 2013); Elizabeth Cafer Du Plessis, "Meatless Days and Sleepless Nights: Food, Agriculture, and Environment in World War I America" (PhD diss., Indiana University, 2009); and Harvey Levenstein, *Revolution at the Table: The Transformation of the American Diet* (Berkeley: University of California Press, 2003).

3. Pete Daniel, *Breaking the Land: The Transformation of Cotton, Tobacco, and Rice Cultures since 1880* (Urbana: University of Illinois Press, 1986), 4; Wayne Flynt, *Poor but Proud: Alabama's Poor Whites* (Tuscaloosa: University of Alabama Press, 1989), 60; Marcie Cohen Ferris, *The Edible South: The Power of Food and the Making of an American Region* (Chapel Hill: University of North Carolina Press, 2014), 98–100. For black farm tenancy statistics, see *Historical Statistics of the United States, Colonial Times to 1970,* Part I, bicentennial ed., Series K 109–53, http://www2.census.gov/library/publications/1975/compendia/ hist_stats_colonial-1970/hist_stats_colonial-1970p1-chK.pdf.

4. Sam Bowers Hilliard, *Hog Meat and Hoecake: Food Supply in the Old South, 1840–1860* (Carbondale: Southern Illinois University Press, 1972; Athens: University of Georgia Press, 2014), 161 (citations refer to the UGA Press edition); Alan L. Olmstead and Paul W. Rhode, "The Red Queen and the Hard Reds: Productivity Growth in American Wheat, 1800–1940," *Journal of Economic History* 62, no. 4 (December 2002): 942–43.

5. Few works on food conservation during World War I focus on professional farmers. Some recent works on food conservation more generally include Rae Katherine Eighmey, *Food Will Win the War: Minnesota Crops, Cooks, and Conservation during World War I* (St. Paul: Minnesota Historical Society Press, 2010); Rose Hayden Smith, "Sowing the Seeds of Victory: National Wartime Gardening Programs in the United States during World War I" (PhD diss., University of California, Santa Barbara, 2010); Erika Janik, "Food Will Win the War: Food Conservation in World War I Wisconsin," *Wisconsin Magazine of History* 93, no. 3 (Spring 2010): 16–27; and Angela Jill Cooley, "Home, Hearth, and Hoover: The Politics of Food in Alabama, 1896–1919," *Southern Historian* 27 (2006): 38–58.

6. "Lever Food Control Act," Public Law 65–41, U.S. Statutes at Large 40 (1917): 276; Woodrow Wilson, Executive Order 2679-A (1917); Mullendore, *History of the United States Food Administration,* 56; "Food Act in Congress," *Washington Post,* May 1, 1917.

7. J. Smith, "Cultivating Intelligent Consumption," 26–27.

8. "Lever Food Control Act," 276–87; "Wilson Asks Hoover to Control All Food," *Washington Post,* May 20, 1917.

9. "Senate Quashes Ban on Grain for Liquor," *Washington Post,* May 15, 1917; "Drive by Wilson on to Pass Food Laws," *Washington Post,* May 16, 1917; "Wilson Asks Hoover to Control All Food," *Washington Post,* May 20, 1917.

10. 55 Cong. Rec. 5746–5747 (1917). See J. Smith, "Cultivating Intelligent Consumption," 24, 40–42, 47–48, for an in-depth discussion of the debate surrounding passage of the Lever Food Control Act. Smith frames the opposition as a contest between autocracy and democracy.

11. George H. Nash, *The Life of Herbert Hoover: The Engineer, 1874–1914* (New York: W. W. Norton, 1983), 4–31; George H. Nash, *The Life of Herbert Hoover: Master of Emergencies, 1917–1918* (New York: W. W. Norton, 1996), 5.

12. A list of all state food administrators can be found in Mullendore, *History of the United States Food Administration,* 359–60. Professions for the referenced food administrators were identified using the following sources: "Richard M. Hobbie, 1897," *University of Alabama Alumni News,* March 1918, 70; Ancestry.com, 1910 United States Federal Census (database on-line) (Provo, UT: Ancestry.com Operations Inc., 2004), http://search.ancestrylibrary.com/; Ancestry.com, 1920 United States

Federal Census (database on-line) (Provo, UT: Ancestry.com Operations Inc., 2004), http://search
.ancestrylibrary.com/; Nathaniel F. Mcgruder, "Robert Newton Page," NCpedia (1994), http://
ncpedia.org/biography/page-robert-newton; *Knoxville City Directory* (Knoxville: City Directory
Co., 1925), 1104, http://search.ancestrylibrary.com/. The description of August Kohn can be found
in William Elliott to Herbert Hoover, no date [ca. February 1918], Box 1413, Folder 3, South Carolina
Federal Food Administrator General Correspondence 1917–1919, RG 4, National Archives, Morrow,
Georgia (hereinafter referred to as SC Food Admin. Gen. Corr.).

13. *Farm Organizations, Before the Committee on Banking and Currency, House of Representatives,* 66th Cong. 78 (WDC: GPO, 1922) (statement of Charles A. Lyman).

14. Mullendore, *History of the United States Food Administration,* 66–73.

15. William Elliott to J. W. Hallowell, February 13, 1918, Box 1437, Folder Substitutes—50–50 Plan,
SC Food Admin. Gen. Corr. See also, e.g., A.P. Meeks to [SC Food Administrator], February 8, 1918,
Box 1414, Folder Aiken County—Aiken, SC Food Admin. Gen. Corr., referencing a news article in
which Willet says incorrectly that farmers can exchange cornmeal for wheat flour.

16. Mullendore, *History of the United States Food Administration,* 72.

17. Mary Feminear, "Report of Home Demonstration Work in Alabama 1918," *Alabama Polytechnic Institute Circular* 27 (February 1919): 5–6. For more on home demonstration work during
World War I, see Lynne Anderson Rieff, "'Rousing the People of the Land': Home Demonstration
Work in the Deep South," (PhD diss., Auburn University, 1995), 90–99.

18. Ferris, *The Edible South,* 97–98; Hilliard, *Hog Meat and Hoecake,* 66–69.

19. "Launch State-wide Campaign to Get More Food Raised," *Birmingham Age-Herald,* April 8,
1917; "Earnest Work Is Begun to Raise Big Food Crops All Over Alabama," *Birmingham Age-Herald,*
April 13, 1917; "Henderson Issues Proclamation to Farmers of State," *Birmingham Age-Herald,*
April 7, 1917; "Alabama Facing Situation More Serious Now Than during Civil War," *Birmingham
Age-Herald,* April 7, 1917; "Men, Women and Things," *Birmingham Age-Herald,* April 10, 1917.

20. Food Administrator for South Carolina [David R. Coker] to Hoover, September 28, 1917,
Box 1413, Folder 3, SC Food Admin. Gen. Corr.

21. *Production and Conservation of Food Supplies: Grain for Distilling Purposes, Parts 1–5, Before
the Comm. on Agriculture and Forestry,* 65th Cong. 485 (1917) (statement of John E. Milholland).

22. *Historical Statistics of the United States, Colonial Times to 1970* (WDC: United States Department of Commerce, 1975), 465, https://www.census.gov/history/pdf/histstats-colonial-1970
.pdf. For a state-specific study, Martin T. Olliff describes how tenancy disproportionately affected
black farmers in Alabama in "Introduction: Alabama, April 1917," in *The Great War in the Heart
of Dixie: Alabama during World War I,* ed. Martin T. Olliff (Tuscaloosa: University of Alabama
Press, 2008), 8.

23. Daniel, *Breaking the Land,* 4.

24. Isabel Wilkerson, *The Warmth of Other Suns: The Epic Story of America's Great Migration*
(New York: Vintage, 2010).

25. *Production and Conservation of Food Supplies: Grain for Distilling Purposes, Parts 1–5, Before
the Comm. on Agriculture and Forestry,* 65th Cong. 511 (1917) (G. W. Koiner to T. P. Gore, April 30,
1917).

26. *Production and Conservation of Food Supplies: Grain for Distilling Purposes, Parts 1–5, Before the Comm. on Agriculture and Forestry*, 65th Cong. 7 (1917) (statement of David F. Houston); John R. McCain to John H. Bankhead, February 22, 1918, Box 26, Folder 3, John H. Bankhead 1842–1920, LPR 49, Alabama Department of Archives and History, Montgomery, Alabama (hereafter referred to as "Bankhead Papers, ADAH").

27. H. Alexander Smith to Richard M. Hobbie, February 7, 1918, Box 16, Folder 266, Correspondence of Richard M. Hobbie, Federal Food Administrator for Alabama 1917–1919, RG 4, National Archives, Morrow, Georgia.

28. N. L. Willet to A. M. Soule, January 15, 1918, Box 1, Folder 111A-A1 W, Georgia General Correspondence Enforcement Division 1917–1919, RG 4, National Archives, Morrow, Georgia (hereafter referred to as Ga. Gen. Corr. Enforcement Div.).

29. "Earnest Work Is Begun to Raise Big Food Crops All Over Alabama," *Birmingham Age-Herald*, April 13, 1917; SC Food Administrator [William Elliott] to Herbert Hoover, no date [ca. January 1918], Box 1413, Folder 3, SC Food Admin. Gen. Corr.

30. "Negroes Pledge Loyalty in War by Resolutions," *Birmingham Age-Herald*, April 8, 1917; "North Alabama Negro Shows His Patriotic Spirit," *Birmingham Age-Herald*, April 8, 1917; "Negroes of State Will Aid in Food Campaign Started," *Birmingham Age-Herald*, April 8, 1917.

31. Wilson Fallin, Jr., argues that black Baptists in Alabama balanced their loyalty to the nation during World War I with calls for equality. See "Alabama's Black Baptist Leaders, the Progressive Era, and World War I," in Olliff, *The Great War in the Heart of Dixie*, 66–80. David Alsobrook agrees that black Alabamians generally responded patriotically to the war, although he identifies some discord among African Americans in response to white hostility and suspicion. See "A Call to Arms for African Americans during the Age of Jim Crow: Black Alabamians' Response to the U.S. Declaration of War in 1917," in Olliff, *The Great War in the Heart of Dixie*, 81–100.

32. "President's Proclamation Calling on Citizens for Meatless, Porkless and Wheatless Periods," *New York Times*, January 27, 1918; "Hoover Decrees 'Victory Bread' and Cut Rations," *New York Times*, January 27, 1918.

33. "Georgians Warned Against Hoarding," *Atlanta Constitution*, January 15, 1918; "Food Act in Congress," *Washington Post*, May 1, 1917.

34. Woodrow Wilson, "A Proclamation," January 17, 1918, in Arthur S. Link, ed., *The Papers of Woodrow Wilson*, vol. 46: *January 16–March 12, 1918* (Princeton, NJ: Princeton University Press, 1984), 19–21; "Food Rations Coming," *Washington Post*, January 26, 1918; "Hoover Decrees 'Victory Bread' and Cut Rations," *New York Times*, January 27, 1918; "Atlanta Placed on War Footing," *Atlanta Constitution*, January 28, 1918.

35. For middle-class women and food, see Angela Jill Cooley, *To Live and Dine in Dixie: The Evolution of Urban Food Practices in the Jim Crow South* (Athens: University of Georgia Press, 2015), 19–42; Elizabeth S. D. Engelhardt, *A Mess of Greens: Southern Gender and Southern Food* (Athens: University of Georgia Press, 2011); and Laura Shapiro, *Perfection Salad: Women and Cooking at the Turn of the Century* (New York: Modern Library, 2001).

36. W. T. Johnson to Andrew Soule, February 1, 1918, Box 1, Folder 111A-A1 J, Ga. Gen. Corr. Enforcement Div.; Executive Secretary [D. F. McClatchey] to W. T. Johnson, February 6, 1918, Box 1, Folder 111A-A1 J, Ga. Gen. Corr. Enforcement Div. See also Ferris, *The Edible South*, 100.

37. Lyon, Meritt & Co. to D. F. McClatchey, January 9, 1918, Box 1, Folder 111A-A1 L, Ga. Gen. Corr. Enforcement Div.; Asst. Executive Secretary to Lyon, Meritt & Co., January 11, 1918, Box 1, Folder 111A-A1 L, Ga. Gen. Corr. Enforcement Div.

38. Marcie Cohen Ferris describes the difficulty tenants and sharecroppers had in accessing food, including how a plantation commissary worked in *The Edible South,* 98–102.

39. N. L. Willet to D. F. McClatchey, January 30, 1918, Box 1, Folder 111A-A1 W, Ga. Gen. Corr. Enforcement Div.; Executive Secretary [D. F. McClatchey] to N. L. Willet, February 6, 1918, Box 1, Folder 111A-A1 W, Ga. Gen. Corr. Enforcement Div.; D. F. McClatchey to G. Fears, January 11, 1918, Box 1, Folder 111A-A1 F, Ga. Gen. Corr. Enforcement Div.

40. C. P. Daniel's Sons to Georgia Food Administrator's Office, February 18, 1918, Box 1, Folder 111A-A1 D, Ga. Gen. Corr. Enforcement Div.; W. C. Wright to B. P. Daniel, February 5, 1918, Box 1, Folder 111A-A1 D, Ga. Gen. Corr. Enforcement Div.; R. R. Williams to C. P. Daniel's Sons, February 4, 1918, Box 1, Folder 111A-A1 D, Ga. Gen. Corr. Enforcement Div. Similar letters exist throughout state food administration correspondence files and congressional papers. See, e.g., John Hollis Bankhead, Sr., to Herbert Hoover, March 22, 1918, Box 30, Folder 5, Bankhead Papers, ADAH, requesting an exemption to the fifty-fifty plan on behalf of a constituent.

41. Albert N. Merritt, *Wartime Control of Distribution of Foods: A Short History of the Distribution Division of the United States Food Administration, Its Personnel and Achievements* (New York: Macmillan, 1920), 69–72, 74–75.

42. E. D. Emigh to A. M. Soule, January 31, 1918, Box 1, Folder 111A-A1 E, Ga. Gen. Corr. Enforcement Div.; Executive Secretary [D. F. McClatchey] to E. D. Emigh, February 4, 1918, Box 1, Folder 111A-A1 E, Ga. Gen. Corr. Enforcement Div.

43. Executive Secretary [D. F. McClatchey] to B. C. Wall, January 31, 1918, Box 1, Folder 111A-A1 W, Ga. Gen. Corr. Enforcement Div.

44. E. D. Emigh to A. M. Soule, January 31, 1918, Box 1, Folder 111A-A1 E, Ga. Gen. Corr. Enforcement Div.

45. E. D. Emigh to A. M. Soule, January 31, 1918, Box 1, Folder 111A-A1 E, Ga. Gen. Corr. Enforcement Div.; Ferris, *The Edible South,* 128.

46. J. L. Betto to State Food Administrator [Andrew Soule], January 29, 1918, Box 1, Folder 111A-A1 B, Ga. Gen. Corr. Enforcement Div. In the colonial era and early republic, Americans more generally relied on corn as a staple. As national food systems developed, however, southerners continued consuming significant quantities of corn as Americans in other regions emphasized wheat and other grains. Hilliard, *Hog Meat and Hoecake,* 48–50, 150–51.

47. H. M. Franklin to A. M. Soule, February 2, 1918, Box 1, Folder 111A-A1 F, Ga. Gen. Corr. Enforcement Div.

48. William Elliott to Herbert Hoover, no date [ca. February 1918], Box 1413, Folder 3, SC Food Admin. Gen. Corr.

49. Faircloth to D. F. McClatchey, February 13, 1918, Box 1, Folder 111A-A1 F, Ga. Gen. Corr. Enforcement Div.

50. D. F. McClatchey to J. H. Ewing, February 22, 1918, Box 1, Folder 111A-A1 E, Ga. Gen. Corr. Enforcement Div.

51. Rieff, "'Rousing the People of the Land,'" 49–51.

52. Dorothy Dickins, *A Study of Food Habits of People in Two Contrasting Areas of Mississippi* (State College: Mississippi Agricultural Experiment Station, 1927), 49; Dorothy Dickins, *A Nutritional Investigation of Negro Tenants in the Yazoo Mississippi Delta* (State College: Mississippi Agricultural Experiment Station, 1928), 46.

53. Hilliard uses similar early twentieth-century nutritional studies to estimate southern diets in the antebellum South and suggests farm diets may have deteriorated after the Civil War, especially for African Americans, because of sharecropping and the legacy of slavery: *Hog Meat and Hoecake*, 62–69. Because there is no reason to suggest a significant decrease in nutrition from 1917 to 1928, these studies are helpful to understanding the quality of southern diets during World War I.

54. Ferris, *The Edible South*, 127–30.

55. Woodrow Wilson, "A Proclamation," January 17, 1918, in Link, *The Papers of Woodrow Wilson*, vol. 46 *January 16–March 12, 1918*, 19–21; "President's Proclamation Calling on Citizens for Meatless, Porkless and Wheatless Periods," *New York Times*, January 27, 1918; "Hoover Decrees 'Victory Bread' and Cut Rations," *New York Times*, January 27, 1918.

56. Susan Levine, *School Lunch Politics: The Surprising History of America's Favorite Welfare Program* (Princeton, NJ: Princeton University Press, 2008), 56; David M. Kennedy, *Over Here: The First World War and American Society* (New York: Oxford University Press, 1980), 166n59.

57. Ferris, *The Edible South*, 133–35; Flynt, *Poor but Proud*, 174–77.

58. Mullendore, *History of the United States Food Administration*, 86–87; "Pledge Card for the United States Food Administration," *Home Economists in World War I*, in Division of Rare and Manuscript Collections, Kroch Library, Cornell University, Ithaca, New York, http://exhibits.mannlib .cornell.edu/meatlesswheatless/meatless-wheatless.php?content=two_a (accessed July 28, 2017).

59. D. R. Coker to County Chairman et al., undated [ca. November 1917], Box 1413, Folder 2, SC Food Admin. Gen. Corr.; William Elliott to Herbert Hoover, no date [ca. February 1918], Box 1413, Folder 3, SC Food Admin. Gen. Corr.

60. R. T. Jaynes to A. V. Snell, September 26, 1917, Box 1412, Folder "Pledge Card Campaign," SC Food Admin. Gen. Corr.

61. Because little research exists on these challenges to food conservation in the region, more studies are warranted.

62. In *Rich Man's War, Poor Man's Fight: Race, Class, and Power in the Rural South during the First World War* (Chapel Hill: University of North Carolina Press, 2004), Jeannette Keith argues that, although the southern middle class tended to accept conscription during World War I, there was more dissent in the southern countryside. Keith asserts that World War I "exposed deep fissures in the supposedly Solid (white) South" as fellow white southerners identified those they believed to be traitors to the cause or "pro-German" and brought them to the attention of federal authorities. Food Administration records document a similar experience.

63. E. L. Darling to D. F. McClatchey, February 2, 1918, Box 1, Folder 111A-A1 D, Ga. Gen. Corr. Enforcement Div.; N. L. Willet to D. F. McClatchey, January 28, 1918, Box 1, Folder 111A-A1 W, Ga. Gen. Corr. Enforcement Div.; J. H. Fender to A. M. Soule, January 29, 1918, Box 1, Folder 111A-A1 F, Ga. Gen. Corr. Enforcement Div.; H. S. Jackson to D. F. McClatchey, January 16, 1918, Box 1, Folder 111A-A1 J, Ga. Gen. Corr. Enforcement Div.

64. "Germany's Agents Active in Alabama Says Mrs. Mathis," *Birmingham Age-Herald,* August 10, 1917; D. F. McClatchey to N. L. Willet, February 1, 1918, Box 1, Folder 111A-A1 W, Ga. Gen. Corr. Enforcement Div.; William Elliott to Herbert Hoover, no date [ca. February 1918], Box 1413, Folder 3, SC Food Admin. Gen. Corr.

65. Federal Board of Farm Organizations, "A Petition," February 8, 1918, in Link, *The Papers of Woodrow Wilson,* vol. 46: *January 16–March 12, 1918,* 279–81. Although the petition was not originally preserved with the president's papers, Link located a copy in the *Congressional Record,* 65th Cong., 2d sess., 1979–80.

5

The Call to Duty in the Old North State

Patriotism, Service, and North Carolina Women's Colleges during the Great War

KATHELENE MCCARTY SMITH AND KEITH PHELAN GORMAN

During a series of speeches given in 1919, renowned suffragist Anna Howard Shaw reminded audiences of the tremendous contributions and sacrifices made by women to sustain the American war effort and the eventual Allied victory. She eloquently reminded her audience, "During the war, women were called upon to serve and the response was universal."[1] A key proponent of home-front mobilization, Shaw had witnessed the swift response by women to rally to the cause after the United States declared war on the Central Powers in April 1917. While serving as the head of the Woman's Committee of the Council of National Defense (Woman's Committee), she found herself in a position to encourage women's war work and patriotic sacrifice in an effort to leverage permanent postwar political and social advancement.[2] But Shaw's speeches also capture a broader point about the nature of home-front mobilization in World War I: women were "called . . . to serve," and in response, their service shaped the southern home front.

Women participated in the domestic war effort of World War I for a variety of reasons. For Shaw, and others like her, the war was an opportunity to encourage positive change in the lives of women; thus, after the war, Shaw and others demanded recognition of their service and expected political and social improvements in the lives of women. Yet not all women shared such progressive sentiments. Others served out of patriotism, out of a sense of personal duty, or out of a sense of shared sacrifice with the troops in Europe, sentiments perhaps best expressed in a Presidential Proclamation issued in April 1917, in which President Wilson specifically challenged American citizens to contribute to food production, conservation efforts, and war work.[3] Wilson stated, "The men and women who devote their thought and their energy to these things will be serving the country and conducting the fight for peace and freedom just as truly and just as effectively as the men on the battlefield or in the trenches."[4]

Because women evidenced such a variety of reasons and motivations for their wartime service, and because women held a variety of expectations concerning the legacy of their sacrifice, those, like Shaw, tasked with encouraging participation in the war effort had to depend upon women leaders at the state level to define the message of the war effort and to engage their own networks of organizations, clubs, and educational institutions. North Carolina was no exception, and upon the outbreak of war, state leaders communicated messages of patriotism, sacrifice, and service to women's groups across the state, and specifically to women's colleges. In a region marked by traditional political and social roles for women, college administrators, faculty, and students at North Carolina's women's colleges found the war to be both an opportunity to challenge the status quo and an opportunity to embrace the president's call for service. They crafted their own model of home-front mobilization and in the process, many laid foundations for postwar activism directly connected to their experiences. Drawing on the existing archival records of fourteen North Carolina women's colleges, this study examines how administrators, faculty, and students took up the patriotic call and subsequently fought for the political legacy of their wartime service.[5]

With the declaration of war, Wilson's administration began to mobilize the home front, as well as its military forces, to fight an overseas war in Europe. Faced with a small federal bureaucracy and a sudden labor shortage resulting from enlistment and rapid expansion of industry, Wilson sought the assistance of nongovernment organizations through the Council of National Defense.[6] To establish credibility and to gain access to these organizations, the government appointed influential national leaders to the council, which drew upon civic associations and social networks to rally popular sentiment, consolidate war work, and support government policies.[7] Toward that end, the council turned to women's groups that commanded effective prewar networks of volunteerism. As the country began to mobilize, these national women's organizations pressured the government to define their roles and responsibilities in supporting the war.[8]

Responding to this political pressure, on April 21, 1917, the Wilson administration created the Woman's Committee of the Council of National Defense. This central body recruited "women of national prominence" to assist in "the prosecution of the war" and coordinate the women's preparedness movement.[9] Secretary of War Newton D. Baker, chair of the Council of National Defense, declared that the committee would function as an "advisory" group to the council.[10] Yet, with the committee's vision established and Anna Howard Shaw appointed as its chair, Baker observed that "the committee went straight ahead, perhaps never reading a second time the resolution of the Council of National Defense by which it was created."[11] In a political and bureaucratic gambit to gain more influence, Shaw actively expanded Newton's charge and interpreted the role of the committee to be that of a "central clearinghouse" for women's war work beyond the national and state level. Employing this expanded mission, the Woman's Committee devised a detailed infrastructure that clarified the reporting lines between the group's national leaders, state divisions, and county and local units.

In a 1918 pamphlet illustrating this organizational model, the committee noted that there were 11,276 local social and civic groups across the nation, and they hoped that shortly, "every woman in the United States and its Insular Possessions" would be included in this wartime network.[12] This report identified the subcommittees within the Woman's Committee, such as Registration, Food Production and Home Economics, Women in Industry, Child Welfare, Liberty Loan, Home and Foreign Relief, and News. Also included were the names of the chair of each state committee. By instituting this organizational system at the state and local levels, Shaw met the council's original mission of streamlining communication between the federal government, state agencies, and citizen groups. More importantly, she, at least, took this opportunity to tap into state women's networks and leverage potential war work for the future advancement of women.[13]

In North Carolina, there was a coordinated effort to ensure cooperation between the Woman's Committee and the state's Council of Defense. North Carolina governor Thomas Walter Bickett appointed Laura Holmes Reilley as the sole female representative on the North Carolina Council of Defense.[14] For Bickett, there was both a practical and a strategic reason for his choice. Reilley was a well-known figure within the political and social circles of Raleigh and Charlotte. She was also a prominent member of many women's organizations, including the League of Women Voters, the Charlotte Woman's Club, the Daughters of the American Revolution, and the Equal Suffrage League. Reilley's reputation as a highly effective organizer and her involvement with these women's groups afforded her access to networks of very influential and well-connected North Carolina women.[15] Shortly after her appointment to the state Council of Defense, Reilley was selected as chair of the state's Woman's Committee and the two groups worked closely together, even holding a joint meeting in early October 1917.[16]

In addition to gaining access to existing social and civic organizations, the North Carolina Woman's Committee recruited successful professional women in fields such as education and public health. Indeed, two important members of the committee were connected with women's education. Harriet Elliott, a professor of political science at the State Normal and Industrial College (State Normal), was chosen as the chair of Educational Propaganda, and Lucy Robertson, president emerita of Greensboro College for Women (Greensboro College), was selected as chair of Child Welfare.[17] These two women had the credentials and experience to be effective state representatives and the connections to recruit students and faculty from North Carolina's established network of women's colleges. By 1917, North Carolina boasted thirteen private, religiously affiliated women's colleges, as well as State Normal, which opened in 1892 as the only public women's college in the state.[18] Women's colleges were training grounds for leadership and volunteerism, producing educated and skilled students who would soon be called to serve their country.[19]

These well-trained and organized young women and the professors who taught them were eager participants in mobilization.[20] They made significant contributions to almost every aspect of war work, including fund raising, food conservation, and knitting socks and sweaters for the soldiers. In spring 1918, a report generated by the Division of Women's War Work of the Committee on Public Information titled "War Work of Women in Colleges" gave an account of student war activities.[21] The Woman's Committee contacted college deans and presidents from across the country and sent a detailed questionnaire about their school's participation during the first ten months of the war.[22] The colleges not only reported significant results achieved by their students but also expressed the young women's desire to do more. The Woman's Committee immediately began to recruit students to enter certain areas of study, such as medicine, poultry raising, bee culture, and the sciences.[23] Additionally, the committee asked colleges to provide practical coursework that would help women fill positions vacated by men.[24]

Many organizations considered female students to be ideal for government jobs that required specialized training and attention to detail. College women with an academic background were strongly encouraged to continue their education and move into professions such as stenographers, librarians, lawyers, agriculturalists, doctors, chemists, and nurses. Groups such as the Intercollegiate Intelligence Bureau recruited women for trained positions that were in great demand by the government.[25] In June 1918, the Women's Collegiate Section of the US Employment Service announced a central registration system for students and graduates who had obtained particular skills, as well as work experience, to fill certain positions in case of emergency.[26] For specific training, such as nursing, college-educated young women were promised special consideration for wartime jobs and a role in postwar society. Julia Newton Brooks, head of the Women's Collegiate Section of the US Employment Service, specifically stated that "after the war a nurse will hold a strategic position when it comes to basic social reorganization."[27]

In attempting to fill the many hospital positions vacated by women serving overseas, special emphasis was given to recruiting female medical personnel. Just as men were contributing to the war effort in Europe, the government called for twenty-five thousand women to serve their country by becoming student nurses. Shaw asked the nation's women to "assume their full share of responsibility in winning the world war" and directed them to immediately enter hospital training schools.[28] One of the first assignments of the North Carolina Woman's Committee was to enroll 460 students in nurses' training schools and to encourage others to take courses in related fields, such as biology, chemistry, and medicine. This targeted recruitment of young students affected women's colleges across the nation.

Student recruitment was aided by the Wilson administration's massive propaganda campaign, which generated popular support for the war and created a national narrative of patriotic duty. On many government posters and pamphlets, there was a visual message suggesting that women must play a public role in maintaining morale, producing and conserving food, and contributing to a depleted workforce. In such propaganda, Columbia, the traditional female personification of the United States, was portrayed as either an idealized woman dressed in a classical gown or that of a contemporary American girl. These images appeared throughout the nation, beckoning women to plant war gardens, buy liberty bonds, and preserve food to help Uncle Sam win the fight.

Not surprisingly, the powerful figure of Columbia was a popular choice on the campuses of North Carolina women's colleges. For example, in a Meredith

College yearbook, a female student portraying Columbia was crowned with a crested headband and draped in an American flag, tailored to resemble a flowing classical gown.[29] In a liberty-loan-bond parade in downtown Greensboro, North Carolina, the Greensboro College student body marched wearing "Columbia Caps."[30] At State Normal, students raised money by presenting the pageant "To Arms for Liberty," which featured a classically dressed Columbia. The production also included girls in the "traditional" dress of America's chief allies: Britain, France, Russia, and Japan. In addition to these symbolic national figures, the stage was filled with students serving as representations of American farmers, Red Cross workers, and liberty bond officials. The production ended with Columbia presenting the ultimate gift to Europe—the lives of her young men.[31]

In the case of Greensboro College, the members of the Class of 1918 titled their senior play "Reveille." In this performance, a student dressed as Columbia walks through a peaceful forest before the outbreak of war. Confronted and imprisoned by treacherous "Germany," she finally understands the true nature of her foe and joins the war effort. This elaborate production provided the audience with a scripted history of how America entered the war, supported by students representing a Red Cross worker, a "Farmerette," and members of the Allied Powers.[32] However, to underline the role of America as a victim, the young women also portrayed passengers of the ill-fated ocean liner *Lusitania*.[33] Patriotic sentiments were also evident at Meredith College where young women drew on military themes when organizing their "Class Day" celebration, including a bugler introducing a flag drill, the singing of patriotic songs, and a program featuring a "campfire tableau," during which students reminisced about their college experiences during the war.[34]

Fund raising also became a large part of North Carolina women's college's wartime contribution. Students raised significant funds by sponsoring concerts, holding patriotic events, and donating their personal money to purchase War Savings Stamps and liberty bonds. War bond rallies were occasions for excitement and patriotism. For example, six hundred State Normal students participated in a Third liberty-loan-bond parade on April 12, 1918, that began in downtown Greensboro and ended on the school's athletic fields. The featured draw of the parade was the beloved British actor Charlie Chaplin, who walked the entire route, urging the crowd to buy bonds.[35]

Many organizations raised money for the war effort, and several specifically canvassed college students. The YWCA remained active on campuses by raising money for the Students' Friendship War Fund and encouraging membership in the Patriotic League, which promoted the purchase of liberty-loan bonds. Meredith College students led the campaign among North Carolina Women's Colleges in collecting funds for the United War Work Campaign.[36] Additionally, college alumnae were seen as a source of wartime giving. At Greensboro College, the school instituted a "Selective Draft" as an alumnae fund raiser.[37] Assuming a military organizational structure, the college classified donors by separate military ranks depending on the size of their contribution.

Colleges often invited speakers to inform their students of current events and encourage their patriotic participation in war work. Stories of firsthand wartime experiences deeply moved the impressionable and relatively isolated young students. State Normal hosted British officer David Fallon, who regaled the young students with stories of his exploits in Gallipoli. He ended his presentation by drawing the dramatic comparison of the German kaiser to the Antichrist. His audience responded by enthusiastically singing both "My Country, 'Tis of Thee" and to their guest's delight, a verse of "God Save the King."[38] St. Mary's College's French professor, a Parisian who had been in France before America entered the war, told stories of "cruel parting scenes" at train stations, food shortages, and her traumatic fourteen-hour trip from Paris to Le Havre.[39] Students were affected by her narrative, and everyone eagerly learned the French national anthem, "La Marseillaise."[40] As President Wilson's daughter, Eleanor, was an alumna of St. Mary's College, patriotic sentiments ran particularly high. The students sent their pledges of loyalty and sympathy directly to the president through "Nell," and he sent the St. Mary's College students his deep appreciation in return.[41]

Heeding Columbia's call and showing their earnest commitment to the cause, some students signed school pledges, vowing to cooperate with campus mobilization.[42] Students at Greensboro College, Meredith College, and St. Mary's College wrote patriotic essays and poems for their respective yearbooks. At St. Mary's College, the 1918 yearbook was dedicated to two students who were working as Red Cross workers in France, as well as to all of the students who were supporting the war at home and abroad. The yearbook also included the words and lyrics to St. Mary's College's own patriotic song, "Hail to Our Boys in France," as well as lists of wartime activities. To motivate classmates to give, students assigned clever names to their campus fund-raising groups, such as "Kaiser Killers," "Hun Hunters," and "Lick 'Em."[43] At Salem College and Meredith College, students chose to sew service flags for their schools. Salem College's flag, currently housed in the institution's archive, included eighty-two stars representing fathers, brothers, and sweethearts who were serving in the military.[44]

Almost every campus was involved in Red Cross work; these efforts included knitting socks and blankets and creating surgical dressings for the troops. State Normal and Meredith College formed military "regiments," which drilled regularly on campus and later marched in their town parades.[45] These student "regiments" demonstrated patriotic support and provided physical exercise.[46] Students also created campus clubs that focused on war work. For example, Greensboro College established the "War Knitters" club and the "Liberty Bond Holders" club.[47]

During this period, a sense of wartime appropriateness settled over the campuses, which emphasized moderation and personal sacrifice. Many students gave up new dresses, movies, shopping, and sweets.[48] At State Normal, ten students elected to remain over winter break and contribute their travel money toward the war effort.[49] On several campuses, young women voted to forgo turkey on Thanksgiving. Meredith College students sacrificed personal items, sewed and mended dresses, and more than two hundred girls chose to do their own laundry.[50] Several of the colleges decided not to issue yearbooks and other campus publications during the war years, opting instead to create homemade versions or to eliminate them rather than spend the money on printing. The money saved was directed toward the war effort. In a particularly interesting alternative, Salem College held "*Ivy* Nights," during which students would read aloud all articles and even advertisements in lieu of publishing the student magazine, *The Ivy.*[51]

Responding to campus labor shortages, volunteer activities also included maintaining campus college facilities and grounds. At Meredith College, students volunteered to sweep residence halls and classrooms.[52] St. Mary's College created war gardens and formed a "clean-up" group to help with the grounds. Although other North Carolina women's colleges tended war gardens, State Normal's "Farmerettes" actually worked the campus farm, producing hundreds of bushels of corn and wheat as well as beans and tomatoes for school use.[53] Student "Carpenterettes" on the State Normal campus built a large YWCA hut on campus with only partial assistance from a local contractor. All the women's colleges participated in food conservation programs that stressed meatless and wheatless days.

Most food preservation and conservation efforts fell under the umbrella of the North Carolina College Volunteer Workers and Women's Land Army, headed by the formidable Minnie Lou Jamison, extension director at State Normal. In May 1918, Jamison become secretary of the North Carolina College Volunteer Workers, through the Collegiate Section of the US Food Administration. She had extensive experience directing food conservation programs throughout the state and had previously been the head of State Normal's Domestic Science Department. Her pioneering methods of teaching and interest in community outreach led to an appointment as a home demonstration agent with the North Carolina Department of Agriculture. This position grew out of the Smith-Lever Act and the National Cooperative Extension Service, which appointed agents to give women living in rural parts of the country practical instruction regarding home economics, agriculture, public policy, and other related topics. Jamison traveled throughout the state teaching women how to incorporate healthy diets and meal efficiency in their homes. Determined to educate North Carolina's women regarding food conservation and preservation and to increase civilian morale, Jamison rallied hundreds of young women to volunteer on college campuses and throughout the state.

To help organize the students' efforts and to conduct the most effective outreach, Jamison contacted D. H. Hill, chairman of the North Carolina Council of Defense and a member of the Executive Committee of the North Carolina Division of the US Food Administration. Her July 1918 memorandum to Hill recommended an ambitious plan for students to engage in volunteer efforts in their communities.[54] Naturally, Jamison's first concern was food conservation, a top priority in mobilizing the nation. She encouraged students to observe wheatless and meatless days on their campuses, pointing to national slogans such as "Food Will Win the War" and "'Hold the Bread Line at Home' for Our Fighting Men in France."[55]

Jamison's memorandum recommended that students create a community center at every county school to hold patriotic daytime meetings and evening entertainments. She suggested that the daytime agenda should include demonstrations of home conservation techniques and practical presentations regarding canning, drying fruits and vegetables, and jelly making. She envisioned evening activities that would incorporate speeches on crops and war measures, children reciting patriotic poems, and the singing of popular war songs such as "Over There" and "Pack up Your Troubles in Your Old Kit Bag."[56] The memorandum also proposed that the students approach local movie theaters and suggest that they show war films. Additionally, Jamison recommended that religious leaders give patriotic sermons and sing hymns advocating a "righteous victory." She even suggested that children learn lessons from the Old Testament, focusing on war-related stories and God's presence in a virtuous and moral cause.[57]

It is unclear whether Jamison actually expected all of the tasks to be accomplished by the students who participated in these efforts. In a report that Jamison sent to D. H. Hill, she laments that although she had registered three hundred volunteers, she could have recruited up to a thousand if she had the time to contact all of the state's colleges. Nevertheless, the results were impressive.[58] After Jamison took charge of the state's college volunteers in May 1918, she noted that hundreds of students were helping in their communities. In her final account to D. H. Hill, Jamison reported that students participated in conserving meat, wheat, and sugar; farming and gardening; drying and canning fruits and vegetables; picking cotton; dispensing practical recipes and leaflets; and demonstrating food preparation and conservation. By the end of the war, the US Food Administration informed Jamison that the work of the North Carolina volunteer units had surpassed any other state in the Union.[59]

The most prominently mentioned college in Jamison's report was, not surprisingly, State Normal. As resident director of the college's extension program, she may have considered the school an example of what other state colleges could accomplish. The consensus was that State Normal was certainly doing "their bit." This is evidenced by an address delivered by Archibald Henderson to the North Carolina Literary and Historical Association in November 1920, in which he specifically acknowledged State Normal as "the recognized leader among North Carolina colleges in organizing and stimulating women's war work."[60] State Normal's mission of service and its large student population certainly contributed to their reputation as a top mobilizing force, as did the school's strong organizational structure, enterprising and patriotic students, supportive and well-connected faculty, and college president Julius Foust's understanding of the value of self-promotion.

Whether his actions stemmed from patriotism or pragmatism, Foust propelled the college into the spotlight by staging a one-man writing campaign to the governor, state legislators, and federal officials touting State Normal as the premier North Carolina women's institution for war work. His efforts at promotion may have been, at least in part, an attempt to strengthen his case for legislative support to complete an extensive postwar campus building campaign. Recognizing the power of visual images, he documented the impressive student mobilization with staged photographs of students knitting, canning food, tending the grounds, reaping wheat on the campus farm, and making surgical dressings on Thanksgiving Day. These photographs served as evidence of the students' patriotism and the college's achievement of wartime goals.

One of President Foust's first large mobilization efforts occurred in conjunction with the US Food Administration's push for conservation on all college campuses. As director of the Food Administration, Herbert Hoover made a direct appeal to the nation's women for support, specifically targeting students. Hoover even sent his agency's publication, *Food and the War*, to the "Women of the Universities and Colleges," urging them to pursue food-related studies and train themselves for real leadership.[61] *Food and the War* was to be used as a textbook, instructing students about proper diet and nutrition. Focusing on feeding the Allied Armies and the civilians of Europe, state representatives of the Food Administration reached out to college presidents requesting that faculty prioritize campus conservation initiatives and teaching opportunities. Foust heeded Hoover's call and pursued a vigorous program of food preservation and education at State Normal. His efforts at promoting the national program included erecting a large sign on campus, for which he was commended personally by Hoover.[62]

President Foust made it his personal mission to contact current students, as well as over seven thousand alumnae, encouraging them to sign food pledge cards and to distribute them to their friends and neighbors. He drafted a strongly worded memorandum to alumnae, calling upon the "womanhood of this country" to help make the world "safe for democracy" and to avoid being slackers by "spreading the gospel of food conservation."[63] Alumnae responded from all over the country, acknowledging his efforts and promising their support. Foust promptly reported these results to Herbert Hoover.

Looking to expand State Normal's sphere of influence across North Carolina, Foust asked women to consider the college as "their Institution," promoting food demonstrations, community aid, and war-related lectures from the faculty of the Department of History.[64] Additionally, State Normal offered the study course "Women and the War" to various women's groups. This course focused on American and European women's wartime activities and speculated on the status of women in a postwar society. In response to the request of the US Civil

Service Commission for stenographers and typists, Foust scheduled stenography and typing courses at State Normal in the spring and summer of 1918 and promoted them through the superintendents and principals of public high schools throughout the state.

Even before the Armistice, there was a sense of historical importance attached to the state's home-front mobilization. North Carolina women's colleges were extremely proud of their achievements and several institutions began gathering information from the faculty, students, and alumnae who contributed to the war effort. Salem College noted the wartime contributions of former students in its *Alumnae Record,* and other colleges gave final tallies in their campus publications of money raised, bandages rolled, and socks knitted.[65] Beyond the individual efforts of several colleges to save an account of their wartime accomplishments, state agencies also made plans to retain documents and artifacts relating to the war.

As early as May 16, 1917, Robert Digges Wimberly Connor, secretary of the North Carolina Historical Commission, drafted a memorandum requesting an account of all activities related to the war effort be sent to his agency for the use by future historians.[66] Citing the lack of similar information from the Civil War, he specifically requested materials such as photographs, newspaper clippings, propaganda, and public service documents. Connor subsequently mailed a personal letter to President Foust at State Normal, dated July 9, 1917, requesting all "materials bearing on the war."[67] Specifically, he asked for circulars and reports noting activities undertaken by faculty, students, and alumnae in connection to home-front mobilization.

State Normal was also intent upon preserving material relating to North Carolina's mobilization. It is not known whether this was an attempt to ensure that the narrative of women's war work be recorded for posterity, to bank political capital, or to position State Normal as a repository for these important historical documents. Nevertheless, Walter Clinton Jackson, head of the State Normal's Department of History, began to collect information detailing North Carolina's women's war work. In 1918, Jackson circulated a pamphlet titled "Women and the War in North Carolina: Suggestions for the Collection of Historical Material," designating information that should be assembled and permanently kept at the college, "so when the historian of the future comes to tell the story of this great epoch . . . he will not lack for ample and correct records."[68] Drawing on material gathered from alumnae across the state, the college issued two publications.

The first, "The State Normal and Industrial College and the War," detailed the college's wartime activities, including its work with the Red Cross, the YWCA, and food conservation, as well as war-related lectures presented on campus.[69] It gave specific instances of sacrifice and service, listing students' names at every opportunity. Not surprisingly, this document included a long introduction by President Foust, who praised the State Normal students' virtuous patriotism, even above the tangible product of their wartime activism. Believing in the high idealism of the Great War, he felt that the true responsibility of war work should be shouldered by students and faculty rather than by "the great mass of the people who have not enjoyed the advantages of [a] college education."[70]

The second State Normal publication, "Women and the War in North Carolina," was written by students Mabel Tate and Naomi Neal of the Class of 1918 and reported on the work accomplished by the state's women from April 1917 until April 1918.[71] The students' mission was to collect material from women throughout the state, synthesize it into a concise document, and encourage further war work in the following months. Although admittedly incomplete, the pamphlet reported on fund raising, knitting and sewing, food production, and medical and nursing activities. The publication specifically mentioned the efforts of several educational institutions that had forwarded information, such as Greensboro College, Salem College, and Guilford College.[72] State Normal was represented as well, focusing on the work of the students and faculty. In addition to such details, the authors nestled in the report the mention of what would become one of the most significant legacies of the war—suffrage. The report stated that 576 State Normal students signed a petition asking their two North Carolina senators to vote in favor of women's suffrage. The fact that this petition is mentioned so prominently in a report on women's war work signifies that the students believed the two issues were connected.

Suffrage had been discussed among the women of the state long before the beginning of the Great War. The North Carolina Equal Suffrage Association was founded in 1894, but it was not until 1913, with the founding of the North Carolina Equal Suffrage League, that the women's movement began to gain momentum in the state. As the private women's colleges in North Carolina were all associated with specific religious denominations, it is likely that suffrage was not always overtly popular with many administers, trustees, faculty, or parents.[73]

Historically, southern women had not readily embraced movements such as suffrage and temperance, since these causes were considered somewhat radical and unfeminine.[74] According to historian George Rable, southern women in the late nineteenth century remained suspicious of national reform movements and saw no place for public political discourse.[75] For a number of other historians, Reconstruction and the establishment of Jim Crow had a profound impact on the slow adoption of the suffrage movement among educated white southern women and men. Within more recent studies, historians such as Elna Green argue that the explanation for strong resistance to suffrage must be placed within a broader framework of class, race, educational attainment, and economic advancement.[76] With few remaining records to confirm the public or private platforms of these women's colleges regarding suffrage, it is impossible to know if students were encouraged or discouraged by their institutions to consider their active citizenship and the impending vote.

However, college publications bear out the fact that suffrage was on the mind of some young North Carolina women. In one case, a Greensboro College yearbook captured a student's variety of interests with drawings of a piano, a young man, books, and a "Votes for Women" banner.[77] In a St. Mary's College yearbook, a student stirs a pot labeled "Suffrage."[78] The Peace Institute's senior class prophesied that students Mary Reed Buchanan and Lenoir Mercer would both be instrumental in winning the vote for women, and "Suffrage" was the nickname of choice for a Chowan College student.[79]

The young women kept abreast of women's issues through local and campus speakers and their professors. For example, Harriet Elliott, a political science professor at State Normal, was involved in the suffrage movement and encouraged activism among her students. Elliott resented being grouped "among idiots and criminals [who] were classified as politically incompetent" to vote.[80] She took every opportunity to educate her students about suffrage, the politics of the day, and the responsibility of citizenship. Part of this education included scheduling important and influential speakers to visit the campus. In 1917, Elliott invited Helen Gutherie Miller, vice president of the National American Womans Suffrage Association, to address the State Normal students. Elliott's personal friendship with Anna Howard Shaw facilitated the latter's three visits to State Normal to speak about topics relating to women's rights. Another influential suffragist, Representative Jeannette Rankin, the first woman elected to the United States Congress and a prominent pacifist, visited Salem College and

State Normal.[81] Whether it was Elliott, other independently minded faculty, or the invited speakers who influenced the young women, the students at State Normal had a strong interest in the suffrage movement.

The first significant suffrage event at State Normal took place in 1915 when 250 students participated in a march through campus. Some women played drums and cornets, while others created homemade kazoos with combs and tissue. The rally ended with students giving speeches on women's rights.[82] During the 1915 commencement exercises, the young women showed their growing frustration with the lack of government support of suffrage when they refused to applaud the speaker, Governor Locke Craig, because he spoke against women's rights. Only after he agreed to support the vote for women, did Craig receive a positive response.[83] This type of protest continued against politicians who spoke negatively about suffrage. An alumna from the Class of 1915 remembered an occasion when a legislator who suggested that women did not really want the vote was burned in effigy by students in the campus park.[84] The same year, State Normal students established a suffrage group on campus, arguably the first of its kind in the South.[85]

In 1918, these demonstrations culminated in 576 of the 650 State Normal students signing a petition supporting suffrage, which was sent to both North Carolina senators. Coming from a women's college, this public act generated a great deal of attention, prompting one local paper to comment, "The action of these young women have had much to do with bringing the North Carolina State Normal [and Industrial] College into prominence as representatively progressive and reflecting twentieth century ideals and revised standards."[86] Several months later, Foust wrote to Senator Lee Overman supporting the vote for women, reflecting his own sentiments, as well as those of most of the faculty.[87]

In the days leading up to the Armistice, there was a sense among students on some North Carolina women's college campuses that suffrage was imminent and that the significant service and patriotic citizenship shown by the students during the war could result in the right to vote.[88] Indeed, the president of the North Carolina Equal Suffrage League, Otelia Carrington Cunningham, declared in 1918, "To my mind every stroke given for war work by North Carolina women strengthened our cause in the State just that much."[89] Closer to campus, Harriet Elliott gave an address to State Normal students in June 1918, titled "Women and War," during which she stated that "the demands that have been made upon [women] in the warring nations [included] filling men's places with equal ability." Elliott went on to assure the young women that the "Anthony suffrage amendment" would soon be passed.[90]

In the early morning hours of November 11, 1918, America first learned of the Armistice between the Allied nations and Germany. Students at women's colleges across North Carolina woke up to church bells, whistles, horns, and sirens. When they realized that the war had ended, the young women held spontaneous celebrations. At Queens College, soldiers from Camp Greene arrived in open-backed army trucks to drive the students around town celebrating the Allied victory.[91] St. Mary's College students quickly dressed and danced until breakfast, and then joined the boys from the neighboring State College in an impromptu off-campus parade, an infraction that caused the young women to suffer certain restrictions and to have their grades lowered.[92] Meredith College's students were not allowed to join the downtown parade due to an influenza quarantine, which affected many colleges across the state. Instead, they celebrated by marching around the campus. Fortunately for the State Normal students, President Foust allowed them to break quarantine to join in the victory celebrations. After building a bonfire on the athletic fields and singing "The Star Spangled Banner," "Keep the Homefires Burning," and "The Battle Hymn of the Republic," they joined the citizens of Greensboro for a downtown parade.[93] Local papers described the event as the "Greatest Story since Bethlehem."[94]

Salem College was likewise engaged in a celebration. On hearing of the Armistice, the students cheered, sang, and beat improvised drums. Later that morning, the young women marched around Salem Square, following President Howard Rondthaler, who held the service flag. The procession expanded to include automobiles with a waving "Columbia"; students representing a Red Cross nurse, soldiers, and sailors; and a coffin inscribed "The Remains of Kaiser Bill."[95]

As the nation celebrated, the US government shifted its priorities from winning the war to winning the peace. Moving from the pressing need of mobilizing the home front, groups like the Council of National Defense looked to the challenges of postwar America as they dismantled the wartime organizational apparatus, even before hostilities officially came to an end. Members of the Woman's Committee were surprised to learn that they were not part of the discussions regarding reconstruction. The editors of the Woman's Committee's newsletter suddenly learned that the October issue would be their last.[96] The Field Division of the Council of National Defense replaced the State Councils Section and most of the responsibilities of the Woman's Committee. Such actions demonstrate that even in the transition to peacetime, the government held to an underlying assumption that women's wartime advancement was provisional and that it was now time for them to return to their prewar lives.

In North Carolina, Laura Holmes Reilley, chair of the North Carolina Woman's Committee, prepared her organization to play an active and visible role in reconstruction. Yet Governor Bickett informed Reilley that the state legislature was "indisposed to make any appropriations" to support her committee.[97] The governor formally discharged Reilley and disbanded the North Carolina Council of Defense in February 1919. In March, the North Carolina General Assembly replaced the state's Council of National Defense and established the State Reconstruction Commission. Twenty-five men were appointed to serve on the commission that examined the effects of the war on the state's population, labor, resources, and economy. Women were not offered representation on the commission.[98]

On North Carolina women's college campuses, war-related clubs returned to their prewar missions and activities. By 1919, most of the yearbooks and campus publications did not mention the recent war. Yet those students seeking political advancement in the wake of wartime service persisted, and some campuses were eager to resume the discussion of the vote for women. In fact, such efforts suggest that for some young women, wartime service was not a temporary duty or sacrifice, but an important step in a larger process of reconsidering political and social inequalities. Only months after the Armistice, women's expectations of greater postwar political involvement met a series of obstacles. Denied a significant role in reconstruction and unsure of their social and economic standing in the years following the end of the war, many women began to question their legacy of service.

In the spring of 1919, the senior class of the North Carolina College for Women (formerly State Normal) requested Anna Howard Shaw as their commencement speaker. These students witnessed the European conflict and American intervention throughout their college tenure as the "wartime class," and they were anxious to hear Shaw's vision of the postwar political landscape. As a key proponent of home-front mobilization and the head of the Woman's

Committee of the Council of National Defense, Shaw had found herself in a position to encourage women's patriotic service and sacrifice in an effort to leverage permanent postwar political and social advancement.[99] In retrospect, Shaw considered her involvement in the national war effort to be the "greatest opportunity to work for suffrage" that had ever been open to her.[100] Following the Armistice, Shaw and other suffragists believed that war work represented proof of women's value to the nation; therefore, it should result in full citizenship. Interrupting her national tour to promote the League of Nations, an ailing Shaw traveled to Greensboro from Washington, DC, to speak at the college's 1919 graduation ceremony.[101] In her commencement address, she recognized the impact of women's home-front contributions, declaring "I believe that the world is fast realizing that there is something in women. For years men have loved us, fought for us, bled for us, and died for us; but they did not respect us. Through our choice of the bigger life, we have led them to respect us."[102]

The Wilson administration also acknowledged the importance of women's response to the national "war emergency."[103] Reflecting on the recent conflict, the chairman of the Council of National Defense, Newton D. Baker, called women's transition into war work "pioneering." Additionally, he recognized the Woman's Committee's success at tapping into far-reaching social networks to effectively mount a mobilization campaign, not equaled in the history of the nation.[104] Baker's comments implied that the committee's efforts would lead to greater political gains for women in postwar America.

Many of the students and faculty at North Carolina women's colleges responded to the call for home-front mobilization by embracing food conservation, fund raising for the liberty loan campaigns, participating in Red Cross work, and training for war service in America and Europe, and many anticipated political gains as part of their patriotic legacy. With the failure of North Carolina to ratify the suffrage bill in August 1920, women's hopes for access to political power were thwarted and their service and sacrifice minimized. Although the adoption of the Nineteenth Amendment would ultimately overturn state opposition and grant the vote to women, they still faced significant barriers to political equality. The graduates of the Class of 1919, who had successfully mobilized their North Carolina women's colleges, continued to struggle in the following decades to define and leverage the meaning and memory of their wartime service and campus activism.

NOTES

1. Anna Howard Shaw, *What the War Meant to Women* (New York: League to Enforce Peace, 1920).

2. The Woman's Committee was formed in April 1917 to support the efforts of the Council of National Defense. John P. Finnegan, *Against the Specter of a Dragon: The Campaign for American Military Preparedness, 1914–1917* (Westport, CT: Greenwood Press, 1974).

3. President Wilson's Presidential Proclamation was issued on April 15, 1917. This statement was made shortly after the formal declaration of war and was widely communicated in the American press.

4. Woodrow Wilson, "Do Your Bit for America: A Proclamation by President Wilson to the American People," *National Geographic Magazine*, 31, no. 4 (April 1917): 287–93.

5. In 1917, there were fourteen women's colleges in the state of North Carolina; only two currently remain as women's colleges. Several of these schools closed, and their records appear to be lost. Of the institutions that survive in some form, the records of their wartime experiences are limited or incomplete. There were all-male or coeducational North Carolina colleges that participated in war work, but they are outside the scope of this study.

6. The Council of National Defense was an Executive Branch committee formed in August 1916. Its charge was to conduct an inventory of the nation's resources.

7. It should be noted that as mobilization expanded and accelerated, the Wilson administration created more formal federal government agencies to support the war. These agencies would quickly supplant the Council of National Defense in terms of staffing, bureaucratic influence, and resources. In the case of home-front mobilization, agencies like the US Food Administration, for example, developed their own divisions and sections specifically targeting women.

8. Emily Newell Blair, *The Woman's Committee: United States Council of National Defense; An Interpretive Report: April 21, 1917–February 27, 1919* (Washington, DC: General Printing Office, 1920), 7.

9. Ida Clyde Clarke, *American Women and the World War* (New York: D. Appleton & Company, 1918), 17.

10. Blair, *The Woman's Committee*, 7.

11. Ibid.

12. *The Woman's Committee of the Council of National Defense: Organization Charts, May, 1917–1918* (Washington, DC: Committee on Public Information, 1918).

13. Five of the nine female appointees were connected to the American Suffrage Movement. Breen, *Uncle Sam at Home: Civilian Mobilization, Wartime Federalism, and the Council of National Defense, 1917–1919*, 236. The Woman's Committee was made up of the following: Anna Howard Shaw (honorary president, National American Woman Suffrage Association); Mrs. Philip North Moore (president, National Council of Women of the United States); Mrs. Josiah Evans Cowles (president, General Federation of Women's Clubs);Maude Wetmore (chairman, National League for Women's Service); Carrie Chapman Catt (president, National American Woman Suffrage Association); Mrs. Stanley J. McCormack (vice president, National American Woman Suffrage Association); Mrs. Joseph R. Lamar (president, National Society of Colonial Dames); Mrs. Isaac Lincoln

Funk (Lawyer); Ida M. Tarbell (publicist and writer); Agnes Nestor (vice president, International Glove Workers Union); and Hannah J. Patterson (head of the Pennsylvania Woman Suffrage Party).

14. Clarke, *American Women and the World War,* 354; Report, Woman's Committee, Council of National Defense North Carolina Division, Box 17, Folder 8, NC Council of Defense Records, WWI-I, Military Collection, State Archives of North Carolina C (hereafter referred to as WWI-I, Military Collection);William J. Breen, "Southern Women in the War: The North Carolina Woman's Committee, 1917–1919," *North Carolina Historical Review* 56, no. 3 (July 1978): 251–83.

15. Despite her prominent social status, Laura Holmes Reilley immediately faced resistance to her efforts to clarify the role of the Woman's Committee. Governor Thomas W. Bickett suggested that the work of the Woman's Committee could be carried out by the North Carolina chapter of the Red Cross Society. Bickett noted that the Red Cross had the advantage of an existing organization that spanned most of the state. Breen, "Southern Women in the War," 253–54.

16. Clarke, *American Women and the World War,* 355.

17. The State Normal and Industrial College is now known as the University of North Carolina at Greensboro. It is a coeducational university within the University of North Carolina system. The Greensboro College for Women is now known as Greensboro College. It remains a private college; however, Greensboro College is now a coeducational school. Both institutions are located in Greensboro, North Carolina.

18. Many of North Carolina's small, religious women's colleges struggled with their finances throughout the nineteenth century. By 1917, there were only thirteen: Carolina College for Women (Maxton, NC), Queens College (Charlotte, NC), Chowan College (Murfreesboro, NC), Mitchell College (Statesville, NC), Flora MacDonald College (Red Springs, NC), Greensboro College for Women (Greensboro, NC), Littleton College (Littleton, NC), Meredith College (Raleigh, NC), Oxford Female Seminary (Oxford, NC), Salem College (Winston-Salem, NC), St. Mary's College (Raleigh, NC), Peace Institute (Raleigh, NC), and Scotia Women's College (Concord, NC). The North Carolina General Assembly passed the "Act to Establish a Normal and Industrial School for White Girls" in 1891, which became the only public women's college in the state.

19. Amy Thompson McCandles, "Progressivism and the Higher Education of Southern Women," *North Carolina Historical Review,* 70, no. 3 (July 1993): 302–25.

20. In the limited archival records of the schools discussed in this chapter, there was no evidence found of antiwar sentiment expressed by students, faculty, or administrators.

21. U.S., Committee on Public Information, *War Work of Women in Colleges* (Washington, DC: Government Printing Office, January, 1918); U.S., Committee on Public Information, *War Work of Women in Colleges,* no. 2 (Washington, DC: Government Printing Office, April, 1918).

22. It is difficult to determine whether there were dissenting voices in the faculty or if they were pressured by the administration to support campus war efforts. Available college administration records reflect only the patriotic participation of the faculty and staff.

23. Report, Box 17, Folder 8, WWI-I, Military Collection.

24. Ibid.

25. Memorandum from the Committee on Public Information, Division on Women's War Work, March 12, 1918, Box 3, Folder 3, MSS 025, Harriet W. Elliott Collection, Martha Blakeney Hodges

Special Collections and University Archives, University of North Carolina at Greensboro (hereafter referred to as Elliott Collection).

26. Memorandum from the Committee on Public Information, Division on Women's War Work, June 26, 1918, Box 3, Folder 3, Elliott Collection.

27. Ibid.

28. "To the Young Women of America," *News Letter of the Woman's Committee Council of National Defense,* July 15, 1918, Box 3, Folder 3, Elliott Collection.

29. The young woman who portrayed Columbia was Meredith College student Minnie Mills. This patriotic representation of America was accompanied by the poem "America, I Love You."

30. *Greensboro Daily News,* April 13, 1918.

31. "Patriotic Pageant at State Normal College," College Scrapbooks, Volume 23, April 1917–December 1920, Martha Blakeney Hodges Special Collections and University Archives, University of North Carolina at Greensboro.

32. The term "Farmerette" was coined in Great Britain to describe female farm workers. During World War I, the term referred to the Woman's Land Army in Great Britain. With the creation of the Woman's Land Army of America, the term "Farmerette" was embraced to describe American women who volunteered for farm work.

33. Greensboro College, *The Echo* (Greensboro, NC: Student Association of Greensboro College, 1918), 145.

34. Mary Lynch Johnson, *A History of Meredith College* (Raleigh: Edwards & Broughton Company, 1972), 160. Meredith College continues to offer an undergraduate degree program for women, though graduate degrees are coeducational.

35. *Greensboro Daily News,* April 13, 1918.

36. Johnson, *A History of Meredith College,* 162.

37. "The Alumnae 'Selective Draft,'" *Bulletin, Greensboro College, Alumnae Edition* 6, no. 3 (1919): 3.

38. "David Fallon, British Captain, Is Optimistic about War, Expects End with United Allies Entering Berlin," *Greensboro Daily News,* February 20, 1918.

39. Martha Stoops, *The Heritage: The Education of Women and St. Mary's College, Raleigh, North Carolina, 1842–1982* (Raleigh: North Carolina, 1984), 195.

40. Ibid. St. Mary's College is now a high school for girls, grades 9–12. It is currently known as St. Mary's School.

41. Ibid.

42. The Volunteer War Service League at Salem College asked students to sign a service pledge and listed suggestions on how to volunteer. "Volunteer War Service League," *Alumnae Record, Salem College* 42, no. 347 (1917): 7498; St. Mary's rector suggested that the students sign a mobilization pledge. "The St. Mary's Girls Mobilize for Work," *St. Mary's Muse,* 1919, 207–8.

43. "Hail to the Boys in France!" *St. Mary's Muse,* 1918, 6–7; ibid., 9.

44. Johnson, *A History of Meredith College,* 160. Salem College offers an undergraduate education for women and coeducational graduate programs.

45. Elisabeth Ann Bowles, *A Good Beginning* (Chapel Hill: University of North Carolina Press, 2011), 131; Johnson, *A History of Meredith College,* 162.

46. For formal military service, there were opportunities for women to serve in the Navy, Marines, and the Army Nurse Corps.

47. "The Alumnae 'Selective Draft,'" *Bulletin, Greensboro College for Women, Alumnae Edition* 6, no. 3 (1919): 3.

48. This emphasis on self-sacrifice may have been influenced by both the national call for daily moderation and the patriotic enthusiasm generated on these women's college campuses.

49. "Normal College Girls Sacrifice for Country," *News and Observer,* November 14, 1917.

50. Johnson, *A History of Meredith College,* 162.

51. "Series of *Ivy* Nights at Salem," *Alumnae Record,* Salem College, vol. 41, no. 341 (1917): 7343.

52. Johnson, *A History of Meredith College,* 162.

53. The Farmerettes were a crucial part of the Woman's Land Army of America during a time when women were urged to take their places on farms across the country.

54. Minnie Lou Jamison to D. H. Hill, July 17, 1918, Box 16, Folder 14, WWI-I, Military Collection.

55. Ibid.

56. Ibid.

57. Ibid.

58. Ibid.

59. "College History Manuscript," Box 60, Folder 1, Julius Foust Records, UA 2.2, Martha Blakeney Hodges Special Collections and University Archives, University of North Carolina at Greensboro (hereafter referred to as Foust Records).

60. Archibald Henderson, *North Carolina Women in the World War, an Address.* (Chapel Hill: Academic Affairs Library, University of North Carolina at Chapel Hill, 2002), *http://docsouth.unc .edu/wwi/henderson/menu.html* (accessed August 4, 2017). Henderson was a widely recognized scholar in mathematics at the University of North Carolina at Chapel Hill.

61. Katharine Blunt and Florence Powdermaker, *Food and the War: A Textbook for College Classes Prepared under the Direction of the Collegiate Section of the United States Food Administration* (Boston: Houghton Mifflin, 1918), dedication page.

62. Herbert Hoover to Julius Foust, September 9, 1918, Box 21, Folder 8, Foust Records.

63. Julius Foust and Committee to the Alumnae of the State Normal and Industrial College, July 9, 1917, Box 20, Folder 9, Foust Records.

64. Julius Foust to the Women of North Carolina, January 30, 1918, World War I Subject File, Martha Blakeney Hodges Special Collections and University Archives, University of North Carolina at Greensboro (hereafter referred to as World War I Subject File).

65. Salem College's *Alumnae Record* reported wartime efforts that included instruction for surgical dressings for the American Red Cross, training for ambulance drivers for the League of Woman's Service, and studying at the Marconi Institute to work in the Signal Corps. Additionally, it reported that during the month of April 1918, students produced 11,549 gauze wipes and 349 abdominal bandages for the Red Cross.

66. Memorandum from R. D. W. Connor, May 16, 1917, Box 19, Folder 3, Foust Records. A North Carolina native, Connor was a historian and the first archivist of the United States (1934–41).

67. R. D. W. Connor to Julius Foust, July 9, 1917, Box 19, Folder 3, Foust Records.

68. *Women and the War in North Carolina: Suggestions for the Collection of Historical Material,* 1918, World War I Subject File.

69. *The State Normal and Industrial College and the War,* 1918, World War I Subject File.

70. Ibid.

71. Ibid.

72. It is interesting to note that Guilford College was included in this report, since it was a coeducational college.

73. A. Elizabeth Taylor, "The Woman Suffrage Movement in North Carolina," *North Carolina Historical Review* 38, no. 2 (April 1961): 177. Taylor notes that student efforts to organize suffrage clubs were thwarted by the trustees at various colleges.

74. George C. Rable, *Civil Wars: Women and the Crisis of Southern Nationalism* (Urbana: University of Illinois Press, 1991); Anne Firor Scott, *The Southern Lady: From Pedestal to Politics 1830–1930* (Chicago: University of Chicago Press, 1970).

75. George Rable, *Civil Wars: Women and the Crisis of Southern Nationalism,* 286.

76. Elna C. Green, *Southern Strategies: Southern Women and the Women Suffrage Question* (Chapel Hill: University of North Carolina Press, 1997); Marjorie Spruill Wheeler, *New Women of the New South: The Leaders of the Women Suffrage Movement in the Southern States* (New York: Oxford University Press, 1993); Elizabeth Gillespie McRae, "Caretakers of Southern Civilization: Georgia Women and the Anti-Suffrage Campaign, 1914–1920," *Georgia Historical Quarterly* 82, no. 4 (Winter 1998): 801–28.

77. Greensboro College, *The Echo* (Greensboro, NC: Student Association of Greensboro College, 1917), 67.

78. *St. Mary's Muse,* 1919, 111.

79. Peace Institute, *Lotus,* 35; Chowan College, *Chowanoka* (Murfreesboro, NC: Alathenian and Lucalian Literary Societies, 1917), 43. Peace Institute is now William Peace University (and is coeducational). Chowan College is now Chowan University.

80. *Virginia Terrell Lathrop,* "Harriet Elliott: An Inspiring Teacher Who Taught History and Lived It," *Alumni News, The University of North Carolina at Greensboro* 55, no. 4 (1967); 8.

81. Rankin visited Salem College in October of 1917. *Alumnae Record* (Salem College) 41, no. 339 (1917); and State Normal in 1918. "Plans to Entertain Miss Rankin in City," *Greensboro Daily News,* February 17, 1918.

82. Allen W. Trelease, *Making North Carolina Literate: The University of North Carolina at Greensboro, from Normal School to Metropolitan University* (Durham, NC: Carolina Academic Press, 2003), 68.

83. Ibid.

84. Paula S. Jordan, *Women of Guilford County: A Study of Women's Contributions* (Greensboro: Greensboro Printing Company, 1979), 102.

85. Trelease, *Making North Carolina Literate,* 69.

86. "Normal College Students Unanimous for Suffrage," *Everything,* February 16, 1918.

87. Julius Foust to Senator Lee S. Overman, May 28, 1918, Box 22, Folder 3, Foust Records.

88. This political assessment was overly optimistic. It was not until August 18, 1920, that Congress passed legislation ratifying the Nineteenth Amendment. However, to the disappointment of

the many women of the state who had proved their patriotism and value to their country through their significant war work, North Carolina did not support the amendment. The North Carolina General Assembly did not officially endorse suffrage until 1971.

89. A. Elizabeth Taylor, "The Woman Suffrage Movement in North Carolina," 178.

90. "Address at Normal on 'Women and War,'" *Greensboro Daily News*, June 22, 1918.

91. Camp Greene was a military training facility where some sixty thousand soldiers trained as pilots and airplane repairmen. Jennifer Garner, "The War to End All Wars," in *150 Stories of Queens: 1857–2007 Queens University of Charlotte*, ed. J. Curtis and J. Garner (Evansville: M. T. Publishing Company, 2006), 27. Now Queens University, the school is coeducational.

92. Stoops, *The Heritage: The Education of Women at St. Mary's College*, 207.

93. Bowles, *A Good Beginning*, 131.

94. "Greatest Story since Bethlehem Drives the People Wild with Joy," *Greensboro Daily News*, November 12, 1918.

95. "When the Good News Reached Salem," Senior Clippings, *Sights and Insights* (Salem College) (Winston-Salem, NC: Class of 1919), 150–51.

96. "An Announcement," *News Letter of the Woman's Committee Council of National Defense*, October 1, 1918, Series 2, Box 3, Folder 3, Elliott Collection.

97. Report, Box 17, Folder 8, WWI-I, Military Collection.

98. Report by Joseph Hyde Pratt, History of the North Carolina Council of Defense, Box 1, Folder 1, WWI-I, Military Collection.

99. The Woman's Committee formed in April 1917 to support the efforts of the Council of National Defense. John P. Finnegan, *Against the Spector of a Dragon: The Campaign for American Military Preparedness, 1914–1917* (Westport, CT: Greenwood Press, 1974).

100. William J. Breen, *Uncle Sam at Home: Civilian Mobilization, Wartime Federalism, and the Council of National Defense, 1917–1919* (Westport, CT: Greenwood Press, 1984), 177.

101. While in the capital, she had received the Distinguished Service Medal for her work as the chair of the Woman's Committee of the Council for National Defense.

102. "Seniors of the State College for Women Hear Noted Leader," *Greensboro Daily News*, May 21, 1919.

103. Blair, *The Woman's Committee*, 8.

104. Ibid.

6

The Great War and Expanded Equality?

Black Carolinians Test Boundaries

JANET G. HUDSON

On April 4, 1917, African Americans in Columbia, South Carolina, held a public forum to consider their response to the United States' anticipated entry into the war in Europe. Participants who had gathered at First Calvary Baptist Church discussed the feasibility and desirability of African American men serving as soldiers. Amid the discussion one participant boldly argued, "The white folks have the Winchesters, and you haven't even a little popgun. They'll not ask you whether you want to enlist. They'll just take you out and shoot you, if you don't." Three months later in North Carolina, Dock Jackson "D. J." Jordan, a history professor at North Carolina Agricultural & Technical (A & T) College, commemorated the 4th of July with a scathing criticism of Woodrow Wilson that condemned the president's indifference to the suffering of the nation's twelve million African American citizens. Only two days before his speech, economic competition in the rapidly growing industrial city of East St. Louis, Illinois, provoked a white mob to murder thirty-nine African Americans and burn black-owned homes to the ground. Incensed by the violence, Jordan attributed the mob spirit to Wilson's callous and apathetic administration. In response to the president's concern that the "world be made safe for democracy," Jordon advised that African Americans should be asking, "Is this the kind of democracy I am asked to give my life and fortune to make safe in the world?" Offering further provocation, Jordan mused to the president that it "may not be safe to wait for these people to give their own answer." Both of these public responses from the two Carolinas testify to African Americans' keen awareness of the injustices they routinely experienced. Moreover, the sentiments they shared testify to African Americans' willingness to criticize publicly the national hypocrisy that called for sacrifice in the name of democracy from citizens who were flagrantly denied participation in that democracy at home.[1]

Numerous historians have drawn attention to similar dissenting voices among African Americans during World War I. Those studies, steeped in the use of federal government surveillance records of the era, have emphasized African Americans' skepticism, apathy, and direct resistance to military service and the other demands of war mobilization. This body of scholarship draws heavily from the invasive and obsessive government investigations into rumors of African American dissent and disloyalty. These studies have enriched our understanding of African American responses to the US involvement in the Great War by bringing new voices of protest and dissent to the forefront.[2]

But any assertion that a variety of disparate African American voices accurately characterized the African American wartime response is misleading. There were multiple African American voices, but at least in the South, there was a dominant African American voice, and that dominant voice urged support for the war effort as a strategic means of realizing fuller participation in the American democracy that Wilson (rather hypocritically) celebrated. The dissenting speaker at the April 4 forum in Columbia, who boldly charged that whites would shoot any blacks who evaded the draft, provoked pandemonium as dozens of participants protested their shock and dismay at his statement. In North Carolina, Professor Jordan also faced extensive criticism and public denunciation from his peers for publishing his forthright critique of African Americans' obstacles to democracy. While there were a number of dissenting voices that captured attention, and certainly raised white anxiety, that scattered, weak voice of dissent did not prevail in shaping the dominant approach to the war among black southerners.[3]

Instead, that dominant voice can be found in the works of local and state African American leaders in southern states, where more than 80% of African Americans lived on the eve of World War I. Focusing specifically on the local- and state-level black leadership in North and South Carolina, two neighboring southern states with numerous similarities and yet widely different proportions of black residents, this analysis examines the roles adopted by those leaders and their success in shaping black Carolinians' responses to World War I.[4] Although often invisible in narratives of national black leadership and opinion makers, such leaders did not operate in isolation. Rather, they worked in a complicated political and social environment constructed by the peculiar local dictates of white supremacy, and in a context informed by national and regional ideas that circulated through African American newspapers, alumni associations, religious networks, denominational conferences and literature, fraternities, and vast personal networks that extended across the nation with migration. They not only consumed this assortment of ideas, but also shaped and circulated them in their communities. Local and state southern black leaders engaged in this dynamic and interconnected network, but their work and influence have been largely overshadowed by the more easily documented role of national leaders whose personal correspondence and edited newspapers have survived and become electronically searchable. A directed study of the work of those local and state leaders, and particularly their response to the crisis of World War I, recovers and highlights the influence they wielded within black communities across the South.

As an elite within their community, these southern black leaders enjoyed privileges most African Americans in their state and community did not. Yet as a black elite, they exercised influence in the context of great limitations. They answered not only to their community but also to whites who held the economic and political power they lacked. Accountable to both the black masses and the white elite, African American leaders in the South traversed complicated terrain that required thorough understanding of how to motivate both audiences. While African Americans were rarely leaders of corporations, large landowners, lawyers, or politicians like their white counterparts, African American leaders forged their leadership skills most often in churches and segregated schools, but also in the courtroom, medical practice, mortuary, statehouse, and as business owners and entrepreneurs. On a continuum, black leaders with the greatest economic independence usually had the greatest freedom from white control in their professions.[5]

African American leaders in the two Carolinas confronted war-related challenges even before Congress officially declared war against the Central Powers because they found themselves accused in the national press of disloyalty and cooperation with the enemy. Rumors circulated that German spies had successfully fomented dissatisfaction among African Americans in the South by exploiting their resentment of white power. As the rumors circulated, white southerners intensified their scrutiny of African Americans' activities, doubting their loyalty and anticipating dissent.[6] Black North Carolinians became the initial target of the national frenzy concerning a potentially subversive black population when the *New York Tribune* broke the first national story of German agents working to subvert African Americans concentrated in the southern tobacco and cotton regions. The *Tribune* reported that the small community of Elm Grove, near Greensboro, had become the "chief seeding ground for the propaganda of sedition." Two Germans were reportedly posing as itinerant doctors and attempting to foment disloyalty among black North Carolinians. Accusations also linked the stirring of disloyalty with Immanuel Lutheran College, which educated African Americans. Federal agents investigating the claims added that reports of German activity had also come from North Carolina's most prominent cities: Wilmington, Raleigh, and Charlotte.[7]

This report energized African American leaders in North Carolina to respond quickly with a firestorm of loyalty declarations issued in public rallies, newspapers, and correspondence to white leaders. A local minister from the accused community organized the "Elm Grove citizens" to publish a letter in the *Greensboro Daily News* declaring their loyalty. Resolutions from across the state flooded into North Carolina governor Thomas Bickett's office as African American communities refuted the rumors of black sympathy with Germany. James B. Dudley, president of North Carolina A & T College, corresponded privately with Governor Bickett to assuage any concerns about disloyalty. Additionally Dudley organized a public rally of support in Greensboro at which prominent ministers, educators, and businessmen and -women offered abundant public expressions of loyalty and characterized the reports concerning German agents as false and disrespectful.[8]

African American leaders rallied their communities to not only express loyalty but to link black loyalty with a call for justice. At their public rally, Durham leaders called for the rights they were "justly entitled" to as taxpayers. They emphasized that if employers wanted to avoid losing laborers in the migration north, a constant concern among whites, they needed to pay them decent wages. Dudley also paired his assertions of loyalty with the call for black men's military service, a direct claim on a long tradition of linking military service with the full political rights of citizenship. The emphatic tone of these letters and resolutions also conveyed frustration that such assertions were necessary. The Durham leaders considered the reports of disloyalty to be false and insulting to them as Americans "pure and simple," because black Americans knew "no other country and . . . no other Flag." These leaders consistently claimed their American identity, and they emphasized its deep roots, recalling African Americans' "valor in the war of Independence" and all other wars since the Revolution.[9]

Just five days after the accusations against black North Carolinians hit the national press, reports reached the Justice Department that German agents were in Lee and Hampton counties, South Carolina, organizing the black community to revolt. Lee and Hampton were two of South Carolina's thirty-two black-majority counties. The federal agent assigned to the area found no creditable evidence for an investigation, and no revolts materialized in either county. Such rumors of German subversive agents obviously alarmed the white minority, who feared all threats that might undermine their racial control strategies.[10]

African American leaders in South Carolina responded with the same firm rebuttal to the rumors of German subversion and the same emphatic expressions of loyalty to the US cause. Just as their fellow North Carolinians had, they corresponded with white leaders, held public rallies, wrote letters to the editor, and adopted formal resolutions outlining specific commitments to their loyalty while pointing to their historical record of allegiance. At a public rally, Beaufort's black residents asserted, "We love our country today as in 1775, in 1812, in 1861–1865, in 1898, and in all the years of its existence." Sumter, South Carolina, residents expressed their indignant frustration with a bold declaration of their loyalty, despite slanderous assertions that they had "conspired" and "plotted" with German spies. Intending to distinguish loyalty to the nation at war from satisfaction with injustice, the black citizens of Clarendon County pointed out that while "we are not unmindful of past events bearing on the treatment of 10,000,000 Afro-American people in these United States . . . we stand now with no feeling of hatred or disloyalty to our government." As Dudley and others had in North Carolina, black leaders in Columbia also held a public forum to assert to their governor and President Wilson that African American men should be allowed to serve as soldiers. Charleston leaders took similar actions and petitioned Governor Richard I. Manning to organize a black regiment from South Carolina and give young black men the opportunity to demonstrate their manhood against the enemy. Speaking on behalf of these young men, former South Carolina Republican congressman Thomas E. Miller pledged not only their "fidelity, patriotism, devoted service and courage" but also presented "their manhood for service or for sacrifice upon the alter [sic] of a nation 'conceived in liberty and dedicated to the principle that all men are created equal.'"[11]

The wartime frenzy over accusations that German spies had undermined black support for the war proved a much more accurate measure of white anxiety than of African American susceptibility to enemy manipulation. White southerners' economic, political, and coercive power over African Americans rested on formal and informal authority that they controlled. Thus influences beyond their control, such as German spies or other variables that introduced unanticipated change, fueled their anxiety. Black Carolinians acutely understood white supremacy's grip on their lives, and they did not need prodding from enemy infiltrators to resent it. The developing narrative of African American disloyalty in wartime that emerged from the German spy rumors presented black southern leaders with their first home-front challenge. Black leaders in the two Carolinas met that challenge with a strategically constructed counter-narrative—one of loyalty, cooperation, and enthusiastic patriotism—as their rapid, organized, and multipronged approach demonstrates. Their response must be seen, not as a simplistic "rally 'round the flag" accommodation of white economic and political leaders or an overly naïve assumption of the goodwill such an approach might earn from whites, but as a strategic effort to gain influence and leverage in a restricted world where whites needed their help.[12]

African American leaders in the South navigated between two conflicting worlds with competing expectations. War mobilization widened the intersection of those two worlds, freeing black leaders from some of the usual constraints, since rallying the black community to patriotic action was necessary for successful execution of the war, especially on the home front. White Carolinians cloaked their need for assistance from black leaders with patriotic rhetoric. Black leaders readily accommodated whites' requests for their wartime sacrifice but for different ends than whites intended. They took full advantage of the unique wartime opportunities to parade in the streets, organize mass rallies, and proclaim publicly and frequently that they were fighting for democracy, a rally cry unthinkable before the war. Thus, the rhetoric black leaders used resonated positively with audiences of both races although each constituency understood the message differently. Black leaders heeded the patriotic calls with enthusiasm for both military and civilian service as an investment in a future of greater African American opportunity, and their own, intentional strategy of employing heightened patriotic rhetoric at every turn during the war had a broader purpose. Immediately after the war these southern black leaders worked to advance their rights as full citizens of the nation, and they linked that push directly with their loyal wartime service.

African American leaders from the Carolinas seized the patriotic rhetoric of military service even before Congress mandated the draft. They consciously sought to link African Americans' service in the war, especially the service of combat soldiers, with broad heroic meaning. African American leaders from the Carolinas diligently promoted draft registration. Rev. R. T. Weatherby of St. Matthews Methodist Episcopal, the oldest African American church in Greensboro, North Carolina, noted, "I trust there will not be a single member of my race who will even attempt to evade the registration Tuesday."[13] Despite white concerns about potential black draft delinquency, when the June 5th registration began black Carolinians responded as required and often with enthusiasm. Columbia's draft board reported that African Americans requested exemptions less often than white registrants.

As the draft unfolded, African American communities across North Carolina rallied in support of the newly drafted soldiers with the full pomp and circumstance of loyalty and commitment. Singing patriotic songs, communities ceremoniously offered their admiration for the young men who boarded trains for distant training camps. At the farewell gathering in Winston-Salem, well-known and respected leader Dr. Simon G. Atkins, founder and principal of Slater Industrial Academy, urged the men to give their all and fight for the "land of Democracy" that had given them "freedom and protection." Around the same time Atkins inspired the new inductees from his community, his own son, 2nd Lt. Russell Atkins, had just weeks earlier been sent to France with the 365th Infantry.[14]

These community opportunities for display of patriotic fervor caught the attention of whites as well. "These future soldiers left with smiles on their faces and with a determination, it appeared, to do their part in helping to lick the kaiser [sic]," a reporter observed of the African American men sworn in at the courthouse ceremony in Gastonia. Members of the Winston-Salem exemption board noticed the excitement the local festivities generated, and they commented on the high spirits of the soldiers. "No more determined set of men ever moved against an enemy" than the young black men that assembled and left Winston-Salem that evening. White community leaders, at times, remarked positively on the young men. The local exemption board from Greensboro praised a group of black inductees from their county when every man reported promptly for the 6:00 a.m. swearing-in ceremony even though, as noted, many lived in the distant rural parts of the county and had traveled long distances with transportation challenges.[15]

A majority of South Carolinians and one-third of North Carolinians inducted in the US Army were African American, making their service contribution vital to meeting both states' draft quotas. In both states, black registrants were inducted at a higher rate than their white counterparts. More than twenty-six thousand young black South Carolina men and twenty-one thousand black men from North Carolina served in World War I. While most were drafted, African Americans from the Carolinas volunteered for combat and labor duties despite the federal restrictions and quotas on African American volunteering. More than half of the African American soldiers from the Carolinas served overseas in France and approximately 20% of those who crossed the Atlantic were combat soldiers, including Freddie Stowers of South Carolina, one of only two African American Medal of Honor recipients in World War I. The other Carolina soldiers served in some type of labor unit where they loaded and unloaded ships, constructed and repaired roads, dug graves, and performed other hard-but-necessary tasks in French ports as well as the war-ravaged interior, near and far from the front lines.[16] Dozens of Carolinians were among the 639 African Americans commissioned as officers on October 15, 1917. After attending the segregated Ft. Des Moines officers' training school in Iowa, these officers primarily led men in combat units of the 92nd Division, the segregated combat division created for drafted black soldiers rather than leading the more seasoned National Guard soldiers of the 93rd Division. These officers were also among the Carolinas' most distinguished African American soldiers, and many became accomplished men after the war.[17]

African Americans' military contribution was in spite of significant opposition, criticism, and publicly expressed fear of their participation, particularly as combat soldiers and commissioned officers. Whites' anxiety, coupled with their commitment to white supremacy, shaped all aspects of African American soldiers' experiences, including when they were drafted, where they trained, and how they served. For example, in August 1917, when the War Department announced its plan to train all African Americans living in the South at only three camps, one near Columbia, South Carolina, one near Atlanta, Georgia, and another near Little Rock, Arkansas, South Carolina governor Richard Manning led a delegation of leaders to Washington in protest. The group insisted that African American soldiers from outside the state not be sent to train in the newly constructed Camp Jackson near Columbia for fear of racial violence erupting as it had recently in Houston, Texas, near Camp Logan.[18] Moreover, Secretary of War Newton Baker sent a National Guard unit of black soldiers from New

York, who had been training at Camp Wadsworth near Spartanburg, South Carolina, to France before its training was complete because of opposition from local whites who resented the presence of black combat-ready soldiers who showed no understanding of or deference to informal Jim Crow expectations of submissive behavior. This black National Guard unit became the 369th, one of the most decorated units of American soldiers to serve in the Great War, and one of only four infantry regiments of African American soldiers that made up the 93rd Division.[19]

While three of the four regiments in the 93rd Division were created from black National Guard units, the 371st Infantry stood apart as the only unit of that division composed exclusively of draftees, and it originated at Columbia's Camp Jackson. A strange set of circumstances in the War Department's continually evolving war plans led to the creation of this combat unit, composed overwhelmingly of black South Carolinians. Opposition from white political leaders, who greatly feared and deemed unacceptable the concentration of large numbers of African Americans preparing to be soldiers in arms, derailed the original plan. Consequently, Secretary of War Baker preferred to disband the developing unit at Camp Jackson and instead use them as laborers or combat replacements. But Commander General Bailey, who had worked with the men and believed them capable of becoming effective combat soldiers, made a special request of Baker that they remain a combat unit and the Secretary of War obliged him. Thus, while discriminatory military practices relegated most black soldiers to labor battalions, the 371st became a combat infantry regiment, one of only four combat regiments to serve directly with the French. Ironically, the military plan designed to keep most black soldiers from training in the South facilitated black Carolinians' participation as combat soldiers in this unique unit.[20]

But it was not only military organization and participation that captured the attention of local and state leaders in the Carolinas during the war. Black leaders in both Carolinas organized local branches of the National Association for the Advancement of Colored People (NAACP) during and immediately after the war, clear evidence that they had wartime agendas that extended far outside the bounds of white approval. In 1917, black men and women in Raleigh, North Carolina, and Charleston and Columbia, South Carolina, organized their local branches as they participated in the early efforts of the NAACP to expand membership into southern states. In the fall of 1918, Darlington began a branch. Formal chartering of NAACP branches took great courage, since whites viewed them as unacceptable and "dangerous." African Americans in Durham, North Carolina, and Anderson, Beaufort, Orangeburg, and Florence, South Carolina, chartered new branches immediately after the war, and despite the increased violence and rising spirit of retribution that characterized 1919, membership in all the branches expanded rapidly.[21]

Charleston's African American leaders quickly demonstrated their determination to expand wartime employment options for black workers and they used their newly formed NAACP organization to facilitate it. The Charleston Navy Yard clothing factory immediately needed six hundred new workers. Despite the labor shortage, black women were excluded from the new jobs. The Charleston NAACP immediately fought for an opportunity for black women to obtain these jobs. The persistence and dedication of black Charlestonians to partner with others, locally and nationally, and push through layers of bureaucracy led to the employment of at least 250 black women, who earned collectively an estimated $150,000 a year at the Charleston Navy Yard's clothing factory.[22]

Across North and South Carolina African American leaders met whites' expectations for loyalty and full civilian participation. They served on county councils of defense, organized mass meetings to communicate war needs, rallied support for those meetings, and planted additional food crops, among other supportive actions. Governor Thomas W. Bickett praised black North Carolinians, particularly women, for their tireless efforts with the Red Cross and bond drives. He also commended North Carolina A & T College for cooperating with the War Department to use the college for training nearly a thousand student soldiers in the Student Auxiliary Training Corps (SATC). When tuberculosis was identified as a wartime problem, a prominent black leader from Marlboro County donated land for the site of the first TB sanitarium for South Carolina's black population. African Americans from both Carolinas also responded to state leaders' request for financial contributions by participating in every bond drive with proportionally generous contributions.[23]

In Columbia, African American leaders used their civilian wartime authority to protest the showing of the racially offensive movie *Birth of a Nation*.[24] Strategically, black leaders linked their protest of the film's showing with their proven record of war support. A delegation of thirteen black leaders from Columbia presented their argument against the film's showing, emphasizing that African Americans had been loyal and patriotic and had fostered unity among all South Carolinians. Moreover, the petitioners argued that their sacrifices should not be denigrated nor should existing racial harmony be jeopardized by showing a film that emphasized racial conflict. Their argument prevailed. Local white leaders asked the theater manager to cancel the scheduled showing of *Birth of a Nation* as a gesture of wartime patriotism, and he yielded to the pressure.[25]

African Americans pushed harder and persistently made demands, even as the Armistice approached. During the final months of the war, black leaders from Charleston organized an intensive campaign in their city to reverse a long-standing humiliation. Unlike all other segregated black public schools in South Carolina, where black teachers taught black children, Charleston's public schools for African American students hired only white teachers. Although the anomalous circumstance of whites teaching black children had remained formally unchallenged for half a century, African American leaders, buoyed by the war to "make the world safe for democracy," began experimenting with democracy at home.

Local NAACP members prepared for months. In meetings throughout the city they organized the community to oppose white teachers in black schools. This skillful and stealthy grassroots organization yielded signatures from five thousand heads of household, representing approximately twenty-five thousand black Charlestonians, nearly three-fourths of the city's black population. Additionally, these Charlestonians, with assistance from the Columbia NAACP branch, had to navigate skillfully through local and state politics to prevail. The determination, careful strategy, and sheer boldness of Charleston's black leaders paid off. Beginning September 1, 1920, Charleston public schools no longer employed white teachers to teach black children.[26]

As Armistice celebrations signaled the victorious end to the Great War, black leaders expected tangible results for their loyalty and wartime cooperation. African American leaders in the Carolinas summoned the imagery of freedom and new beginnings on January 1, 1919, as they gathered to celebrate Emancipation Day. More than three thousand black North Carolinians gathered in Raleigh, while a similar crowd of South Carolinians gathered in Columbia. Each group of leaders publicly praised the soldiers' valor and the civilians' cooperation, protested the injustices they suffered, and resolved to change the future. Specifically, they condemned mob violence and lynch law, the inadequate and inferior Jim Crow accommodations, and the meager education appropriations allocated for black schools. More provocatively, they identified the solution for these inequalities: the ballot.[27]

On January 1, 1919, black leaders in Columbia called on whites to live up to the American ideals of freedom and equality. Quoting the Declaration of Independence, they asserted their belief that "governments derive their just powers from the consent of the governed." These black South Carolinians understood that whites had corrupted American political ideals with disfranchisement, which denied consent to a majority of South Carolina's citizens. The North Carolina resolutions attracted praise from the *New York Age* and condemnation from white North Carolinians for their forthright insistence that African Americans' wartime sacrifices deserved better than the same prewar bigotry at home. The editor of the *Winston-Salem Journal* denounced the Emancipation Day resolutions as a "dangerous thing" and stated that "sensible and patriotic negroes" did not demand such "privileges." The *New York Age* retorted that it was precisely the "sensible and patriotic colored people of North Carolina" who had offered the greatest support for the war effort and who now demanded something better.[28] The bold and optimistic assertions black leaders in Raleigh and Columbia made on January 1 signaled the tone they sustained that momentous postwar year.

Throughout 1919 African Americans gathered publicly to restate the postwar agenda adopted on Emancipation Day. For example, just three weeks later, on January 22, a race conference in Columbia began with more than one thousand in attendance. Rev. D. F. Thompson, a minister whom white leaders had praised during the war for his successful fund raising as chair of Columbia's United War Work Campaign, delivered the keynote address. In the war's aftermath these same white leaders responded with alarm to his "Grievances of the Negro," an address that referenced inadequate educational funding, inadequate justice in the courts, inadequate space on the segregated streetcars, excessive labor coercions, the barbarism of lynching, and disfranchisement. Thompson directly linked African Americans' wartime actions with his postwar demands. He longed to make real "the democracy for which the negro fought" and concluded his rousing appeal with an impassioned promise: "We will not be satisfied until we can vote."[29]

Clearly, African Americans' boldest challenge to institutional white supremacy lay in their appeal for the ballot. On February 4, 1919, African American leaders from across South Carolina met in Columbia for a conference where they not only condemned injustices but also affirmed that voting was the best strategy for redressing these injustices. Ministers left the conference with in-

structions to urge members of their congregation who could qualify to register to vote. Knowing the importance of systematic and grassroots actions, the
conference requested that each precinct and ward captain develop a plan for
registering eligible voters within the next year.[30]

The clearest articulation of the argument that African Americans deserved
rewards for wartime service came a few weeks later, on February 21, when thousands gathered in downtown Columbia to cheer returning, battle-hardened
war heroes of the 371st Infantry, the regiment composed of African American
draftees primarily from South Carolina with some from North Carolina. The
men who paraded that February afternoon had fought in the climactic Cham-
pagne offensive in France and demonstrated their valor on the front lines at
Verdun, one of Europe's most infamous dying fields. These returning soldiers
wore American and French military decorations that testified to their battlefield
courage. South Carolinians who assembled in Columbia that day had come to
honor the bravery and sacrifices of these drafted young men who, the previous
year, had trained just miles down the road at Camp Jackson before leaving for
France.[31]

South Carolina's newly inaugurated governor, Robert A. Cooper, and other
prominent white guests spoke to the parading soldiers and accompanying crowd
that gathered at Allen University, an African Methodist Episcopal (AME) educational institution. Following their comments, several prominent African American ministers, including Nathaniel F. Haygood and AME bishop William D.
Chappelle, addressed the expectant crowd. Reverend Haygood assured the men
that they had proven themselves the equal of any soldier. Consequently, he encouraged them to demand and insist the rights denied them; he suggested that
the returning soldiers' mantra become "Give me what belongs to me." Then he
asserted that these young men deserved a "man's place," which he defined as service on grand juries and in local police departments. Bishop Chappelle offered
the frankest conclusion when he declared emphatically, "The war was fought
for democracy. We want democracy in our own country. . . . We want freedom."
The bishop specifically explained that democracy and freedom required access
to the ballot box and the jury pool. While the pomp and circumstance of this
unique occasion enjoyed the official sanction of city, state, and military white
leaders, African American leaders' use of this occasion to present a provocative
wish list linking military service with political rights challenged the parameters
of acceptable public discourse in South Carolina in 1919.[32]

As frequently happened that year when African Americans publically claimed their rights to democracy at home, a white resident quickly and publicly characterized these expectations as extreme and unreasonable, consistent with the "socialistic propaganda that is floating about the world."[33] Whites feared the logic that connected citizenship with honorable military service. Could white control possibly be maintained if they so readily acknowledged the value of such a socially leveling experience as confronting a common enemy on a foreign battlefield?

Calls for voter registration among African Americans did not remain simply rhetorical. In Lexington, North Carolina, soldiers became angry when they were denied voter registration, reporting that other towns allowed "all who served in the army to vote, regardless of color or whether their poll tax had been paid or not." These black soldiers asserted that if they were not allowed to vote, then they would not participate in the welcome home celebration for returning soldiers.[34] Black leaders in Charleston and Columbia began voter registration drives. The Charleston NAACP branch president bragged that on the first Monday of each month, the only day the registrar's office opened, black men lined up halfway around the block waiting to enter the registration office, even though only forty or fifty men managed to enter and register. Columbia NAACP members actively recruited new voters as well. On the first Monday of each month, beginning in February, NAACP members assisted new voters with the complex registration procedures and reading skills, if needed. Their work that spring yielded over three hundred new voters. Proud of this accomplishment, Butler Nance, branch president, touted Columbia's new voters to the national office and assured New York that African Americans in Columbia intended to "fight until every man of color in this southland has a vote."[35]

Nance's aspiration, an articulation of southern black leaders' endgame that every man of color should have a vote, crossed the line of white tolerance and met determined resistance as 1919 unfolded. Alarmed by this persistent voter registration effort, a white attorney from Columbia, who had been monitoring black behavior, informed Governor Robert Archer Cooper of increased African American voter registration. Outraged that Richland County's Board of Registration allowed this, he noted to the governor, "I do not mean the intelligent classes but anyone who appears they register." Increased calls for black voter registration particularly alarmed whites when those expectations were linked with the military service of young black men who had recently returned from France.[36]

Confirming white fears, a *Plaindealer* reporter, A. M. Carpenter, declared "a well defined movement has already been launched" in Carolina to demand the ballot for African Americans, noting that black soldiers' returning from France had brought that "matter to a head."[37] As the year progressed, even talking about black voting rights met swift rebuttal.

Although black Carolinians' raised expectations drove demands for change, opportunities that the war had briefly facilitated rapidly diminished with the Armistice. Rigidity in race relations soon replaced the short-lived fluidity that wartime necessity had created as white leaders labored to reestablish the imagined stability of the prewar racial structure that they readily controlled.

Consequently, racial violence enveloped the nation in 1919, emanating from clashing expectations, dashed hopes, economic distress, and other tensions. Ernest McKissick, black combat soldier from Asheville, North Carolina, who had served in France in the skilled 349th field artillery unit, returned to his home state to find that "democracy wasn't working at all at home 'cause they hadn't done anything for us. We had Jim Crow and all." "They tried to put us down in every way," McKissick lamented. In South Carolina, the black press reported similar frustrations. "There is scarcely a day that passes that newspapers don't tell about a Negro soldier lynching in his uniform. . . . Instead of race prejudice being modified, as some of us fondly hoped, it has become intensified," the *Charleston Messenger* reported. Just one week after the Armistice signing, racial violence erupted in Winston-Salem, North Carolina, when a lynch mob appeared at the city jail for Russell High, a black man. Before the National Guard restored order the next morning, four people had died and numerous others suffered injury from the gun violence initiated by the white mob on November 17, an incident that became known as the Winston-Salem "Race Riot" of 1918. Months later, on a Saturday evening in May 1919 in Charleston, South Carolina, white sailors stationed at the Naval Yard unleashed their frustrations on black civilians, sparking riotous mayhem throughout the city that night, destroying property and engaging in open gunfights that tallied three black men dead and eighteen black men and five white men seriously wounded. These incidents of racial violence in the Carolinas typified the reactionary violence against African Americans and immigrants across the United States in 1919.[38]

As these postwar social forces collided and suggested a social unraveling, thirty-eight prominent African American men and women in North Carolina held a private conference that fall and then later met with Governor Bickett and other key white state leaders to hammer out a racial compromise that they imagined would "allay race friction." Participants from the October conference presented their "Declaration of Principles" as a national, and not simply a North Carolinian, solution to alleviate the rising distrust and to prevent more of the agitation that fueled the recent "race clashes in the country." Billed as comprehensive, the declaration addressed the range of familiar issues: employment and educational opportunity, better living conditions and treatment in the courts, and opposition to the outrage of lynching. The concession African Americans gained in the compromise was the white leadership's promise to actively seek improvement in the areas of employment and educational opportunity, improved living conditions, better treatment in the courts, and opposition to lynching. The concession whites received, and the one that garnered the declaration's approval from politicians and the endorsement from newspaper editors, was to "get rid of the outside agitator" from whom whites imagined all trouble originated. For white Carolinians this meant halting efforts to entice black laborers to migrate to the North and ignoring or silencing voices from the NAACP and any other national advocates of social and political equality, especially demands for the ballot.[39]

Such a compromise may suggest that the wartime strategy of southern black leaders to promote greater equality failed. Instead, it reveals that leaders had found in the unfolding violence and tension of 1919 the limits of the equality they could attain. The editor of the *Winston-Salem Journal* noted that the black leaders who offered the compromise were the same leaders from "whose lips the word 'fight'" had recently been heard.[40] The swift and ruthless reaction that came in 1919, a year for pervasive violence and increased oppression of blacks, testifies to the success African American leaders had enjoyed by tying wartime service to greater opportunity. Whites recognized that African Americans were seeking to cash in on their investment and they were determined to deny the reward.

A distant and general summary of twentieth-century history of the American South might characterize the Great War as a momentary ripple in the long history of Jim Crow that left the repressive legal structure of white supremacy securely in place for another half century. Such a broad-spectrum summary, however, relies on the wisdom of hindsight to minimize the anticipated possibility that the war might offer an opportunity to alter race relations and obscures the intentional strategy southern black leaders employed in search of that possibility. Black leaders from both Carolinas worked to bring some tangible meaning to the lofty ideal of making the world "safe for democracy" as they quickly rallied their communities to support the US war effort. The majority of African Americans overtly demonstrated their patriotism with active support on the home front and compliance with the draft registration and service. Most importantly, black Carolinians linked their patriotic wartime behavior with calls for greater equality. They created and joined new chapters of the NAACP, organized Emancipation Day rallies, wrote petitions, sought new employment opportunities, organized voter registrations, and migrated north. Each challenge required negotiating an environment marked by a white power structure that resisted every challenge to white supremacy, thus raising the stakes of resistance and necessitating creativity. Yet southern black leaders, who had always operated within a system of oppression, crafted a public message which was pitched to different listeners and which asserted a single intention with differing purposes. They understood well that whites posed formidable obstacles but, at times, whites could unwittingly become conduits for change.

South Carolina minister John McClellan articulated an imagined future facilitated by the war: "We pray God, in the midst of shot, blood shed and shells, that out of this great struggle for democracy, a new democracy may be born which shall measure a man by his mind and not by his face."[41] African American leaders had a keen awareness of the powerful obstacles they faced but also a vision of hope that the war presented an opportunity to challenge these barriers. Half a century later McClellan's vision seemed to have found resonance in another southern minister's dream, providing evidence that while the strategic campaign southern black leaders waged in World War I suffered a bitter defeat in 1919, it never died.

The engaging experience of war mobilization, for soldiers and citizens, transformed many African Americans even if it failed to alter the tangible reality of their Jim Crow existence. The doing and hoping of the war years reconnected African Americans with the promise of Reconstruction and reengaged their sense of possibility that seemed to have eroded with the early twentieth-century expansion and solidification of Jim Crow. The World War I experience served as an incubator for succeeding decades of challenges to Jim Crow, challenges that continually matured through the actions of participants as well as their children. North Carolina combat veteran Ernest B. McKissick's son, Floyd S. McKissick, became the first African American to attend the University of North Carolina

Law School, an education that prepared him for an accomplished career and civil rights activism. A number of World War I veterans became civil rights activists, such as Charles Hamilton Houston, Medgar Evers, Amzie Moore, and South Carolina's own Osceola McKaine; studies have shown that the war nurtured, if not inaugurated, their activism. Two prominent young women from South Carolina, Modjeska Simkins and Septima Clark, emerged into adulthood during the war campaign that failed to make democracy accessible to them. Yet both women devoted their lives in the struggle for African Americans' full citizenship rights, employing the strategies they first learned in the war. Simkins and Clark's consistent and devoted practice of honing these same strategies, which had disappointed their parents, succeeded at making democracy a reality for the next generation.[42]

NOTES

1. *State,* April 5, 1917; *Greensboro Daily News,* July 17, 1917. Jeffrey J. Crow, Paul D. Escott, and Flora J. Hatley, *A History of African Americans in North Carolina* (Raleigh: Office of Archives and History, North Carolina Department of Cultural Resources, 2002), 125; Robin D. G. Kelly and Earl Lewis, eds., *To Make Our World Anew: A History of African Americans* (London: Oxford University Press, 2000), 396–97; James B. Dudley to Governor T.W. Bickett, August 6, 1917, Box 370, Governor Thomas W. Bickett Papers, North Carolina Department of Cultural Resources, Division of Archives and History (hereafter cited as NCDAH), Raleigh, NC. For an extensive analysis of rural southern dissent, see Jeanette Keith, *Rich Man's War, Poor Man's Fight: Race, Class, and Power in the Rural South during the First World War* (Chapel Hill: University of North Carolina Press, 2004).

2. For described studies, see Mark Ellis, *Race, War, and Surveillance: African Americans and the United States Government during World War I* (Bloomington: Indiana University Press, 2001); Theodore Kornweibel, Jr., *"Investigate Everything": Federal Efforts to Compel Black Loyalty during World War I* (Bloomington: Indiana University Press, 2002); Keith, *Rich Man's War, Poor Man's Fight.*

3. The most prominent voices of African American dissent came from national leaders, particularly those editors with the black press, but their audience and purpose were very different than those of southern black leaders. Moreover, that voice has received much attention. For a thorough examination of that perspective, see William G. Jordan, *Black Newspapers & America's War for Democracy, 1914–1920* (Chapel Hill: University of North Carolina Press, 2001).

4. South Carolina was a black majority state at the time of the war whereas in North Carolina, the African American population was just under one-third of the state's total.

5. See Glenda Gilmore, *Gender and Jim Crow: Women and the Politics of White Supremacy in North Carolina, 1896–1920* (Chapel Hill: University of North Carolina Press, 1996), for her characterization of the black elite as the "Best Men," those African Americans whom whites preferred to lead and even control their communities.

6. This heightened anxiety facilitated development of a wartime bureaucracy that investigated allegations of German subversion and provided close scrutiny of possible draft evasion. Known as the "Old German" series in the Justice Department's Bureau of Investigation, this file housed investigation records of suspected German subversion of African Americans. Theodore Kornweibel, in *"Investigate Everything,"* analyzes these voluminous records nationwide.

7. *New York Tribune* story of April 4, 1917, printed in full in *Greensboro Daily News,* April 5, 1917; Ellis, *Race, War, and Surveillance,* 5–6.

8. Petitions from Washington, Durham, Shaw University, Goldsboro, Pantego to Governor T. B. Bickett; James B. Dudley to Governor Bickett, April 7, 1917, Folder "Correspondence April 3–30, 1917," Box 369, Governor Bickett Papers, NCDAH; *Greensboro Daily News,* April 5, 8, 10, 11, 1917.

9. *Greensboro Daily News,* April 5, 8, 10, 11, 1917.

10. B. F. McLeod to Department of Justice, April 9, 1917; Agent Branch Bocock reports, May 10, 23, 1917, OG 3057, RG 65, Bureau of Investigation, reel 8; Theodore Kornweibel, Jr., ed., *Federal Surveillance of Afro-Americans 1917–1925: The First World War, the Red Scare, and the Garvey Movement* (Frederick, MD: University Publications of America, 1986).

11. *Charleston News and Courier,* April 8–9, 18, 1917; *State,* April 5, 22, 24, 1917.

12. David Alsobrook observes similar responses of African Americans in Alabama. See his essay "A Call to Arms for African Americans during the Age of Jim Crow: Black Alabamians' Response to the US Declaration of War," in Martin Olliff, ed. *Great War in the Heart of Dixie: Alabama during World War I* (University of Alabama Press, 2008), 81–100.

13. *Greensboro Daily Record,* May 28, 1917.

14. *Greensboro Daily Record,* March 29, 31, April 4, 27, 1918; *Winston-Salem Journal,* July 19, 1918. *Winston-Salem Registrar,* J. S. Kuykendall's summary notes on "Mobilization," Winston-Salem bound volume, 166–68, Box 2, V. Local Draft Boards, World War I Papers, Military Collection, NCDAH.

15. *Charlotte Observer,* July 20, 1918; *Greensboro Daily Record,* April 27, 1918; *Winston-Salem Journal,* July 19, 1918.

16. Recent studies that address the national African American experience in World War I include Chad L. Williams, *Torchbearers of Democracy: African American Soldiers in World War I Era* (Chapel Hill: University of North Carolina Press, 2010); Nina Mjagkij, *Loyalty in Time of Trial: The African American Experience in World War I* (Lanham: Rowman & Littlefield, 2011); Adriane Lentz-Smith, *Freedom Struggles: African Americans and World War I* (Cambridge: Harvard University Press, 2009); Jennifer Keene, *Doughboys, the Great War, and the Remaking of America* (Baltimore: Johns Hopkins University Press, 2001). Yet none of these studies address the experience of black Carolinians specifically. See Arthur E. Barbeau and Florette Henri, *The Unknown Soldiers: African-American Troops in World War I* (1974, repr., New York: Da Capo Press, 1996), 36.Tables on data by state and race found in United States Provost Marshal General's Bureau, *Second Report of the Provost Marshal General to the Secretary of War on the Operations of the Selective Service System to December 20, 1918* (Washington, Government Printing Office, 1919), 458–59; for a thorough discussion of North Carolina soldiers' experiences, see Janet G. Hudson, "Black North Carolinians as Soldiers in the Great War: Microcosm of the National African American Experience," in *North Carolina during the First World War, 1914–1922,* University of Tennessee Press. forthcoming. Stowers

received the Medal of Honor posthumously in 1991. In 2015, President Barack Obama posthumously awarded William Henry Johnson, of the 369th Infantry Regiment, the same rare and coveted Congressional Medal of Honor. Johnson was from Winston-Salem but was inducted in New York, where he lived when the war began.

17. A list of the commissioned officers is found in Emmett J. Scott, *Scott's Official History of the American Negro in the World War* (1919, repr., New York: Arno Press, 1969), 471–81. There were two all-black divisions organized in World War I—the 92nd and 93rd. The 92nd Division was created with drafted soldiers and the 93rd with National Guard units. For a discussion of African American officers, see Williams, *Torchbearers of Democracy*, 38–51.

18. On August 23, 1917, approximately one hundred African American soldiers from the 24th Infantry, who had been moved recently from New Mexico to Houston to guard the construction of Camp Logan and who had encountered racial hostility and discrimination from white civilians, marched to Houston armed and angry. The details and provocation are disputed but at the conclusion of two hours, sixteen whites, including five police officers, and four black soldiers had been killed. For a thorough exploration, see Robert Haynes, *A Night of Violence: The Houston Mutiny of 1917* (Baton Rouge: Louisiana State University Press, 1976).

19. Janet G. Hudson, *Entangled by White Supremacy: Reform in World War I Era South Carolina* (Lexington: University Press of Kentucky, 2009), 89–97. See also Janet G. Hudson, "Black North Carolinian Soldiers in the Great War: A Microcosm of the National African American Experience," chapter in *North Carolina during the First World War, 1914–1922*, University of Tennessee Press, forthcoming.

20. From April through October 1917 numerous internal committees within the War College Division (planning unit) of the War Department circulated internal memos drafting, critiquing, and revising plans for what they termed "Utilization of colored men drafted for the National Army." The correspondence reveals frequently changing recommendations and suggests that a host of pressures within and outside the War Department influenced the decision makers. Two lengthy memos, with attachments, document some of this history. Memorandum for the Adjutant General of the Army from the Chief of Staff, War College Division, August 1, 1917, File #8142–13; Memorandum for the Secretary of War, August 24, 1917, File #8142–17, National Archives Microfilm Publication M1024, Correspondence of the War College Division and Related General Staff Officers 1903–1919, Army War College and the War College Division 1900–1948, Records of the War Department General and Special Staffs, Record Group 165 (hereafter as M1024/RG 165), Memorandum for the Adjutant General, November 23, 1917, File #45–3188, "Colored Organization of the U.S. Army" Folder, Records of the Historical Section (Entry 310), Army War College and the War College Division 1900–1948, Textural Records RG 165 (hereafter Entry 310/RG 165), National Archives at College Park, MD (hereafter as NACP); Barbeau and Henri, *Unknown Soldiers*, 80–83. The 371st Infantry Regiment joined the other regiments created from National Guards and formed the 93rd Division.

21. Branch Files, Group I, boxes G196-G197, Papers of the NAACP, LC. The growth of the NAACP in the Carolinas supports the argument made by Lee Sartain in his chapter "'The Race's Greatest Opportunity since Emancipation'" in this volume.

22. For a thorough discussion, see Hudson, *Entangled by White Supremacy*, 110–11.

23. *Greensboro Daily News,* December 4, 1918; Theodore Hemmingway, "Prelude to Change: Black Carolinians in the War Year 1914–1920," *Journal of Negro History* 65 (Summer 1980): 216–17; *State,* June 22, November 14. 1918; *Greenville News,* November 9, 1918.

24. For a discussion of the controversy surrounding *Birth of a Nation*'s initial release, see Thomas R. Cripps, "The Reaction of the Negro to the Motion Picture *Birth of a Nation,*" *Historian* 25 (1963): 344–62; *State,* May 24, 1918.

25. *State,* May 24–25, 1918; *Columbia Record,* May 24, 1918.

26. "Colored Teachers in Charleston Schools," *Crisis,* June 1921, 58–60; Hudson, *Entangled by White Supremacy,* 116–19.

27. *Greensboro Daily News,* January 3, 5, 1919; *State,* January 2, 1919.

28. *State,* January 2, 1919; *Winston-Salem Journal,* January 8, 1919; Crow et al., *African Americans in North Carolina,* 125–26.

29. *State,* January 23, 1919, November 14, 1918.

30. *State,* February 4, 1919.

31. *State, February* 21–22, 1919. Robert J. Dalessandro and Gerald Torrence, *Willing Patriots: Men of Color in the First World War* (Atglen, PA: Schiffer Publishing, 2009), 106–9; For the names of soldiers, see W. J. Megginson, "Black South Carolinians in World War I: The Official Roster as a Resource for Local History, Mobility, and African-American History," *South Carolina Historical Magazine* 96 (1995): 153–73; For a contemporary's assessment of the experience, see Chester D. Heywood, *Negro Combat Troops in the World War: The Story of the 371st Infantry* (Commonwealth Press, 1928; repr., New York: AMS Press, 1969).

32. *State,* February 22, 1919. Parts of this and the preceding paragraph are drawn directly from Hudson, *Entangled by White Supremacy,* 11–14.

33. *State,* February 26, 1919.

34. *Greensboro Daily News,* April 26, 1919.

35. E. A. Harleston Address and Butler W. Nance Address, Tenth Anniversary Conference of the NAACP, Report of Branches, June 28, 1919, pt. 1, reel 8; Mrs. R. T. Brooks to James W. Johnson, March 8, 1919; Butler W. Nance, "Notes from the Columbia Branch," May 20, 1919, Part 12-A (Selected Branch Files), reel 18, Papers of the NAACP.

36. Graydon, attorney of Logan & Graydon, to Robert A. Cooper, July 26, 1919; Philip G. Palmer to Robert A. Cooper, October 3, 1919, Robert A. Cooper Papers, South Carolina Department of Archives and History, Columbia, SC.

37. *Plaindealer* (Topeka, KS), April 18, 1919.

38. Transcript of Ernest McKissick Oral History Interview by Dr. Louis Silveri, August 2, 1977, Southern Highlands Research Center, UNC-A. Retrieved from http://toto.lib.unca.edu/findingaids/oralhistory/SHRC/mckissick_ernest.pdf. Also see Robert T. Kerline, *The Voice of the Negro 1919* (New York: Arno Press, 1968), 37–38. For a thorough analysis of the violence in Winston-Salem, see Joanne Glenn, "The Winston-Salem Riot of 1918" (M.A. thesis, University of North Carolina at Chapel Hill, 1979); for Charleston race riot, see Hudson, *Entangled by White Supremacy,* 140–41.

39. *Charlotte Observer,* October 1–2, 1919: *Greensboro Record,* October 2, 1919; *Greenville Daily News,* October 3, 1919; *Winston-Salem Journal,* October 7, 10, 1919.

40. *Winston-Salem Journal,* October 8, 1919.

41. Arthur Bunyan Caldwell, *History of the Negro and His Institutions,* Vol. 3, *South Carolina* (Atlanta: Caldwell Publishing, 1919), 190.

42. Adriane Lentz-Smith and Chad Williams argue that the wartime, and particularly military experiences, galvanized a generation of African Americans to struggle for full citizenship rights. See Lentz-Smith, *Freedom Struggles;* Chad Williams, "Vanguards of the New Negro: African American Veterans and Post-World War I Racial Militancy," *Journal of African American History* 92 (2007): 347–70, who argues that World War I veterans were active shapers of the New Negro movement. Abstract from Ernest B. McKissick Paper, 1918–1924, Southern Historical Collection, University of North Carolina University Libraries, http://www2.iib.unc.edu/mss/inv/m/McKissick,Ernest_B .html. Simkins' mother was a charter member of the Columbia NAACP and she began teaching in 1920. Clark participated in the Charleston campaign to secure signature on the petition to hire black teachers. See Hudson, *Entangled by White Supremacy,* 311–12.

7

"The Race's Greatest Opportunity since Emancipation"

The National Association for the Advancement of
Colored People, the Great War, and the South

LEE SARTAIN

When World War I broke out in Europe in 1914, the National Association for the Advancement of Colored People (NAACP) was a fledgling organization, a mere five years old. Emerging in response to the Springfield, Illinois, riot of 1908, the NAACP sought to address a number of pressing issues for African Americans, including voting rights, lynch mob violence, and racist depictions (the latter most notably in protests against the popular film *Birth of a Nation*). Yet, at the outset of the Great War, the organization had yet to make its mark on the national consciousness as the foremost civil rights organization of the twentieth century. Moreover, while the organization's genesis came in response to northern violence, its leaders needed to design a strategy to address the specific problems of the South, a region marked by a large African American population living and working under the oppressive conditions of segregation and disfranchisement. World War I provided an opportunity for the NAACP to emerge as an effective campaigning organization, able to navigate strategically the federal system, to speak to the tribulations facing southern black communities, and to move beyond an era marked, most notably, by Booker T. Washington's conservatism to become a recognizably modern civil rights organization.[1]

Today, the NAACP has become synonymous with organizational civil rights, yet the group was not assured survival or longevity at any stage of its early development. The Niagara Movement, established in 1905, failed to cohere around a permanent liberal program and did not demonstrate the ability to sustain itself financially. In fact, other groups had dissipated in the late nineteenth century that could be seen as forerunners of the NAACP, such as the Afro-American League, the National Afro-American Council, and the Committee of Twelve.[2] Indeed, in 1916, the NAACP was still arguing over what to call itself.[3] Moreover, many opponents of segregation did not back the work of the organization; Booker T. Washington, for instance, saw the NAACP as a threat to his own power base and believed that northern elites could not understand or represent black lives in the rural South. Before his death in 1915, Washington embodied an era in which black leaders sought to address segregation conservatively; the NAACP's leadership and their approach to inequality which suggested that African Americans should demand rights with greater immediacy were relative outliers in the national conversation on civil rights and justice.

World War I provided an opportunity for the NAACP to address those problems and concerns. The United States' involvement in the conflict allowed the NAACP to coalesce its tactical approaches at a time of increasing federal power, in a manner which related to the condition of the majority of African Americans who lived in the South. Furthermore, the NAACP was able to gain some traction as the country reckoned with the state of African American life after the war. During the war, the NAACP developed a national and international strategy that replaced Booker T. Washington's conservative model, which was marked by a gradualist, integrationist approach limited by white intransigence, with its own more radical approach. In doing so, the NAACP paved the way for the modern civil rights era.[4]

Given that the war provided an opportunity for the advancement of the NAACP's mission, it is, perhaps, surprising that its founders divided over support for the war. Some of its leaders, such as its first president, Moorfield Storey, and activist Mary White Ovington, did not support the war effort due to their pacifist beliefs. Oswald Garrison Villard, chair and treasurer of the early NAACP, put it as a personal "matter of record" at a board of directors discussion that the NAACP's call for black men to enlist as equal to whites "in no way implies support of conscription or any military system."[5] Yet others argued that African Americans should fight for their country, with the defense effort serving as a way to assert patriotism and make a case for the extension of equal rights. For example, W. E. B. DuBois, a founding member of the Niagara Movement and the first African American to earn a PhD from Harvard, issued a "closed ranks" plea in the NAACP journal, *The Crisis* (which he edited from 1910 to 1934), that asked blacks to assist in the war effort in order to advance their civil rights. However, DuBois was heavily criticized for "selling out" when it became known that he was offered a captaincy in the Military Intelligence Branch.[6]

Yet, as American participation in the war escalated, the organization's leaders came around to DuBois's point of view; as the pacifist Storey put it, if the African American population was "needed in war they are just as much needed in peace" and should be given their American constitutional rights.[7] Similarly in 1917, James Weldon Johnson, appointed acting secretary of the NAACP in that year, saw that "the Negro is becoming an increasingly important factor in the United States. Colored men and women are entering factories and workshops that were completely closed to them three years ago. This is certain to create race friction, but it is equally certain to secure higher Negro manhood, a more self-reliant, industrious type of black men."[8]

Once the war began, the NAACP sought to make clear the link between American citizenship and military service, and the board of directors voted to "oppose and take every feasible step to prevent any discrimination against Negroes in any volunteer or compulsory military act." And, the organization stated, "the Negro must demand this evidence of citizenship on exactly the same terms as other American citizens."[9]

The NAACP's encouragement of black enlistment brought an immediate problem: segregation in the US military. Given President Woodrow Wilson's approval of the segregation of the federal bureaucracy in 1913, this issue proved particularly difficult.[10] The association confronted an unpalatable choice: either have no black officers due to segregated training facilities (leaving black regiments to be led entirely by white officers) or have separate officer training and thereby maintain (and seemingly condone) segregated military units. DuBois resolved to the board of directors that the NAACP "believes that colored officers ought to be provided for the colored regiments already ordered." And, he continued, while the NAACP remained "thoroughly opposed" to segregated training camps, the organization would prefer separate camps to having no training camps for black officers. The resolution was only carried after "considerable discussion" and sat uneasily alongside NAACP political stridency on integration more generally.[11]

On the home front, the central focus of the NAACP's wartime campaigns was its efforts to stop lynching, particularly in the South. NAACP press releases during this time regularly highlighted the crime of lynching and white mob violence, unfavorably comparing the practice with the patriotic participation of

African Americans in the war. The organization singled out Louisiana as having "the unenviable record of having lynched eleven Negroes without trial, six of those lynchings having occurred since January 1 [1918]." Such pronouncements show that the NAACP saw President Wilson's declaration of war on April 2, 1917, and its prodemocratic rhetoric as a "year zero" for black rights and American politics—a point by which the US government could redeem itself from the history of slavery and the abandonment of Reconstruction-era policies supporting black rights. A telegram sent to Louisiana governor Ruffin G. Pleasant exemplifies the NAACP's effort to conflate black rights and the global war, calling out southern states specifically for inequality during a war fought (at least rhetorically) for democracy and freedom. The NAACP declared that "Louisiana is in the position of embarrassing the nation in its death struggle against autocratic powers."[12]

The NAACP conducted in-depth studies of lynching and proclaimed that contrary to the South's standard argument on mob violence toward blacks, the protection of white women from black savages was rarely directly used to legitimize the specific acts. Instead, the organization argued that upholding white supremacy and economic inequality were the major catalysts for lynching and racial violence. Through the studies, the association sought to highlight the contradictions and hypocrisy of the South's actions toward blacks, noting how such arguments diametrically opposed President Wilson's call to make the world "safe for democracy." Indeed, John Shillady, NAACP executive secretary, proclaimed that during the war in "the case of the Negroes who have been lynched no question of loyalty to their country has been raised in any case."[13]

Efforts to address injustices at home allowed the NAACP to gradually formalize and ritualize the kinds of protests, like marches and mass meetings, that eventually became a mainstay of the movement for civil rights. The "Negro Silent Protest Parade," which occurred in New York City on July 28, 1917, used a public march in order to portray southern race crimes as a national problem incompatible with American war aims. Officially sanctioned banners such as "Memphis and Waco—Centers of American Culture?" and "Make America Safe for Democracy" clearly presented southern injustices as a point of national (and, indeed, international) concern.[14]

The organization juxtaposed the dignity of the Silent Parade with white, segregationist mob rule in the South, all couched in the imagery of an international effort to defend democracy. As an NAACP official pamphlet observed, "The children will lead the parade followed by the Women in white, while the Men will bring up the rear. The labourer, the professional man—all classes of the Race—will march on foot to the beating of muffled drums. The native born, the foreign born, united by ties of blood and color, all owing allegiance to the Mother of races will parade silently with the flags of America, England, Haiti and Liberia." This symbolism of race, gender, and nationality (balancing white and black republics in the publicity) was set alongside the war aims of President Wilson to "make impossible a repetition of Waco, Memphis and East St. Louis, by rousing the conscience of the country and bring the murderers of our brothers, sisters and innocent children to justice . . . We march because we want our children to live in a better land and enjoy fairer conditions than have fallen to our lot."[15]

In fact, the specific reference to race riots in both the North and the South (East St. Louis in the North, Waco and Memphis in the South) strategically illustrated that the race issue was a national problem and not simply a regional one. The East St Louis, Illinois, massacre of 1917, in which up to two hundred African Americans were murdered, spoke to the conflict that emerged as southern blacks migrated to northern cities for greater opportunities and more freedom. The "Waco Horror" referred to the lynching of a black man, Jesse Washington, in 1916, demonstrating the lack of equal justice for blacks in the United States. Ell Persons had been lynched by a white mob in Memphis, Tennessee, in May 1917, after confessing, under extreme duress and despite a lack of evidence, to the murder of a sixteen-year-old girl. Persons's death was investigated by James Weldon Johnson of the NAACP, who published details of the injustice in *The Crisis*. Taken together, these cases demonstrated that Wilson's "war for democracy" abroad was not being practiced on the home front.[16]

Moreover, the organization's statement describing the parade specifically noted that the "children will lead." The deployment of youth in civil rights rhetoric, especially during wartime conscription, was symbolic of the hope for American racial progress in the future. References to youth also indicated an innocence untainted by worldliness or corruption—itself a symbol of American faith in its exceptionalist national destiny. John Shillady stated that African Americans were willing to sacrifice this innocence "to make the world safe for democratic government. One hundred thousand of the best colored youth of the land have responded to the call of the country and are preparing to give their lives in its defense and in support of the cause upon which it is embarked."[17] The initial optimism and idealism of the war was, in this manner, to sweep through the racist and autocratic South and bring justice and democracy to all.

The NAACP experienced some limited success petitioning President Wilson on the matter, and he denounced mob violence in his appeal to "keep the nation's fame untarnished," identifying the domestic terrorism "of the mob" as a "betrayer of democracy" as part of an international propaganda battle. In his efforts, James Weldon Johnson found Wilson to be "surprisingly interested and engaged" in the issues of black soldier life and lynching. As Wilson was the first southerner to be president since Andrew Johnson, the potentially national unifying symbol of the chief executive also brought race back to the forefront of the national debate as well as reflecting the growing power of the federal government. However, Johnson was to be disappointed in Wilson's enthusiasm on the race issue, which was directly reflective of his southern upbringing (indeed DuBois had similarly misplaced faith by favoring Wilson's candidacy in the 1912 election). Indeed Wilson's segregation of the federal bureaucracy, citing that racial separation was to the benefit of both races, and his public adoration of *Birth of a Nation* (1915), reflected these southern sensibilities.[18]

In addition to its national efforts to bring attention to southern racial injustices in the context of the global struggle for democracy, the NAACP also founded a proliferation of local branches across the South, though they tended to be small bastions of black middle-class resistance that often did not survive for long due to the social and economic pressures of Jim Crow on black communities, the geographic isolation of many areas of the South, and a lack of coherent black middle-class political consciousness.[19] In other cases, though, African American soldiers in the South boosted branch membership, such as in Texas, although these numbers were fragile because of local oppression of the organization and its membership and the linking of black militancy to the war effort.[20]

In the more successful southern branches, the wartime economic stimulus, expansion of federal power and an overt emphasis on patriotism and ideals of democracy and liberty translated into a notable push for greater black citizenship. The New Orleans NAACP branch, in its short-lived city newspaper *The Vindicator,* stated that the war was "the race's greatest opportunity since emancipation. The race is on trial, and it is up to us to prove ourselves equal to the task before us. . . . The Kaiser and Kaiserdom must be crushed everywhere. . . .

The black man joins hands in the great fight against Autocracy. He prays for a Democracy that will give to every man his just desserts . . . our first duty is to help win the war."[21]

For many local branches, the most pressing concern was suffrage, particularly among those African Americans actively serving their country. Black soldiers in training camps were not always given access to the ballot, and if they had access then it was not always clear that their votes were counted. The NAACP sent a letter to President Wilson claiming "that in many Southern States Negro electors [in training camps] have been prevented from casting their ballots." Despite their efforts, Secretary of War Newton D. Baker rejected federal oversight of elections.[22] The administration considered the ballot a state issue, and some believed that stepping in would align Wilson with Reconstruction-era policies that might alienate his base in the Democratic South. The administration claimed that its decision was made in the interest of racial "justice . . . to see the [segregation] matter settled in a way to make the least friction." Nevertheless, the NAACP's willingness to reach out to the highest office in the nation demonstrates its desire to use the war as a means of obtaining integration and full constitutional rights via federal action.[23]

In addition to limited access to the ballot, the NAACP addressed the second-class conditions that black soldiers faced at home and abroad. It reported that the US government provided African American servicemen substandard training, used them as menial laborers, and delayed granting commissions to black officers.[24] NAACP secretary John Shillady took the issues up with Secretary of War Baker, asserting that "a disproportionate number of colored soldiers [were] in industrial battalions rather than in combative service" and that "colored officers or soldiers would be forced into Jim Crow cars in the South while on official business." While there was an unofficial promise to transfer black troops to the front, Baker stated "that he would take no action regarding the Jim Crow car question, repeating his well-known attitude that his job was to get the largest and best army he could to France and that he was not going to deal with the race question."[25]

This litany of issues, which were often but not exclusively in a southern context, gave evidence that civil rights for African Americans was, in fact, a national issue and that the federal government, already using its broad war powers, could solve critical problems of the age. The experience of Lieutenant Charles A. Tribbett exemplifies this. Tribbett, from New Haven, Connecticut, earned a degree in electrical engineering from Yale University and graduated from an officers' training camp in Des Moines, Iowa. While Tribbett was on duty and in uniform, he was arrested in Oklahoma for riding in a Pullman coach with white people. Despite protesting that he was traveling in pursuit of government business, he was jailed and fined. The case was contested because it dealt with interstate travel and Tribbett was therefore not subject to state law, but Tribbett, on advice from his attorney, paid his bail and resumed his official duties.[26] The attempt to nationalize civil rights in this way during the war securely established the NAACP tactic of pursuing rights through legal challenges and constitutional law, although it found an even less receptive political situation during the 1920s.

When the NAACP sought to highlight events in the South, it attempted to place blacks' second-class citizenship into a national framework of wartime campaigning. Publicity given to soldiers, such as those stationed at Camp Alexander, Virginia, was part of the attempt to federalize black rights and to return to a framework of Reconstruction-era politics in which federal action superseded state laws that did not protect all citizens. This included the recurrent issue of travel on "the cars that run into the camp," on which there were reports of "daily disturbances on account of Jim Crowism." African American sergeant Bernard Henderson wrote to DuBois that the men at Camp Alexander were given inadequate amenities and some claimed that "last winter men died in this camp like sheep." The soldiers felt "that the part they have played in this war is commendable as the men that have been to the front. They are the ones that have loaded ships with food and ammunition and made it possible for those that have been sent over, and for Pres. Wilson's democracy, which they believe to be a farce." Many of the African American men in the camp were trained professionals, in fields such as dentistry and medicine, but were not promoted beyond the rank of sergeant. Additionally, Henderson reported that black soldiers were "cursed, kicked and often beaten."[27]

African American women, too, suffered from the effects of state-sponsored prejudice. Some women were subject to forced labor laws at the state level, reminiscent of slavery and the black codes in the immediate aftermath of the Civil War. The organization reported an attempt by the state of Arkansas to implement "compulsory work laws which are applied against colored women only" that would force them to work on cotton plantations during the conflict. The NAACP responded in a telegram to Arkansas governor Charles H. Brough that there was no attempt "made to conscript [the] labor of white women. The nation as a whole will regard [this] attempt to conscript colored women as in the nature of peonage. Negroes of the country are serving loyally in [the] nation's armed forces and on its industrial battlefields."[28] Here again, the NAACP made painfully clear the dissonance between the wartime rhetoric of "democracy" and the treatment of African Americans in the segregated South.

In fact, the NAACP viewed military camps, in particular, as sites where soldiers and laborers might prepare to become active citizens and to become aware of the broader civil rights struggle. As such, the organization demanded that the government provide training and education that might allow for personal advancement. For instance, Sergeant Henderson complained specifically to the NAACP that in Camp Alexander, no "provisions are made . . . for night schools as in some camps," while socially they were ostracized as the YMCA was closed to them; "guards are stationed to prevent us from entering," and "Sundays are not regarded here."[29]

Such criticism sometimes brought recrimination. In late 1918, S. A. Brown, pastor of Gillfield Baptist Church in Petersburg, Virginia, attempted to reach across the color line by arranging a meeting between white and black unionized carpenters after thirty-six black carpenters were turned away at the building of the barracks at Camp Lee when whites refused to work with them. Brown argued that such "prejudice is unfair, unjust, undemocratic. These men are loyal, patriotic, natural born citizens of Petersburg." Highlighting the contradiction between US war aims and the unequal treatment of American citizens, he asked, "Is this what we are buying Bonds for? Is this what our best boys are in France for?"[30] Others, however, declared that such critics of discrimination were "agitators and radicals" who would negate the "good work" and influence that blacks had contributed to during wartime.[31]

And those who complained about such conditions could face disciplinary action. Stanley Moore was arrested for writing to his sister about the "cruel and brutal treatment the Negro soldiers were undergoing" at Camp Travis, Texas. At Camp Alexander, Virginia, a noncommissioned black officer who had questioned a white officer for "cursing blacks . . . was arrested and charged with trying to incite mutiny among the men . . . for trying to be smart."[32]

While the organization's efforts to demand equal treatment at training camps emerged directly from the dislocations that appeared during the war effort and appealed to the charged rhetoric of the Wilson administration, certain NAACP campaigns predated American involvement in the war. These pre-existing programs were nevertheless integrated into the war effort and attached to wartime concepts, such as sustaining national morale. The campaign against the D. W. Griffith film *Birth of a Nation* was such a national campaign. Since the film's first release in 1915, the NAACP attempted to get the movie, which depicted a racist interpretation of slavery and Reconstruction, either banned, censored, or retold to reflect the actual history; soon, the NAACP began to argue that the film undermined the war effort.[33] The campaign reflected the tactical approach of combining local and national appeals for change while situating those protests in the wartime lexicon of patriotism and democracy. The NAACP board of directors thought that the federal, or at least the respective state governments, might be receptive to censoring or banning such an alienating film to keep African Americans "to a man, unfaltering in their loyalty to the program the Government has asked its people to follow in order to win this great war."[34]

As in other wartime campaigns, the NAACP took a multilayered approach to censoring or removing the film from public viewing. The NAACP called on Griffith and the film studios to create more positive black images and to remove the worst excesses of *Birth of a Nation*. With a degree of success, the association also lobbied politicians at the state level across the nation. Due to NAACP pressure, the governor of Ohio, James M. Cox, asked the producers of *Birth of a Nation* "to withdraw the film for the period of the war." In a press release, the NAACP reported that in the interests "of national unity [the NAACP] has begun a nation-wide campaign against certain movie plays which serve to stir up race antagonisms between white and colored people and against unduly offensive caricatures of colored people."[35] Shillady stated, "At the present time when colored people are performing their full share of patriotic service both in the fighting forces of the nation on the battle fronts of Europe and at home, and when national unity and not race differences and antagonisms should be accentuated, it is important to the national morale that all divisive influences be subordinated to the common good."[36] Besides Ohio, the NAACP had some success with curtailing the showing of the film in West Virginia.

Deeper into Dixie, however, the NAACP met with more predictable intransigence and deliberate misunderstanding. Governor Theodore G. Bilbo of Mississippi declared that he would not follow Governor Cox's example:

I beg to state that this film has already been widely exhibited in Mississippi, in fact it has been presented at every play house in the state, I believe and I question whether it is the intention of the producers to show it again. However, I will say that the showing of this picture was not objected to so far I ever heard, by the colored people in Mississippi and caused no friction between the races. As it has been shown, as stated, and is not likely to be shown generally, again, I do not see the necessity for requesting The D. W. Griffith Corporation, No.1476 Broadway, to withdraw it.[37]

As the efforts to ban *Birth of a Nation* suggest, the war brought up issues of morality, patriotism, and conformity across the South in the search for unity of national purpose. The NAACP highlighted the case of Dr. J. A. Miller of Vicksburg, Mississippi, who had refused to purchase an excessive number of "War Savings Stamps upon demand of the Vicksburg War Saving Committee" and "was tarred and feathered by Vicksburg people, among whom . . . were police officers." The NAACP reported that Miller was ordered to leave the city "by the Mayor, and . . . his house was broken into and goods stolen. Dr. Miller states that he had agreed to buy $150 worth of War Saving Stamps, which was all that he could afford to purchase."[38]

This high profile patriotism, often enforced, was used to maintain the status quo and was specifically directed at the black middle class and those who had money and might be susceptible to NAACP values and appeals. Indeed, Dr. Miller had organized and was president of the Vicksburg NAACP branch in 1918, which was the first in the state and which had thirty-six members; therefore, the unreasonable demands made upon him were a direct attack on his political activities. This also reflects the impossible standards of patriotism that the black population saw themselves needing to attain in order to win their rights.[39]

Indeed, the NAACP was particularly concerned about the issue of "moral problems" within the black community, especially issues of sexuality and behavior that might tarnish the group's status in the view of white people. When authorities arrested two black soldiers for drunkenness at Camp Bowie, Texas, black organizations used the incident to criticize such activities: "Colored men have done boot-legging principally among white soldiers. Some colored men [were] arrested for bringing [a] coffin filled with whiskey into Camp. Rules against gambling seldom enforced." Women, black and white, were also arrested in the camp for prostitution and were examined for venereal diseases.[40]

In New Orleans, there were similar attacks on immoral behavior, attacks which the local NAACP branch enthusiastically embraced. Although the "red light district" in the city, informally known as Storyville, had been officially closed in 1917, raids continued throughout 1918 against "Society ladies" in what was called the "War on Joints." The Central Congregational Church in the city formed a committee "for the purpose of establishing a rescue home for fallen women and girls." The New Orleans branch publication, *The Vindicator*, detailed that

> large numbers of women of both races have been arrested recently because of their failure to comply to our country's call for a higher standard of morality— a better way of living. . . . This movement, if successfully carried out, is going to mean much to our whole city. The morals of our boys and girls will be safeguarded and a better standard of living assured. . . . This work cannot be done by the civil authorities alone. There must be a united effort on the part of those who live on a higher plane. Much can be accomplished if each one of us, considering ourselves a committee of one, seizes every opportunity to lift our fallen sisters out of the mire.[41]

This moral impulse in American politics was part of the NAACP creed and the organization believed that the fate of the black population as a whole was tied to this American "national morale." Winning the war, John Shillady stated in 1918, "will demand not alone military resources, but industrial efficiency, moral cohesion and social stamina."[42]

The NAACP believed that the effects of its wartime campaigns would result in marked improvements in the lives of African Americans in the postwar years. In fact, such "industrial efficiency" and "social stamina" might translate into peacetime gains, particularly in terms of economic opportunity. Yet as the United States prepared for the transition, black troops were once again the victims of discriminatory preferences; white troops demobilized first, providing a distinct advantage for postwar job opportunities. Walter White, the assistant NAACP national secretary, called this preference a "deliberate move" that gave white veterans "a chance to secure the best positions, so that when colored troops of any great numbers are released from the army, the most advantageous jobs will all have been taken." White also noted a "second possibility," one that spoke more directly to the inequalities that black soldiers faced during their years of service. Delayed demobilization for African American servicemen and -women meant that they would be "held in camp to do the hard and unpleasant work of cleaning up and taking down of those camps which are not to be permanent."[43] This latter critique certainly was in keeping with the idea that black soldiers were laborers and that such work should be left to them.

With demobilization came a greater impetus for blacks to leave the South and migrate toward cities and the North where more economic opportunities and more liberal social conditions existed. The Great Migration was "not new, but only accelerated by the War emergency"; according to John Shillady, it was part of "an ancient quest for a larger life whose chief manifestation has been in the trend from country to city, so characteristic of our machine and factory age." He added, "But more potent than economic or health factors as affecting Negro migration . . . are those that touch the soul—the things that afford or deny him the deep human satisfaction of life as more than meat and raiment. I refer to those unsatisfied and unwelcomed yearnings for spiritual and mental participation in the life of the Soul."[44]

For some members of the NAACP, both nationally and locally, this shift toward urban centers across the South and the widespread northward migration was not necessarily a positive development. Shillady believed that African Americans could assist in moving the South into the modern era if white businessmen provided economic opportunities that would entice them to stay in the region. Like other civil rights activists in the period, Shillady saw a blend of fiscal and social reasons for "Negro labor's disquietude," but he argued that there was a spiritual direction, too, in the impetus to go North and westward. The New Orleans NAACP branch believed that to stop the exodus, African Americans required a "square deal" to "make the South fit for the black man to live in and we can . . . honestly tell our people from the pulpit and from the platforms to remain in Dixie and make the cotton fields bloom and the cane fields wave [and] the factories roar and the gins and steamers whistle as the black man in contentment and satisfaction sings his cornfield songs and plantation melodies, in the balmy breezes of Dixie's Land and under Dixie's blue skies."[45]

Cities were often an identifiable "American frontier" to many black people in the South who sought better prospects, and the Great Migration led to the emergence of areas of economic opportunity in southern cities. Baltimore, Maryland, for example, underwent a 32% increase in its black population in the decade containing the Great War, the largest net increase in the city since 1840–50. The Baltimore NAACP branch in 1917 gave "a hearty welcome to our brethren from the South who have recently come to . . . industrial centers in this vicinity." However, such migration could also contribute to challenges for the NAACP, due to the appeal of the Universal Negro Improvement Association (UNIA) as wartime beliefs of integration gave way to Black Nationalism, particularly among urban populations. Marcus Garvey, founder of the UNIA, criticized the NAACP for its intellectual and urban leadership, which he asserted was divorced from the majority of black people's lives. In turn, the NAACP asserted that Garvey exploited the uneducated black masses by promoting unachievable and fanciful goals, such as continued black separatism and migration to West Africa. Garvey's message, however, grew in popularity during the 1920s as African Americans became disillusioned with the false promise of greater equality they thought would come because of their service in the Great War. New Orleans was seen as a "Mecca for Garveyites," with five thousand UNIA members by 1925, whereas the NAACP could muster a mere 206.[46]

Nevertheless, membership in the NAACP increased dramatically during World War I, from a reported 8,710 at the start of 1917 to 35,898 in July 1918 and pushing to over 40,000 by the time peace was declared that November. The association continued to develop its branch system across the country, and by 1919, embodying James Weldon Johnson's belief that a civil rights organization should reflect those it was trying to empower, the NAACP membership in the South exceeded that of the North for the first time. However, the NAACP message reached further than its actual membership, as indicated by the success of *The Crisis* magazine, which had an estimated circulation of approximately 100,000 by March 1918.[47]

Perhaps more than any other individual, James Weldon Johnson represents the transformational experience of the NAACP's wartime efforts. Born in Jacksonville, Florida, Johnson spent his formative years in the South before finally settling in the burgeoning cultural metropolis of Harlem. Initially a proponent of Booker T. Washington's accommodationism, Johnson became increasingly involved with the NAACP with a particular focus on expanding its reach and membership into the South. Johnson became acting secretary in 1917 and spent his time traveling through the southern states, documenting incidents of violence that he used to publicize the gap between the rhetoric of wartime democracy and the realities of racial inequality. Johnson became the organization's first black executive secretary in 1920, and in addition to his efforts to build the NAACP's southern membership, he encouraged political activism. His work to address lynching resulted in the Dyer Anti-Lynching Bill, which passed the House of Representatives in 1922 but was halted by a filibuster in the Senate.

Such campaigns turned the NAACP into an overwhelmingly black membership organization, making it slightly less dependent on individual contributions of white liberals. The organization was also more focused on establishing branches in areas where the majority of blacks actually lived, investigating local civil rights grievances, and advancing a growing black cultural movement in the 1920s.[48]

Historians traditionally situate the emergence of the NAACP as the preeminent national force for civil rights in the World War II years. Certainly, the organization took advantage of the fight against fascism and Nazism to confront Jim Crow, and the postwar era saw a more responsive federal government, particularly the Supreme Court, that proved more sympathetic to the organization's political and legal strategies. Yet the World War I era, too, was important to the development of the organization, in ways that have been largely overlooked and misunderstood. That war effort provided the NAACP with its first real opportunity to push into the South, addressing the most egregious instances of segregation and discrimination while building an organizational structure that might continue the struggle beyond the war years. Moreover, the rhetoric of Wilson's war to make the world "safe for democracy" combined with the mobilization of the federal government to provide an opportunity for the organization to employ a political and legal strategy to address inequality. Though that strategy met resistance at every level, it came to embody the NAACP's approach to civil rights and was foundational for later victories. World War I may not have brought the victory over segregation that the NAACP's leadership so stridently worked to realize, but the effort did provide a "great opportunity" for growth. In fact, the historical victories of the post–World War II era were, in many ways, indebted to the transformational experience of the Great War and the possibilities it presented in the assault on racial discrimination.[49]

NOTES

1. Risa Goluboff, *The Lost Promise of Civil Rights* (London: Harvard University Press, 2007), 9, 235; Harvard Sitkoff, *A New Deal for Blacks: The Emergence of Civil Rights as a National Issue* (New York: Oxford University Press, 2008); Richard Dalfiume, "The 'Forgotten Years' of the Negro Revolution," *Journal of American History* 55, no.1 (June 1968): 90–106; Patricia Sullivan, *Lift Every Voice: The NAACP and the Making of the Civil Rights Movement* (New York: New Press, 2009), 48–49; Kevern Verney and Lee Sartain, eds., *Long Is the Way and Hard: One Hundred Years of the*

National Association for the Advancement of Colored People (Fayetteville: University of Arkansas Press, 2009), 9–10.

2. Shawn Leigh Alexander, *An Army of Lions: The Civil Rights Struggle before the NAACP* (Philadelphia: University of Pennsylvania Press, 2012), xii, 42.

3. The board of directors approved of a change of name but remained divided on what was appropriate. The Garrison-Douglass Association was voted down 9 to 3. NAACP minutes of the meetings of board of directors, December 11, 1916, NAACP Papers, Group I, Box a-8, NAACP, Library of Congress, Washington, DC (LOC).

4. Sullivan, *Lift Every Voice*, 2–7.

5. NAACP Minutes of the meetings of board of directors, April 9, 1917, NAACP Papers, Group I, Box a-8, LOC; Charles Flint Kellogg, *NAACP: A History of the National Association for the Advancement of Colored People, Volume 1* (Baltimore: Johns Hopkins University Press, 1973), 272; William B. Hixon, *Moorfield Storey and the Abolitionist Tradition* (New York: Oxford University Press, 1971), 39.

6. Mark Ellis, "'Closing Ranks' and 'Seeking Honors': W. E. B. DuBois in World War I," *Journal of American History* 79, no. 1 (June, 1992), 96–124. Some criticized Du Bois for "selling out" when it became known that he was offered a captaincy in the Military Intelligence Branch.

7. Address by Moorfield Storey, Anti-Lynching Conference, May 6, 1919, NAACP Papers, Group I, Box 334, Folder 5, LOC.

8. James Weldon Johnson to Julius Rosenwald, September 1, 1917, NAACP Papers, Group I, c-66, Reel 3 (microfilm), LOC.

9. NAACP minutes of the meetings of board of directors, April 9, 1917, NAACP Papers, Group I, Box a-8, LOC.

10. Sullivan, *Lift Every Voice*, 27.

11. NAACP minutes of the meetings of board of directors, May 14, 1917, NAACP Papers, Group I, Box a-8, LOC.

12. NAACP press release, April 24, 1918, NAACP Papers, Group I, Box c-336, Folder 13, LOC. Tennessee, by comparison, counted five lynchings since the American declaration of war.

13. Open letter from John Shillady to Atty. General Thomas W. Gregory, May 10, 1918, NAACP Papers, Group I, Box c-336, Folder 13, LOC.

14. Negro Silent Protest Parade, July 28, 1917, flyer, NAACP Papers, Group I, Box c-334, Folder 12, LOC; Memorandum for NAACP branches: Mottoes used in the Negro Silent Parade, New York, ibid.; James Weldon Johnson to branch secretaries, August 9, 1917, ibid.; Anti-Lynching Conference program, May 6, 1919, ibid., Folder 5, LOC.

15. Negro Silent Protest Parade, July 28, 1917, flyer, NAACP Papers, Group I, Box c-334, Folder 12, LOC.

16. Open letter from John Shillady to Atty. General Thomas W. Gregory, May 10, 1918, NAACP Papers, Group I, Box c-336, Folder 13, LOC; *The Crisis*, July 1916; *The Crisis*, August 1917; Williams, *Torchbearers for Democracy*, 28, 65; Sullivan, *Lift Every Voice*, 65–66.

17. Open letter from John Shillady to Atty. General Thomas W. Gregory, May 10, 1918; Anna Hartnell, *Rewriting Exodus: American Futures from Du Bois to Obama* (London, Pluto Press, 2011), 18.

18. NAACP Official Bulletin, July 26, 1918, NAACP Papers, Group I, Box c-336, Folder 2, LOC; Sullivan, *Lift Every Voice*, 72, 75; Manning Marable, *W. E. B. Du Bois: Black Radical Democrat* (Boulder, CO: Paradigm, 2005), 90; Gloria J. Browne-Marshall, *The Voting Rights War: The NAACP and the Ongoing Struggle for Justice* (Lanham: Rowman & Littlefield, 2016), 64.

19. Kevern Verney, "'To Hope Till Hope Creates': The NAACP in Alabama, 1913–1945," in Verney and Sartain, *Long Is the Way*, 106; Lee Sartain, *Invisible Activists: Women of the Louisiana NAACP and the Struggle for Civil Rights, 1915–1945* (Baton Rouge: Louisiana State University Press, 2007), 54–56; Dorothy Autrey, "'Can these bones live?': The National Association for the Advancement of Colored People in Alabama, 1918–1930," *Journal of Negro History* 82, no.1 (Winter 1997): 1, 4.

20. Sullivan, *Lift Every Voice*, 77, 86, 99. In her chapter in this volume, entitled "The Great War and Expanded Equality?" Janet Hudson documents the emergence of active local branches in the Carolinas, and she notes particularly effective campaigns against the film *Birth of a Nation* and against white teachers in black schools (see above).

21. *The Vindicator*, September 3, 1918, Selected Branch Files, 1913–1939, Part 12, series A, Reel 14, NAACP Papers, microfilm, Cambridge University Library, England (CUL); Sartain, *Invisible Activists*, 52–53.

22. NAACP minutes of the meetings of board of directors, November 11, 1918, NAACP Papers, Group I, Box a-8, LOC.

23. Sullivan, *Lift Every Voice*, 27–28.

24. Report of the Director of Publications and Research, NAACP minutes of the meetings of board of directors, October 8, 1917, NAACP Papers, Group I, Box a-8, LOC.

25. NAACP minutes of the meetings of board of directors, March 11, 1918, NAACP Papers, Group I, Box a-8, LOC; E. J. Scott, "The American Negro in the World War; What the Association Did," membership flyer, 1918, NAACP Papers, Group I, Box c-374, Folder 1, LOC.

26. E. J. Scott, "The American Negro in the World War; What the Association Did," membership flyer, 1918, NAACP Papers, Group I, Box c-374, Folder 1, LOC; Chad L. Williams, *Torchbearers of Democracy: African American Soldiers in the World War I Era* (Chapel Hill: University of North Carolina Press, 2010), 85–86.

27. Sgt. Bernard O. Henderson to W. E. B. Du Bois, December 18, 1918, NAACP Papers, Group I, Box c-374, Folder 1, LOC; Williams, *Torchbearers of Democracy*, 110.

28. NAACP press release, September 24, 1918, NAACP Papers, Group I, Box c-319, Folder 3, LOC.

29. Sgt. Bernard O. Henderson to W. E. B. DuBois, December 18, 1918, NAACP Papers, Group I, Box c-374, Folder 1, LOC.

30. S. A. Brown to John Shillady, October 17, 1918, NAACP Papers, Group I, Box c-319, Folder 4, LOC; Brown to Shillady, November 8, 1918, ibid.

31. William Dobson, secretary, Bricklayers, Masons and Plasterers International Union, to Frank Morrison, secretary, AFL, n.d., 1918, NAACP Papers, Group I, Box c-319, Folder 3, LOC.

32. Miss Haydee Moore to John Shillady, December 30, 1918, NAACP Papers, Group I, Box c-374, Folder 1, LOC; Sgt. Bernard O. Henderson to W. E. B. Du Bois, December 18, 1918, NAACP Papers, Group I, Box c-374, Folder 1, LOC.

33. *New York Age,* May 18, 1918, NAACP Papers, Group I, Box c-301, Folder 5, LOC; Jenny Woodley, "In Harlem and Hollywood: The NAACP's Cultural Campaigns, 1910–1950," in Verney and Sartain, *Long Is the Way,* 20.

34. NAACP minutes of the meetings of board of directors, October 14, 1918, NAACP Papers, Group I, Box a-8, LOC; *New York Age,* May 18, 1918.

35. NAACP Press Release, October 9, 1918, NAACP Papers, Group I, Box c-301, Folder 5, LOC.

36. John Shillady to 'dear sir,' October 10, 1918, NAACP Papers, Group I, Box c-301, Folder 5, LOC.

37. Governor T. G. Bilbo to John Shillady, October 15, 1918, NAACP Papers, Group I, Box c-301, Folder 5, LOC.

38. The NAACP documents suggest that Dr. Miller was ordered to buy $1,000 of War Savings stamps which, if correct, was an extortionate amount and (if true) was perhaps demanded to catch out members of the NAACP in the state in order to suppress black agitation; NAACP minutes of the meetings of board of directors, September 9, 1918, NAACP Papers, Group I, Box a-8, LOC; October 14, 1918, ibid.; Sullivan, *Lift Every Voice,* 86.

39. Branches authorized during the year of 1918 report, NAACP Papers, Group I, Box A-23, Folder 5, LOC; Memorandum on Investigations into Social and Religious Conditions of Certain Camps, by Charles H. Williams, physical director at Hampton Institute (Colored), December 20, 1918, NAACP Papers, Group I, Box c-374, Folder 1, LOC.

40. Memorandum on Investigations into Social and Religious Conditions of Certain Camps, by Charles H. Williams, physical director at Hampton Institute (Colored), December 20, 1918, NAACP Papers, Group I, Box c-374, Folder 1, LOC.

41. "Social worker delivers address to colored citizens of N.O.," *The Vindicator,* August 20, 1918, Selected Branch Files, 1913–1939, Part 12, series A, Reel 14, NAACP Papers, CUL; "War on Joints," ibid., September 12, 1918; "A necessity for social workers," ibid.

42. Summary address of John R. Shillady at a meeting of committee of Memphis, Tennessee, Chamber of Commerce, April 13, 1918, NAACP Papers, Group I, Box c-74, reel 9 (microfilm), LOC.

43. Memorandum re: attached letter of complaint from Negro soldiers, Walter White, December 18, 1918, NAACP Papers, Group I, Box c-374, Folder 1, LOC.

44. Summary address of John R. Shillady at a meeting of committee of Memphis, Tennessee, Chamber of Commerce, April 13, 1918, NAACP Papers, Group I, Box c-74, reel 9 (microfilm), LOC. See also James N. Gregory, *The Southern Diaspora: How the Great Migrations of Black and White Southerners Transformed America* (Chapel Hill: University of North Carolina Press, 2005); and Isabel Wilkerson, *The Warmth of Other Suns: The Epic Story of America's Great Migration* (New York: Random House, 2010). Gregory argues that the earliest waves of black migrants sought "opportunities, both economic and social." Gregory, *Southern Diaspora,* 24.

45. *The Vindicator,* August 20, 1918, 1; Selected Branch Files, 1913–1939, Part 12, series A, reel 14, NAACP Papers, microfilm, CUL; W. A. Lewis, "The Present Necessity of Vocational Training," ibid., 2.

46. Baltimore NAACP flyer, Mass Meeting, Metropolitan Methodist Episcopal Church, January 1, 1917, NAACP Papers, Group I, Box g-84, Folder 9, LOC; Report by Bureau Agent Harry D.

Gulley, January 16, 1923, New Orleans, in Robert A. Hill, ed., *The Marcus Garvey and Universal Negro Improvement Association Papers*, vol. 5 (Berkeley: University of California Press, 1990), 178; New Orleans NAACP membership lists, NAACP Papers, Part 12: Selected Branch Files, 1912–1939, Series A, reels 13–15: The South, Louisiana, microfilm, CUL; Mary G. Rolinson, *The Universal Negro Improvement Association in the Rural South, 1920–1927* (Chapel Hill: University of North Carolina Press, 2007), 18–19, 162–63, 170–71; Lee Sartain, *Borders of Equality: The NAACP and the Baltimore Civil Rights Struggle, 1914–1970* (Jackson: University Press of Mississippi, 2013), 16.

47. There is some discrepancy between membership numbers during the war. The minutes of the board of directors suggest fewer members than later statistics suggest. Either the membership more than quadrupled or increased just under tenfold. NAACP minutes of the meetings of board of directors, September 17, 1917, NAACP Papers, Group I, Box a-8, LOC; July 8, 1918, ibid.; November 11, 1918, ibid.; NAACP minutes of the meetings of board of directors, March 11, 1918, ibid.; Membership Growth, 1912–1957, NAACP minutes of the meetings of board of directors, n.d., NAACP Papers, Group III, Box a-37, LOC.

48. Verney, "To Hope Till Hope Creates," 106; Jonathon Watson, "The NAACP in California, 1914–1950," in Verney and Sartain, *Long Is the Way,* 189; Sullivan, *Lift Every Voice,* 61–63, 80; Gilbert Jonas, *Freedom's Sword: The NAACP and the Struggle against Racism in America, 1909–1969* (New York: Routledge, 2007), 21–23.

49. Sullivan, *Lift Every Voice,* 100; Glenda Elizabeth Gilmore, *Defying Dixie: The Radical Roots of Civil Rights, 1919–1950* (New York: W. W. Norton, 2008), 300, 312, 346.

8

Cotton's Chaotic Home Front

The First World War and the Southern Textile Industry

ANNETTE COX

During World War I, chaos and disruption proved to be the norm for the southern textile industry. The British shipping blockade that began in 1914 drove down the average price of raw cotton to nine cents per pound, creating panic among growers. Watching this decline, mill owners also worried, knowing that their cloth inventories might have to be sold at a loss. Once European and military cloth orders poured in, however, raw cotton rose to thirty-one cents, and the rush overwhelmed the southern cotton industry and its rail system, leading to massive delays. In 1917, North Carolina towel manufacturer James W. Cannon complained that "we have to fight all the time without any let up to get cars and material." Once the United States entered the war, labor shortages loomed, leading southern textile publisher David Clark to warn in the spring of 1917 that there were 37,000 textile workers who could be drafted. In desperation, a few hosiery mill owners turned to young African American females.[1]

However, no matter how frustrated or beleaguered mill owners became, they did sell more goods than ever at extraordinary prices. In the fall of 1914, the sale of goods needed immediately in Europe, such as towels, socks, and denim, boomed. In October, the British government ordered 12 million towels from mills in North and South Carolina. At the same time, the US Navy awarded Durham Hosiery Mills a contract for 300,000 pairs of cotton socks, and the J. P. Morgan Bank notified North Carolina's Cone Mills that Great Britain wanted a half million yards of its denim. During the period 1914 to 1919, the nominal value of unfinished cotton cloth produced in South Carolina tripled from over $193 million to almost $610 million. At Dan River Mills in Virginia, the average selling price of dyed cloth rose from thirty-six cents in 1914 to $1.24 in 1920.[2]

Historians of the southern textile industry have paid little attention to World War I. A significant number of them have focused instead on the relationship between antebellum plantation slavery and the New South's factories and mill villages, stressing control and paternalism, strategies pursued by both slave masters and mill owners. No doubt, the latter were dedicated to low wages and domination of their workforce, but other historians find important differences between the two regimes. Most prominently, C. Vann Woodward argues that mill owners constituted a new, rising group in the South, the town builders. He characterizes them as captives of northern business interests, operating in what amounted to a "colonial" economy. David Carlton refines Woodward's thesis with a detailed examination of South Carolina mills that identifies considerable northern investment and partnership but supports the overall thesis that these factory owners were not primarily cotton planters transferring their capital to factories, but a new elite of small town businessmen and professionals. In *Old South, New South,* Gavin Wright closes the discussion by pointing out substantial differences between the antebellum and New South economies.[3]

Once scholars turn away from the industry's links to the past, they are quick to portray the industry of the early twentieth century as dysfunctional and on the brink of disaster. Writing in 1930, economist Claudius T. Murchison warns that "King Cotton is sick. . . . He has not been a well monarch since 1923. From that time to the present . . . he has been steadily growing worse." Murchison argues that the cause of this crisis was the industry's lack of integration, its cut-throat business practices, and the lack of institutional solutions for downturns. He portrays the industry as a collective of mostly small firms narrowly focused on their own advancement without regard to any wider interest. Agreeing with Murchison, Jack Blicksilver, the author of the standard history of the industry, characterizes the interwar period as one "great, long textile depression." In a study of the US economy during the 1930s, Michael Bernstein concurs with these diagnoses, concluding "for the textile industry, the Great Depression was almost fatal," a time when "textiles no longer occupied a central place in American manufacturing."[4]

During the 1980s, labor historians begin to question the stereotype of southern textile workers as docile and anti-union. Led by the authors of *Like a Family,* they find World War I to be a key turning point, the seed bed of increased worker militancy. As demand for cloth collapsed during the postwar period, the industry, according to these historians, went into a "tailspin," forcing cutbacks that triggered worker resistance and instigating owner crackdowns. During the 1920s and 1930s, workers, as *Like a Family* asserts, were "emboldened by the democratic rhetoric of the Great War and angered by the deterioration of shop floor life." As a result, labor conflict erupted on "an unprecedented scale."[5]

However, World War I affected more than labor relations. It brought one crisis after another, putting pressure on the industry's infrastructure and systems. Railroad delays, hurricanes, and the flu distracted and harried mill owners, who thought of only immediate problems and not those of the long term. They spent hours solving urgent problems with shipments of cotton and cloth, dye shortages, and labor scarcity. Too many times, they had to raise prices and wages without regard for the consequences. Even large, modernized firms had to struggle to manage the onslaught of events. High returns kept the system from going under during the war, but when abnormal wartime sales disappeared, overexpansion, fragmentation, price volatility, and the lack of industry integration led to the disaster of the 1920s and 1930s. The chaos and disruption brought on by the war did nothing to solve the industry's woes, but only shed more light on its fault lines, weaknesses that would prove nearly fatal during the Depression.

During the war's first few chaotic months, some textile-mill owners anticipated a lucrative market for their products, but the events of 1914 seemed to indicate the opposite. On July 28, 1914, one day after Serbia and Austria-Hungary declared war, US raw cotton investors panicked, causing "smart declines" at the Chicago Board of Trade, where brokers worried about the demand for the South's primary crop. Three days later, on Friday, July 31, New York's cotton exchange opened briefly but after a half hour of "sensational" trading, it closed its doors. Cotton trading floors in New Orleans, Chicago, and Charlotte also discontinued their operations. Without any hope for profits, several brokers declared bankruptcy, including the prominent firm S. H. P. Pell & Company, which the *Atlanta Constitution* described as "the leading firm on the long side of the cotton market," with "enormous commitments" when the war began. It had to sell over 140,000 bales of cotton at sharply reduced prices. In New Orleans, the head of one large cotton exporting business, Simon Steinhardt, committed suicide, having become "increasingly agitated" about falling prices. The US cotton exchanges did not reopen until November 16.[6]

Southern cotton farmers also feared the European war would ruin them because they exported almost two-thirds of their crop, significant portions of which went to the combatants Great Britain, France, and Germany. In 1913, of the 14.1 million bale output, 9.5 million was sold abroad.[7] Export figures for the next five years reveal that the conflict eventually cut the cotton trade with Europe in half (table 1). The year that ended on June 30, 1914, saw the export of 4.8 billion pounds of US cotton. That figure declined to 4.4 billion in 1915, to 3 billion in 1916 and 1917, and to the low point of 2.1 billion in 1918. During the years 1916, 1917, and 1918, no US cotton reached Germany, and exports to France fell by nearly half. Sales to Great Britain, the South's leading customer, also decreased as wartime exigencies cut into its cloth production, and as its cotton imports from Egypt increased. Japan bought more southern cotton, but not enough to replace European losses.

Table 1. US Raw Cotton Exports to Selected Nations, 1913 to 1920, in Pounds

	FRANCE	GERMANY	ENGLAND	JAPAN	TOTAL
1913	537,493,608	1,221,943,252	1,828,026,526	198,389,341	4,562,295,675
1914	569,699,520	1,442,161,777	1,759,647,396	176,720,057	4,760,940,538
1915	313,813,995	145,166,718	1,933,090,896	214,403,214	4,403,578,499
1916	338,418,027	0	1,372,703,281	251,538,465	3,084,070,125
1917	331,068,078	0	1,426,105,888	265,445,968	3,088,080,786
1918	271,436,451	0	1,176,220,005	299,728,224	2,118,175,182
1919	395,124,968	77,757,100	1,617,461,328	440,520,341	3,367,677,985
1920	333,534,482	371,358,816	1,299,456,427	335,880,918	3,179,313,336

Sources: Bureau of Foreign and Domestic Commerce, Department of Commerce, Foreign Commerce and Navigation of the United States for the Fiscal Year 1914 (Washington, DC, 1915), 401–2; Foreign Commerce and Navigation of the United States for the Fiscal Year 1919 (Washington, DC, 1917), 438–39; Foreign Commerce and Navigation of the United States for the Calendar Year 1921(Washington, DC, 1922), 379–80.

Note: These figures include both Sea Island cotton and Upland. The figures for 1910–1914 also include linters. After 1914, linters were counted separately.

As cotton prices fell in the first months of the war, southern textile-mill owners worried about their inventories. (table 2). In August 1914, William A. Erwin, the manager of the cotton mills owned by the Duke brothers James and Benjamin, whose fortune rested on cigarette manufacturing, reassured his bosses that "we are running our mills with all the prudence and economy that conditions enable us to do in these war times." He predicted that he had cotton on hand to last until October and that raw cotton prices were "hardening" at around eight-and-a-half cents.[8]

Table 2. Prices of Middling Upland Spot Cotton in New York, 1912–1932

| | PRICE IN CENTS PER POUND | | |
CROP YEAR	HIGHEST	LOWEST	ANNUAL AVERAGE
1912–1913	13.40	10.75	12.30
1913–1914	14.50	11.00	13.11
1914–1915	11.00	7.25	9.10
1915–1916	13.45	9.20	11.98
1916–1917	27.65	13.35	19.28
1917–1918	35.05	21.20	29.68
1918–1919	38.20	25.00	31.00
1919–1920	43.75	28.85	38.29
1920–1921	40.00	10.85	17.89
1921–1922	23.75	12.80	18.92
1922–1923	31.30	20.35	26.30
1923–1924	37.65	23.50	31.11
1924–1925	31.50	22.15	24.74
1925–1926	24.75	17.85	20.53
1926–1927	19.20	12.15	15.15
1927–1928	23.90	17.00	20.42
1928–1929	21.65	17.65	19.73
1929–1930	19.99	12.45	16.60
1930–1931	13.15	8.25	10.38
1931–1932	8.15	5.00	6.34

Source: H. E. Michl, *The Textile Industries: An Economic Analysis* (Washington, DC, 1938), 113.

Note: From 1910–1911 to 1913–1914, the crop year began September 1, and in subsequent years, the crop year began on August 1.

In response to the cotton panic, southern mills initially reduced production. The *Wall Street Journal* reported on August 17 that mills in Charlotte, North Carolina, were operating only three days a week. In Anderson, South Carolina, the Orr Cotton Mills closed for two weeks. In some places, demand for goods did not improve for months. It was not until January 1915 that the large Fulton Bag Company in Atlanta announced that its workforce of thirteen hundred was again employed full time. The next month, Gunby Jordan, the president of the Eagle and Phenix Mills of Columbus, Georgia, declared that his factories had finally resumed their former production levels.[9]

To rescue farmers, some urged keeping cotton off the market until prices rose. On September 15, an associate warned Erwin that the cotton business "is completely blocked by the almost hysterical holding movement. The farmers have forgotten apparently that cotton sold a few years ago at seven and eight cents." Southern politicians such as Georgia's Senator Hoke Smith pressured the State Department to demand that the British keep the cotton trade open. In October 1914, the British announced that they would allow US cotton to reach continental ports. That promise only lasted six months before the British announced another blockade in March 1915. But before the southerners could again urge the reopening of cotton trade, Britain announced on August 21, 1915, an absolute ban on cotton for European ports. This blockade led towel manufacturer James W. Cannon to predict rock-bottom cotton prices, a situation that would create a surplus so great that it could not be absorbed by domestic mills. He cautioned his managers to buy cotton very slowly and methodically, believing that at any point its price might fall dramatically. The eventual increase in prices did not allay Cannon's fears. He remained nervous about cotton prices throughout the war. In November 1916, he wrote to one of his clients that "things are getting so high I am getting fearful. I do not know what is going to happen." At Dan River Mills, a dyed-cloth manufacturer in southern Virginia, management built more storage space for raw cotton to allow flexibility during buying season. Despite the lobbying efforts, neither Congress nor the president regulated raw cotton prices.[10]

The British blockade of the Atlantic also eliminated the importation of German synthetic dyestuffs, introducing even more uncertainty into the cloth trade. The South's denim sector was particularly hard hit by the loss of blue dyes for overalls. Of the 8.1 million pounds of synthetic indigo imported in 1914, 7.4 million was from Germany. In 1916, 1917, and 1918, the Commerce Department recorded no German indigo imports.[11] As early as August 1914, Erwin warned Benjamin Duke that nearly all his dyes were German in origin. Managers at Dan River found foreign brokers to be unreliable when, after buying five casks of Chinese indigo, they opened them to find nothing but mud. Executives at

Cone Mills became obsessed with the blue dye. One of its top New York agents, Saul Dribben, spent most of the war frantically searching for indigo and its substitutes. In February 1916, he expressed his determination to Julius Cone: "I am going to try to get hold of every single ounce of color" and warned, "I am beginning to feel . . . that there will be the greatest kind of a famine in all colors."[12] Cone and other denim manufacturers were fixated on indigo because manufacturers of overalls were convinced that customers would not accept any other choice. When Dribben took a survey of New York overalls manufacturers in 1917, he reported that "they all have a feeling that they are going to cut indigo denims as long as they can get them. Price seems to be no object." In June 1915, Dribben accused an agent of Massachusetts Mills of hoarding indigo.[13]

While textile men agonized about dyestuffs, the domestic chemical industry saw the shortage as an opportunity to develop its own products and began promoting a tariff to protect itself from future German competition. Southern mill men were divided about the tariff. Opposed to a duty on dyes, Caesar Cone traveled to Washington in July 1916 to lobby against it but found little support for his cause. In contrast, most other southern mill owners supported a tariff campaign led by a chemistry professor at the University of North Carolina, Charles Herty. Georgia's Gunby Jordan, in a letter to the *Atlanta Constitution,* urged Congress to find a way to protect domestic dyestuffs makers. One tariff supporter darkly predicted that if the country did not protect itself from German dyestuffs, "we might ultimately have to change the colors in the American flag." With this support, a tariff on dyes passed in September 1916. Wartime dye prices continued to worry the mill men, but the tariff did eventually lead to the development of a robust US dyestuffs industry.[14]

Railroads, central to the functioning of the southern textile industry, failed to keep up with shipping demands during the war. In David Kennedy's study of the home front, he concludes that the US rail infrastructure suffered from inadequate equipment, poorly maintained tracks, and ineffective management. In 1917, as a large volume of goods including textiles moved north and east to major Atlantic ports to be loaded for Europe, the system buckled. Experts estimated that the railroads needed 100,000 to 150,000 more cars than were available. When the draft began in 1917, a labor shortage developed. To resolve these problems, President Woodrow Wilson put the railroads under federal control in December 1917, in what Kennedy calls "the most drastic mobilization measure of the war."[15]

Weather also disrupted southern railroad lines. In July 1916, two hurricanes converged over the southern states, closing the main line to northern cotton and cloth markets. During this storm, the Catawba River, the waterway at the heart of the Piedmont textile belt, rose to forty-seven feet above flood level and destroyed all nearby rail, telephone, and telegraph lines. The flood washed away one mill in North Carolina along with its warehouse, company store, and one thousand bales of cotton. In another incident, at least ten people died when a rail bridge near Charlotte, North Carolina, collapsed. As a result, all railway traffic north ceased, cutting off mills in Alabama, Georgia, South Carolina, and parts of North Carolina from New York. Factories away from the rivers also stopped because the storm disabled the hydroelectric plants. The stoppage had an immediate effect on the cloth markets, driving up prices for sheeting and duck. The railroads and the Southern Power Company responded quickly by hiring large repair crews. The *Textile World Journal* described the effort as one where "great armies of laborers are being mobilized, and the work of rebuilding is going on at a rate that is nothing short of miraculous."[16]

Despite the emergency repair effort, shortages continued. While electricity was scarce, some mills switched from electric power back to steam, forcing them to buy more coal. In August 1916, the *Textile World Journal* reported that since the storm, "all coal produced has been consumed as fast as mined and hauled away. It is this state of affairs which makes the freight car shortage the governing factor of the coal situation." A coal strike in Tennessee in September 1917 caused another shortage and led the national rail board to refuse fuel to mills without military contracts. As a result, one North Carolina hosiery mill announced that it was almost entirely out of coal and had none for employees to burn in their houses. The strike had a significant effect on nearby Asheville where there were "desperate circumstances" and "no relief in sight until the strike is settled."[17]

Wartime conditions also contributed to a labor shortage that forced mill owners to accept drastic changes to their traditional workforce practices. The situation was so dire that a few hosiery-mill owners began hiring young, female African Americans, a practice normally taboo under white supremacy. These factories needed black workers because whites were leaving for more rewarding jobs in spinning. George T. Andrews, the manager of North Carolina's Rocky Mount Hosiery Company, claimed to prefer African Americans over whites: "The colored girls make as much progress in learning and actual efficiency in four days, as some of the white employees had made in four weeks." Despite his enthusiasm, he was careful to keep his new workers segregated in buildings separate from whites. In a 1918 speech, prominent Georgia cotton-mill owner Fuller Callaway defended the practice as patriotic while inexplicably labeling it "synthetic labor," an example of the war "bringing us closer together."[18]

Soon after the United States entered the war, David Clark's *Southern Textile Bulletin* began reporting labor shortages and printing advertisements from mills looking for workers. Some mills resorted to bragging about their facilities, listing amenities such as electric lights in every room and "splendid" city water in every house. Clark predicted that labor shortages would be "getting worse and may become very severe" as workers returned to farms for the spring planting, as a new 1916 child labor law took effect, and as the draft sent men into the army. He recommended turning again to the mountains that he described as "our logical point for securing labor" and using a newspaper publicity campaign to show readers "the advantages of cotton mill life."[19]

In May 1918, a Cone Mills executive reminisced about the low wages the firm had once paid in Greensboro, recalling that in 1904 unskilled labor earned only eighty-five cents per day. By 1914, wages had risen to $1.15. He lamented that the war had pushed the daily wages as high as $3.15. At nearby Dan River Mills, management chose not to raise wages and instead instituted a bonus system that increased pay 242% from April 1917 to April 1920. Dan River and the Marshall Field operations in Spray, North Carolina, also tried to lure away Cone's workers with handbills lauding their high wages.[20]

When confronted with labor demands, some mill managers turned hostile and bitter. One southern mill man denounced workers who changed jobs as unpatriotic, a familiar wartime tactic. In a speech to a textile conference, W. M. Sherard of North Carolina recommended that something be done because "the habit of moving from one mill to another breeds discontent. A laborer dissatisfied and disappointed infects other people with his spirit of unrest." He proposed that the mills start a campaign to educate workers on how much it cost to change jobs because that "represents just so much waste, pure and simple—a waste, which at this critical time in the affairs of the nation, is almost criminal." In the Dan River community, mill management and local town leaders exasperated by the labor shortage and absenteeism tried to intimidate residents with a handbill entitled "Go to Work or Go to Jail."[21]

In the fall of 1918, mill work schedules were disrupted by the influenza pandemic. For example, in Concord, North Carolina, all the mills, schools, and theaters were ordered closed for one week in October. In Gaston County, conditions were so bad that the local Board of Health ordered all the mills shut as well as the churches and schools. The textile press reported that "gruesome details are given in certain communications that indicate a particularly gloomy frame of mind." The quarantine lasted much of the month of October. A mill in Covington, Georgia, had half of its workforce out with the flu. All the mills in Manchester, Georgia, stopped, along with its churches, schools, and movie theaters. The largest mill town in the state, Columbus, reported five thousand flu cases, including seventy-three deaths, and responded by closing its public gathering places.[22]

The signing of the Armistice on November 11, 1918, brought even more confusion to the textile industry. The next day, the US government abruptly began cancelling orders. Southern mill men objected to the suddenness of the decision, arguing that once raw cotton prices fell again, they would be left with yarn, cloth, and hosiery manufactured at high wartime costs. In November 1918, Cannon warned one of his selling agents that the move was dangerous because it might cause "textile semi-panic," but he did expect there to be some compensation from the government. Other mill men warned of labor unrest if contracts were cancelled too quickly. They also worried that the government might honor some contracts and not others and feared that the military would dump its surplus uniforms on the market. The government did settle some cloth contracts by offering a few cents on the dollar, but mills only suffered temporarily because of the pent-up demand of domestic and foreign customers.[23]

The war took southern mill owners on a wild ride. The constant disruptions in cotton prices, supplies, and transportation did indeed make life difficult for them. However, no matter how frustrated or even hysterical they became, they did earn higher profits. At Dan River Mills, the returns on stockholder investment ranged from 14.1% in 1915 to 24.9% in 1918. Sales at Cannon Mill totaled over 5 million in 1915 and advanced to 16 million by 1918; its returns on sales were 7.5% in 1915, 16.3% in 1916, and 9.3% in 1917. In July 1914, Durham Hosiery Mills had almost $3 million dollars in assets, a figure that grew to over $6million by December 1917. In Dalton, Georgia, the Crown Mills saw an astounding 40% return on capital from 1915 to 1919.[24]

The largest sector of the southern industry, plain, unfinished cloth, brought profits without any increase in production. In 1914, the five leading southern textile states, South Carolina, North Carolina, Georgia, Alabama, and Virginia, produced three billion square yards of coarse cloth, about half of the national total (table 3). South Carolina led the region in the prewar years, weaving over one billion square yards in 1914, 20% of the national total. Five years later in 1919, South Carolina's cloth production fell slightly but it still led the South and nationally ranked only behind Massachusetts. While production held steady, prices boomed, causing cloth values to increase threefold from over $193 million in 1914 to almost $610 million in 1919. In 1914 dollars, the value of the 1919 cloth would have been $342 million.[25]

Table 3. Southern Cloth Production in Square Yards and Dollars,
over Twelve Inches in Width, 1914, 1919

1914 PRODUCTION IN SQUARE YARDS	VALUE IN DOLLARS	1919 PRODUCTION IN SQUARE YARDS	VALUE IN DOLLARS
1,343,606,006	70,579,894	1,283,490,769	204,648,028
748,119,020	50,221,104	769,846,326	172,488,385
569,279,930	43,279,755	553,862,081	140,726,106
246,512,045	19,525,519	268,585,986	60,578,243
137,932,424	9,962,298	149,706,553	31,501,391
3,045,449,425	193,568,570	3,025,491,715	609,942,153
6,813,540,681	489,985,277	6,317,397,984	1,489,610,779

Source: Bureau of the Census, Department of Commerce, *Fourteenth Census of the United States Taken in the Year 1920, Volume X, Manufactures 1919, Reports for Selected Industries* (Washington, DC, 1923), 169.

The war also reinforced major structural changes in the textile industry. Most importantly, capital for expansion shifted south, seeking lower costs, particularly in labor. As equipment manufacturers sold more knitting machines, spindles, and looms to meet the demand for war goods, their management and the banks that financed them chose to invest in the South. As a result, the two major clusters of northern cotton production—New England's bulk goods factories and Philadelphia's specialty manufacturers—conceded further ground. In New England, the industry was older, had more access to capital, built large mills, and marketed its goods in nearby New York and Boston. In Philadelphia, the factories were smaller, pursued flexible production strategies, and produced a variety of more expensive consumer goods such as hosiery, other knit goods, and carpets. Before World War I, the South built factories that made basic, unfinished goods but, lacking extensive capital, did not match New England in capacity nor did it rival Philadelphia in specialization. Further away from New York, Boston, and Philadelphia, most southerners had to rely on northern commission houses and equipment manufacturers for marketing expertise.[26]

Overall, the number of spindles in five leading southern textile states, grew from 6.7 million in 1914 to 8.2 in 1919 while wage earners increased from 151,000 to 178,000 (tables 4 and 5). Before the war, South Carolina led the South in the number of spindles, with over 4.5 million. The next two leading states were North Carolina and Georgia, in that order, trailed by Alabama with almost 1 million spindles and Virginia with nearly half a million. South Carolina's mills had the region's largest capacity because they were erected during the 1880s and 1890s when exports to China seemed promising. However, during the war expansion appeared in more diversified North Carolina, where output also included towels, fine combed yarns, hosiery, and denim, products in demand during the war. This output meant that the state could attract more capital for expansion, raising the number of spindles by one quarter from 1914 to 1919. The state also had more native capital to invest in textiles because its mill owners could draw on lavish profits of the tobacco industry. The Duke and Carr families were the two most important examples of cigarette manufacturers that invested their profits in textiles. Their expertise in marketing also contributed to the state's increase.

Table 4. Cotton Spindles in United States and Leading States, 1909–1927

	1909	1914	1919	1927
United States	27,395,800	30,815,731	33,718,953	33,607,939
South Carolina	3,754,251	4,552,048	4,949,225	5,422,526
North Carolina	2,908,383	3,703,482	4,622,714	6,073,027
Georgia	1,747,483	2,043,386	2,459,123	2,921,349
Alabama	885,803	998,836	1,108,933	1,447,441
Virginia	316,970	499,144	560,280	679,280
Total in Five Southern States	5,541,669	6,745,704	8,190,770	10,441,817

Table 4 (*continued*)

	1909	1914	1919	1927
Massachusetts	9,372,364	10,556,867	11,206,855	8,818,981
Rhode Island	2,338,689	2,339,844	2,512,283	2,209,116
New Hampshire	1,318,932	1,340,753	1,336,797	1,297,205
Connecticut	1,241,524	1,276,148	1,256,776	1,072,872
Maine	1,020,688	1,098,142	1,091,991	1,021,607
Total in Five New England States	15,292,197	16,611,754	17,404,702	14,419,781

Sources: Bureau of the Census, Department of Commerce, *Fourteenth Census of the United States Taken in the Year 1920, Volume X, Manufactures 1919, Reports for Selected Industries* (Washington, DC, 1921), 176; and *Biennial Census of Manufactures, 1927* (Washington, DC: Government Printing Office, 1930), 258.

Table 5. Wage Earners in Cotton Goods in Five Leading Southern Textile States and Massachusetts, 1909, 1914, 1919, 1921

STATE	1909	1914	1919	PERCENTAGE INCREASE, 1914–1919	1921
North Carolina	47,231	53,703	67,297	25.31	66,316
South Carolina	45,454	46,448	48,079	3.51	51,509
Georgia	27,803	30,719	38,283	24.62	35,237
Alabama	12,731	13,697	18,102	32.16	18,275
Virginia	5,057	6,310	6,518	0.03	7,395
Subtotal	138,276	150,877	178,279	18.16	178,732
Massachusetts	108,914	113,559	124,150	9.33	107,488
Total U.S.	371,182	379,366	430,966	13.6	412,058

Sources: Department of Commerce, Bureau of the Census, *Census of Manufactures, 1914, Volume II, Reports for Selected Industries and Detail Statistics for Industries by States* (Washington, DC, 1919), 18; *Fourteenth Census of the United States Taken in the Year 1920, Volume X, Manufactures 1919, Reports for Selected Industries* (Washington, DC, 1921), 162; and *Biennial Census of Manufactures: 1921* (Washington, DC, 1924), 182.

As the war years brought growth in southern spindles, the other regions either saw slower expansion or loss of equipment. The national leader in spindles, Massachusetts, grew at only 6% during the war while Rhode Island increased at just over 7%, but there were decreases in New Hampshire, Connecticut, and Maine (table 4). The number of knitting machines in Pennsylvania increased by only 12% during World War I while those in North Carolina rose by 30%, and in Tennessee by 92% (table 6). During the war, mill men might have installed even more spindles and knitting machines, but it was difficult for equipment companies to provide them because after April 1917, the government directed raw materials and labor to other, more vital industries. For example, at the Whitin Machine Works in Massachusetts, an important southern supplier, the country's entry into the war brought raw material shortages, labor scarcity, and shipping disruptions.[27]

Table 6. Cotton Hosiery Production in Dozen Pairs by States
and Knitting Machines, 1914, 1919

STATE	DOZEN PAIRS		KNITTING MACHINES	
	1914	1919	1914	1919
Pennsylvania	23,383,766	17,722,549	51,422	57,508
North Carolina	8,746,982	9,431,825	10,959	14,234
Tennessee	5,426,052	8,643,319	6,749	12,986
Georgia	4,651,961	4,967,042	4,699	5,834
Massachusetts	3,791,779	1,990,675	10,209	10,755
Wisconsin	2,567,571	3,654,564	6,820	8,367
Virginia	1,524,174	1,387,716	1678	2,043
South Carolina	983,871	1,012,533	1,015	1,985
Alabama	586,334	1,108,379	635	1,257
U.S. Total	61,409,575	60,613,342	142,240	172,365

Source: Bureau of the Census, Department of Commerce, "Knit Goods," Fourteenth Census of the United States Taken in the Year 1920, Volume X, Manufactures, 1919, Reports for Selected Industries (Washington, DC, 1921), 200, 207.

Note: Knitting machines in Pennsylvania, Massachusetts, and Wisconsin also made hosiery from wool and silk while the southern machines were almost all of cotton. The production figures in dozen pairs are just cotton hosiery.

One southern sector that grew significantly during the war was fine yarn production. Coarse yarn output had already moved to the South, and during the war, its fine yarn segment grew at an astounding rate. From 1914 to 1919, for example, North Carolina raised its output from 14 million pounds to 24 million, an almost 75% increase (table 7). For the most part, North Carolina spinners sold their output to hosiery and knit goods producers in Philadelphia, in part replacing goods once imported from Germany.[28] Yarn mills in Gaston County, North Carolina, emerged as a center of low-cost fine yarn production, replacing a rival in New Bedford, Massachusetts. Gaston County's success rested not only on its lower wages but also on the introduction in 1905 of a new simplified cotton comber for inexperienced workers. Gaston County's mills were unusually small, even for North Carolina, but among them were four chains, Separk-Gray, Armstrong, Rankin, and Lineberger-Stowe, that operated as single entities when buying cotton, purchasing equipment, and marketing goods.[29]

Table 7. Fine Yarn Production, No. 41 and Over, in Pounds, 1914, 1919

	1914	1919
Alabama	639,881	997,902
Georgia	255	333,275
North Carolina	14,002,981	24,426,690
South Carolina	10,212,247	16,414,041
Virginia	292,986	275,000
Subtotal	25,148,350	42,446,908
Massachusetts	**83,656,591**	**78,934,942**
Rhode Island	**21,103,257**	**18,781,946**
Connecticut	**16,199,989**	**12,898,651**
Total U.S.	154,857,886	161,392,158

Source: Bureau of the Census, Department of Commerce, *Fourteenth Census of the United States Taken in the Year 1920, Volume X, Manufactures 1919 Reports for Selected Industries* (Washington, DC, 1921), 173.

Note: Figures in bold are decreases.

At the start of the war, another up-and-coming southern sector was seamless cotton hosiery, where the region was also beginning to supplant northern production. Seamless hosiery was made possible by a circular knitting machine introduced in the late nineteenth century that produced it as a tubular web. The machine could be operated by unskilled labor, making it a perfect piece of equipment for the South. Among the first to use the new machinery was Julian S. Carr of Durham, North Carolina, who, along with his sons, managed Durham Hosiery Mills. Carr had been a success in the tobacco business, then sold out his interests to the Dukes and reinvested part of that fortune in hosiery. Because he had thrived in the highly competitive cigarette business, he understood that controlling one's own marketing was essential, and he started his own commission firm in New York City.[30] There was another important concentration of hosiery production in Tennessee (see table 6). In that state, the number of workers in knit goods rose from 5,690 in 1914 to 10,308 in 1919, located primarily in Chattanooga and Knoxville. The number of knitting machines rose from 6,749 in 1914 to 12,986 in 1919. The value of Tennessee knit goods, primarily cotton hosiery, rose from $7,522, 846 in 1914 to $32,052,349 in 1919. Even converting the latter figure to 1914 dollars ($17,900,000) demonstrates that the state experienced a considerable step up in manufacturing.[31]

Despite labor shortages, southern mill managers did find more and more workers to run their equipment (see table 5). North Carolina, with the largest number of workers, saw its workforce increase over 25%. Alabama's numbers rose the most, 32% between 1914 and 1919. Georgia saw almost the same level of growth as North Carolina but began from a much lower level. Overall, by 1919 there were 18% more workers on the payroll in the five leading southern states. However, southern mill owners did not turn to child labor, on which they had once relied, because Congress passed a law restricting it in 1916. As a result, during the war, there was a significant decrease in the number of North Carolina workers under the age of sixteen. For example, the percentage of children under sixteen in that state's mills dropped from 13.3% in 1914 to 5.9% in 1919. In raw numbers that meant that child labor in North Carolina's mills decreased from 7,142 in 1914 to 3,971 in 1919. At the same time, both male and female adult workers increased their numbers, with women finding work at a slightly higher rate.[32]

Differences in textile distribution also explain in part why North Carolina expanded so much more than the other southern states. Textile mills with their own salesmen in New York knew more about customer demand, could better calibrate their own factory production schedules, and search out elusive supplies of indigo. Mills that relied on outsiders had much less market intelligence. For example, in South Carolina, two New York selling houses, Woodward, Baldwin & Company and Deering, Milliken & Company dominated the marketing of the state's unfinished cloth and saw little need to expand their capacity during the war (table 8). The two firms together controlled the distribution of 45% of the state's spindles. In 1914, Woodward, Baldwin & Co. represented 25% of the state's total while Deering, Milliken & Co. sold goods for thirteen South Carolina mills, 19% of the total. Most of these mills were located along the rail line that ran through the northwest counties of Anderson, Spartanburg, Greenville, and Pickens. The cotton mills of Georgia and Alabama did not ally themselves with any one particular commission house, and few sold their own goods.[33]

Table 8. South's Largest Cotton Goods Distribution Networks,
1913–1914, 1918–1919

	SPINDLES	
	1913–1914	1918–1919
Woodward, Baldwin	1,259,484	909,568
Deering, Milliken	849,632	1,068,360
Cannon	483,504	556,366
J. P. Stevens	359,642	398,504
Dan River	240,000	348,912
Joshua Baily (Dukes)	232,084	259,668
Cone	225,996	366,524
Combed Yarn Mills—		
Gaston County, North Carolina	112,832	379,334

Sources: Davison's Textile Blue Book 1913–1914 (New York, 1913), 141–72, 472–78; *Davison's Textile Blue Book 1918* (New York, 1918), 257–92, 644–55. For listing of Cannon's holdings and clients, see letterhead, January 2, 1917, Folder "New York Correspondence - 1916," Box 9, Cannon Papers.
Note: The Gaston County combed yarn mills used four selling agents in Philadelphia to market their goods. J. P. Stevens represented firms in South Carolina.

While North Carolina had mills relying on New York commission houses, the state also had two especially aggressive chains of cotton mills, Cannon and Cone, which did their own selling. Cannon Mills was the largest textile firm in North Carolina, operated fifteen mills of its own and, by 1918, had seven other mills as clients. During the war, the company wove a considerable amount of toweling, but its output also included hosiery yarns and sheeting. Cone Mills, originally a selling house, set up its first factories in Greensboro, North Carolina, and by 1914 had established a significant foothold in denim for men's work clothes. By 1918, Cone owned six mills of its own and sold goods for six more. The companies provided their clients with direct access to the New York cloth markets and expert sales staff. Of the state's 3.7 million spindles in 1914, almost 20% (Cannon, 13%, Cone, 6%) were managed by those two.[34]

Nearby in southern Virginia, there was another textile firm with marketing expertise rivaling that of Cannon and Cone. Dan River Mills, a colored-goods manufacturer, operated 240,000 spindles in 1914, about half of the total in the entire state, and ran its own selling operations through an office in New York. The combed yarn chains of Gaston County had close relationships with Philadelphia selling agents who distributed their yarn to nearby knitting mills.[35]

But no matter how knowledgeable these distribution operations were, they were no match for the conditions that led to collapse during the early 1920s. These firms may have expanded during the war, but the bulk of the industry was still fragmented and lacked the marketing expertise to navigate the era's turbulence. Helpless when confronted with volatile raw cotton or cloth prices, they could not make well-informed decisions about production. While an automobile or chemical manufacturer could control the price and volume of his supplies and the flow of his distribution, cotton-mill owners were subject to abrupt changes in the weather, international cloth market gyrations, and consumers' fashion decisions.

One strategy that might have saved southern textiles was exports, but this was one time when even the savviest of firms failed. During and immediately after the war, Cannon, Cone, and Dan River had a promising opportunity when European manufacturers were unable to operate or were rebuilding. United States mill owners could have replaced them in Asia, Africa, and Latin America. During the early years of the twentieth century, the United States had found one rewarding market in China, but after 1906, it lost much of that trade to Japan. When World War I began, US overseas sales began to grow again, increasing 55% in yardage from 1913 to 1917 (table 9). Since it took time for European mills to resume operations after the war, US cloth exports peaked in 1920 at 819 million square yards. After that year, exports never reached even 600 million yards, and after 1930, never reached half that amount.

Table 9. US Cotton Cloth Exports, 1900–1930

YEAR	TOTAL, IN SQUARE YARDS	TOTAL, IN DOLLARS
1900	352,194,989	18,068,934
1901	251,503,351	14,136,037
1902	504,773,813	25,861,196
1903	495,379,197	25,352,584
1904	247,380,737	14,696,199
1905	694,500,715	41,320,542
1906	711,493,054	43,181,860
1907	326,340,329	21,239,247
1908	214,994,812	14,268,083
1909	367,631,542	21,693,080
1910	396,944,195	19,971,431
1911	346,590,169	24,387,099
1912	476,778,499	31,388,998
1913	444,729,241	30,668,234
1914	414,860,013	28,844,627
1915	396,944,195	28,682,515
1916	550,571,720	46,381,389
1917	690,193,296	72,608,110
1918	544,174,574	107,519,333
1919	683,045,326	151,997,817
1920	818,750,954	238,153,557
1921	551,512,942	71,573,875
1922	587,492,532	85,232,112
1923	464,520,397	79,357,337
1924	477,815,408	78,204,177
1925	543,316,851	85,011,749
1926	513,300,000	74,589,000
1927	565,022,000	76,756,000
1928	546,847,000	79,298,000
1929	564,448,000	79,411,000
1930	416,283,000	51,385,000

Source: Annette Cox, "Imperial Illusions: The New South's Campaign for Cotton Cloth Exports," *Journal of Southern History* 80 (August 2014): 613–14.

At the beginning of the war, some US textile leaders believed that the conflict offered a unique opportunity in Latin America since its location gave them an advantage over the Europeans. The United States exported little cloth there before the war because Great Britain and Germany already dominated that region, relying on its preference for inexpensive colored cloth and generous credit terms.[36] As soon as fighting began in Europe, US textile publications began promoting this opening. In the fall of 1914, New York's *American Wool and Cotton Reporter* published three issues in Spanish and Portuguese and called for the US textile industry "to go after Latin American business." In October 1914, the Atlanta Chamber of Commerce hosted a conference to explore how southerners could steal Latin American trade from the Europeans. In January 1915, a steamship company invited Benjamin Duke on a voyage to explore the export "possibilities" in the region's ports.[37]

When Cone Mills received orders from Argentina in 1915, Caesar Cone advised his staff to remain cautious, ordering them not to ship anything until they were sure of the terms. Despite his initial skepticism, Cone was so intrigued that in 1916 he personally visited Havana. After his trip, he concluded that a Cone salesman in Cuba could sell $1 million worth of cotton goods and be able to "dump" goods unsold at home. He also recognized that US producers faced significant hurdles because Cuba's population could only afford "cheap" cotton goods. He warned that Cuban brokers will "talk different when they can again get what they want in England and other European countries." Cone proved to be prescient because after the abnormally high postwar year of 1920, when Cuba bought over 160 million square yards, US exports declined below 65 million.[38]

The campaign to capture more of the Latin American market failed. United States' textile manufacturers did very little to attract more Latin customers because goods sold so easily at home. There was also a shortage of the dyes popular in Latin American markets because the British blockade had choked off that trade. After the war, the Japanese moved aggressively into the region, and the British recaptured a share of the Argentine market. By 1930, US cotton cloth exports were half what they had been in 1920.[39]

Unable to turn to foreign markets for relief, cotton-mill owners during the 1920s found themselves vulnerable as the cotton textile industry suffered one setback after another. Their overcapacity crippled profits as robust wartime sales did not persist. Mills in New England and the mid-Atlantic states closed or transferred equipment to southern locations. Even in the lower-cost South, returns on investment lagged. There was a host of other reasons for this down-turn. Harsh weather and boll weevil infestations caused raw cotton prices to vary significantly from one growing season to another, constantly endangering inventory valuations. As the 1920s and 1930s wore on, there were more and more alternatives to cotton as US consumers turned to other fibers. Fashionable women bought silk dresses and hosiery and then rayon. The decline of immi-gration took the edge off what had been a booming domestic market. During the 1920s, any profit in the apparel industry often went into the hands of the increasingly powerful middlemen called converters, garment manufacturers, and retailers.[40]

Once frantic to attract workers, mill owners quickly found themselves forced to fire employees and cut wages. Desperate to protect their wartime gains, work-ers resisted by joining unions and striking. In a business where labor control and paternalism had been the byword, employers could no longer rely on past practices. In 1919, workers in Columbus, Georgia, and the Horse Creek Valley of South Carolina demanded union recognition. The unrest spread to North Carolina. In February 1919, when owners decreased wages, strikes erupted in Charlotte and then spread to nearby towns. As labor activism rose during the summer of 1919, unions claimed that they had signed up forty thousand work-ers. The unrest appeared again in the fall of 1920 after another round of wage and hour cuts. In June 1921, strikes led by the United Textile Workers again began in Charlotte and extended to the Cannon mills in Concord and Kannap-olis. Although mill owners successfully ended these strikes, worker militancy continued to serve as a constraint on their options. No longer able to rely on child labor, owners struggled to meet the demands of an adult workforce. To try to increase productivity, owners eventually turned to scientific management techniques, a course that only caused further unrest.[41] Even though African American workers might have worked for lower wages, there were no further attempts to bring them into southern hosiery mills. After the war, racial repres-sion took a violent turn as white southerners grew determined to perpetuate their control over blacks and wipe out aspirations brought on by wartime ad-vances.

What had begun in 1914 as panic and then proceeded to unprecedented profit became something quite different after the war. Determined to overcome wartime obstacles, some mill men modernized their operations, but their efforts failed to stop the oncoming crisis. The 1920s saw the beginning of a long-term cotton textile depression with sales declines, bankruptcies, and high unemployment. An industry that had once been the hope of a new industrialized South fell victim to the disruptive forces of war and postwar readjustment. The dismal situation that settled on southern cotton textiles in the years following World War I lasted until another war again brought prosperity.

An examination of the textile industry during World War I reveals an industry overwhelmed with daily problems brought on by the conflict and by the strain on its infrastructure. Rushing from one crisis to another, some caused by war, some by weather or pandemic, textile managers had little time to reflect or little time to make reforms. Buying more equipment, hiring more workers, and raising wages were decisions made with immediate goals in mind. Large integrated firms like Cannon, Cone, and Dan River might have made better decisions cognizant as they were of market conditions in New York. However, the steady drumbeat of war and the constant upheavals of the years 1914 to 1918 meant that few had the time or energy to analyze the long-term condition of the southern textile industry.

NOTES

1. H. E. Michl, *The Textile Industries: An Economic Analysis* (Washington, DC: The Textile Foundation, 1938), 113; James W. Cannon to T. C. Thompson, May 25, 1917, Box 2, Cannon Mill Records, David M. Rubenstein Rare Book and Manuscript Library, Duke University, (hereafter Cannon Papers) [There are no folder numbers in this collection], quoted in Timothy W. Vanderburg, *Cannon Mills and Kannapolis: Persistent Paternalism in a Textile Town* (Knoxville: University of Tennessee Press, 2013), 43; David Clark, *Southern Textile Bulletin* 13 (June 28, 1917): 12; and "Southern Negro Help," *Textile World Journal* 51 (August 26, 1916): 57. In real dollars, an average price per pound of thirty-one cents during the 1918–19 growing season translates to twenty cents in 1914 dollars. See Samuel H. Williamson, "Seven Ways to Compute the Relative Value of a U.S. Dollar Amount, 1774 to Present," *MeasuringWorth*, 2017 [URL: www.measuringworth.com/uscompare/]. I have cited the nominal amounts in this paper to show the figures that textile mill owners, brokers, and workers would have encountered during the war and noted real values in the notes.

2. "Southern Export Orders," *Wall Street Journal*, October 7, 1914, 5; "Durham Plant Gets Order for 300,000 Pairs of Socks," *Greensboro Daily Record*, September 23, 1915, 1; L. H. Sellars to Caesar Cone, September 1, 1915, Folder 34, Box 4, Cone Mills Corporation Records, 5247, Southern Historical Collection, Louis Round Wilson Special Collections Library, University of North Carolina at Chapel Hill (hereafter Cone Papers); Douglas Flamming, *Creating the Modern South: Millhands and Managers in Dalton, Georgia, 1884–1984* (Chapel Hill: University of North Carolina Press, 1992), 136; and Robert Sidney Smith, *Mill on the Dan: A History of Dan River Mills, 1882–1950* (Durham,

NC: Duke University Press, 1960), 151. In 1919, the real value of the cotton goods produced in South Carolina was $342 million. For the price of Dan River cloth, the price of $1.24 in 1920 would have been sixty cents in 1914 in real terms. See Williamson, *Measuring Worth*.

3. Works that stress the continuity between slavery and New South textiles include W. J. Cash, *The Mind of the South* (New York: Alfred A. Knopf, 1941), 209–10, 214–17, 224–26; Jonathan Weiner, *Social Origins of the New South: Alabama, 1860–1885* (Baton Rouge: Louisiana State University Press, 1978), 186–211; Dwight B. Billings, Jr., *Planters and the Making of a "New South": Class, Politics, and Development in North Carolina, 1865–1900* (Chapel Hill: University of North Carolina Press, 1979), 42–95; and Jay Mandle, *The Roots of Black Poverty: The Southern Plantation Economy after the Civil War* (Durham, NC: Duke University Press, 1978), 3–51. Woodward's thesis is found in *Origins of the New South, 1877–1913* (Baton Rouge: Louisiana State University Press, 1951), 131, 133, 308. Also see David Carlton, *Mill and Town in South Carolina, 1880–1920* (Baton Rouge: Louisiana State University Press, 1982), 13, 61; and Gavin Wright, *Old South, New South: Revolutions in the Southern Economy since the Civil War* (New York: Basic Books, 1986), 17–50.

4. Claudius T. Murchison, *King Cotton Is Sick* (Chapel Hill: University of North Carolina Press, 1930), 1, 361; Jack Blicksilver, *Cotton Manufacturing in the Southeast: A Historical Analysis* (Atlanta: Bureau of Business and Economic Research, School of Business Administration, Georgia State College of Business Administration, 1959), 89; and Michael A. Bernstein, *The Great Depression: Delayed Recovery and Economic Change in America, 1929–1939* (Cambridge: Cambridge University Press, 1987), 75.

5. Jacqueline Hall et al., *Like a Family: The Making of a Southern Cotton Mill World* (Chapel Hill: University of North Carolina Press, 1987), 183.

6. "Panic Is Caused by the War News Exchanges," *Atlanta Constitution*, July 29, 1914, 1; "War Sends Stock to New Low Levels," *New York Times*, July 29, 1914, 3; "Markets Close All Over the World," *Greensboro Daily Record*, July 31, 1914, 1; "Security Markets of World Closed To Stop Unloading," and "Brokers Unable to Stand Pressure," *Atlanta Constitution*, August 1, 1914, 1; "War News Forces Four Firms to Quit," *New York Times*, August 1, 1914, 3; and "War News Causes Suicide," *New York Times*, August 2, 1914, 11.

7. Gilbert Fite, *Cotton Fields No More: Southern Agriculture, 1865–1980* (Lexington: University Press of Kentucky, 1984), 91.

8. William A. Erwin to Benjamin N. Duke, August 4, 1914, Folder "August 1–17, 1914"; and September 12, 1914, Folder "September 4–14, 114," Box 55, Benjamin N. Duke Papers, David M. Rubenstein Rare Book and Manuscript Library, Duke University (hereafter B.N. Duke Papers).

9. "Cotton Mills on Half Time," *Wall Street Journal*, August 17, 1914, 7; "Southern Cotton Mills Running to Supply Demand," *Wall Street Journal*, September 1, 1914, 5; "Cannon Cotton Mills Run on Short Time," *Greensboro Daily News*, August 15, 1914, 1; "Cotton Mills to Curtail," *Greensboro Daily News*, August 1, 1914, 3; "Fulton Cotton Mills Runs Full Capacity, " *Atlanta Constitution*, January 12, 1915, 8; and "Eagle and Phenix Is to Operate on Full Time," *Atlanta Constitution*, February 4, 1915, 4.

10. Alexander Sprunt to Erwin, September 15, 1914, Folder "September 15–30, 1914," Box 55, B. N. Duke Papers; Fite, *Cotton Fields No More*, 91–95; James W. Cannon to N. B. Mills, October 10, 1916, and November 4, 1916, Folder "M," Box 3, Cannon Papers; and Smith, *Mill on the Dan*, 147. Also see "War's Grave Effect on Cotton Industry," *Greensboro Daily News*, September 15, 1914, 9; "Reassur-

ance Comes from Senator Smith," *Greensboro Daily News,* August 26, 1915, 2; and Dewey Grantham, Jr., *Hoke Smith and the Politics of the New South* (Baton Rouge: Louisiana State University Press, 1958), 277–91, 324–26." Ryan Floyd discusses the so-called "Cotton Crisis" and its impact on southern agriculture in his chapter in this volume, "'A Diarrhea of Plans and Constipation of Action.'"

11. Bureau of Foreign and Domestic Commerce, Department of Commerce, *Foreign Commerce and Navigation of the United States for the Year Ending June 30, 1918* (Washington, DC: Government Printing Office (GPO), 1919), 53.

12. William A. Erwin to Benjamin N. Duke, August 4, 1914, Box 55, B.N. Duke Papers; Smith, *Mill on the Dan,* 146; and Saul Dribben to Julius Cone, February 11, 1916, Box 5, Folder 52, Cone Papers.

13. Saul Dribben to Julius Cone, June 28, 1915, 159, Box 5, Folder 51, Cone Papers.

14. Caesar Cone to Julius Cone, July 25, 1916, Folder 41, Box 4, Cone Papers; "Gunby Jordan Wants Congress to Consider Dyestuff Problem," *Atlanta Constitution,* September 20, 1915, 4; "Attacks Dye Exemption," *New York Times,* February 23, 1917, 11; John Corrigan, Jr., "Crisis in Dyestuff Industry Must Be Averted by Congress—and Congress Only Can Do It," *Atlanta Constitution,* February 24, 1916, 8; David A. Hounshell and John Kenly Smith, Jr., *Science and Corporate Strategy: Du Pont R&D, 1902–1980* (Cambridge: Cambridge University Press, 1988), 78–97; Kathryn Steen, "Confiscated Commerce: American Importers of German Synthetic Organic Chemicals, 1914–1929," *History and Technology* 12 (1995): 261–84; and Kathryn Steen, *The American Synthetic Organic Chemicals Industry: War and Politics, 1910–1930* (Chapel Hill: University of North Carolina Press, 2014), 138–71.

15. Austin Kerr, *American Railroad Politics, 1914–1920: Rates, Wages, and Efficiency* (Pittsburgh, PA: University of Pittsburgh Press, 1989), 39–71; Steven W. Usselman, *Regulating Railroad Innovation: Business, Technology, and Politics in America, 1840–1920* (Cambridge: Cambridge University Press, 2002), 375–78; and David Kennedy, *Over Here: The First World War and American Society* (Oxford: Oxford University Press, 1980), 252–53.

16. *The Floods of July 1916: How the Southern Railway Organization Met an Emergency* (Washington, DC: Southern Railway Company, 1917), 7–16; *The North Carolina Flood: July 14, 15, 16, 1916* (Charlotte: W. M. Bell, 1916); "Crops Destroyed in South Georgia," *Atlanta Constitution,* July 12, 1916, 3; "Walls of Water Swept the Valley of French Broad," *Atlanta Constitution,* July 17, 1916, 2; "Southern Floods Will Raise Prices," *New York Times,* July 21, 1916, 10; and "Actively Rehabilitating Flooded Mills," *Textile World Journal* 51 (July 29, 1916): 11,16.

17. *Textile World Journal* 51 (August 26, 1916): 57; "Little Encouragement for Towns That Are Out of Coal," *Greensboro Daily News,* September 27, 1917, 1; and "New Handicaps," *Textile World Journal* 53 (October 6, 1917): 73.

18. "Southern Negro Help," *Textile World Journal* 51 (August 26, 1916): 57; and Fuller E. Callaway, "Synthetic Labor," *Textile World Journal* 54 (November 23, 1918): 43, 47. The Carrs, owners of Durham Hosiery Mills, pioneered in the hiring of African Americans even before the war when they opened a new factory using all-black labor in 1902. See Mena Webb, *Jule Carr: General without an Army* (Chapel Hill: University of North Carolina Press, 1987), 183–84. In June 1918, the company announced that they were building a new mill in Goldsboro, "in which they will employ negro labor exclusively." See "New Mill to Hire Negroes," *Textile World Journal* 53 (June 1, 1918): 83. Also see "Employing Negroes," *Textile World Journal* 53 (January 5, 1918): 49. The workers never shared the same factory floors with whites; new buildings were erected for them.

19. "Help Wanted," *Southern Textile Bulletin* 10 (January 27, 1916): 17; Classified Advertisements, *Southern Textile Bulletin* 13 (June 7, 1917): 17; and David Clark, "Labor Supply," *Southern Textile Bulletin* 13 (April 26, 1917): 12. The Supreme Court declared the 1916 child labor law unconstitutional in 1918.

20. J. E. Hardin to Saul Dribben, May 1, 1918, Folder 53, Box 6, Cone Papers; Smith, *Mill on the Dan*, 165; and Dribben to Julius Cone, April 26, 1918, Folder 53, Box 6, Cone Papers. Greensboro textile wages of $3.15 per day would have been $1.81 in 1904 dollars and $2.03 in 1914 figures. See Williamson, *Measuring Worth.*

21. "Problem of Labor Shortage Discussed," *Textile World Journal* 53 (June 29, 1918): 41, 43; and Smith, *Mill on the Dan*, 164.

22. "Closes Textile Mills," *Textile World Journal* 54 (October 12, 1918): 69; "Spinners Hard Hit; So. Mills Stopped," *Textile World Journal* 54 (October 26, 1918): 82, 256; "Churches, Schools, and Picture Shows Closed," *Gastonia Gazette,* October 9, 1918, 1; "Gastonia Still in Grip of Influenza," *Gastonia Gazette,* October 16, 1918, 1; "Quarantine Ends Tomorrow Night," *Gastonia Gazette,* November 1, 1918, 1; "Flu Situation about the Same," *Atlanta Constitution,* October 18, 1918, 5; and "Columbus Lifts Ban on the 'Flu' Epidemic," *Atlanta Constitution,* November 2, 1918, 10.

23. James W. Cannon to Leslie, November 20, 1918, Box 9, Cannon Papers; Grantham, *Hoke Smith,* 326–27; and "The Difficult Process of Demobilizing Industry," *Textile World Journal* 54 (November 23, 1918): 36–37.

24. Smith, *Mill on the Dan*, 151, 113; Vanderburg, *Cannon Mills and Kannapolis*, 41–46; "Durham Hosiery Mills," *Moody's Analyses of Investments, Part II, Public Utilities and Industrials* (New York: Moody's Investors Service, 1917), 2000–2001, and (New York: Moody's Investors Service, 1918), 1934–1935; and Flamming, *Creating the Modern South*, 136.

25. Williamson, *Measuring Worth.*

26. Philip Scranton, *Figured Tapestry: Production, Markets, and Power in Philadelphia Textiles, 1885–1941* (Cambridge: Cambridge University Press, 1989), 7–16.

27. Thomas R. Navin, *The Whitin Machine Works since 1831: A Textile Machinery Company in an Industrial Village* (Cambridge: Cambridge University Press, 1950), 314–18.

28. Imports of German cotton thread and yarns in 1913 amounted to 1,169,879 pounds; there were no German imports in 1918 and 1919. German hosiery imports also declined. In 1914, the United States imported 2,375,494 dozen pairs from Germany, a figure that fell by half the next year, then took a precipitous fall in 1916 and 1917, and disappeared completely in 1918. Bureau of Foreign and Domestic Commerce, Department of Commerce, *Foreign Commerce and Navigation of the United States for the Year Ending June 30, 1918* (Washington, DC: GPO, 1919), 89; and *Foreign Commerce and Navigation of the United States for the Calendar Year 1921* (Washington, DC: GPO, 1922), 64.

29. Robert Allison Ragan, *The Textile Heritage of Gaston County, North Carolina, 1848–2000: One Hundred Mills and the Men Who Built Them* (Charlotte: R. A. Ragan and Company, 2001), 88–91, 190–94; Navin, *The Whitin Machine Works,* 223–35; and Seymour Louis Wolfbein, *The Decline of a Cotton Textile City: A Study of New Bedford* (New York: Columbia University Press, 1944), 59–90.

30. Pamela C. Edwards, "Entrepreneurial Networks and the Textile Industry: Technology, Innovation, and Labor in the American Southeast, 1890–1925," in Susanna Delfino and Michele Gillespie, eds., *Technology, Innovation, and Southern Industrialization: From the Antebellum Era to the Computer Age* (Columbia: University of Missouri Press, 2008), 151–60.

31. Bureau of the Census, Department of Commerce, *Fourteenth Census of the United States Taken in the Year 1920, Manufactures 1919, Reports for the States, With Statistics for Principal Cities* (Washington, DC: GPO, 1923), 1418–1419, 1428, 1430–1431; Williamson, *MeasuringWorth*.

32. Bureau of the Census, Department of Commerce, *Fourteenth Census of The United States, State Compendium, North Carolina 1919* (Washington, DC: GPO, 1925), 7.

33. Mary Baldwin Baer and John Wilbur Baer, *A History of Woodward, Baldwin & Co.* (Annapolis, MD: Baer, 1977), 20–24; and Carlton, *Mill and Town in South Carolina*, 57–59.

34. Timothy W. Vanderburg, *Cannon Mills and Kannapolis*, 37–46; Bryant Simon, "Choosing between the Ham and the Union: Paternalism in the Cone Mills of Greensboro," in Jeffrey Leiter, Michael D. Schulman, and Rhonda Zingraff, eds., *Hanging by a Thread: Social Change in Southern Textiles* (Ithaca, NY: ILR Press, 1991), 83–89; and Cone Corporation, *The Story of Cone Denim* (Greensboro, 1950), 4–6.

35. Smith, *Mill on the Dan*, 36.

36. Louis Bader, *World Developments in the Cotton Industry with Special Reference to the Cotton Piece Goods Industry in the United States* (New York: New York University Press, 1925), 32–43; Lars G. Sandberg, *Lancashire in Decline: A Study of Entrepreneurship, Technology, and International Trade* (Columbus: Ohio State University Press, 1974), 97–199; and D. A. Farnie, *The English Cotton Industry and the World Market, 1815–1896* (New York: Oxford University Press, 1979), 93–96. Also see "Wartime Exports of Cotton," *Textile World Journal* 54 (August 24, 1918): 86, 202.

37. *American Wool and Cotton Reporter* 28 (September 10, 1914): 14, 15; "Dixie Seeks Trade of South America," *Atlanta Constitution*, October 13, 1914, 12; and Travel Department, Fidelity Trust Company of Baltimore to Benjamin Duke, November 3, 1914, Box 56, B. N. Duke Papers.

38. Caesar Cone to Saul Dribben, August 26, 1915, Box 5, Folder 51, and Caesar Cone, "Report on Havana," February 19, 1916, Box 4, Folder 33, Cone Papers; W. A. Graham Clark, *Cotton Goods in Latin America, Part I, Cuba, Mexico, and Central America*, Special Agents Series #31, Department of Commerce and Labor (Washington, DC: GPO, 1909), 6–14; "Opportunity to Expand as Export Call Broadens," *Textile World Record* 51 (January 22, 1916): 39; and A. J. Marrison, "Great Britain and Her Rivals in the Latin American Cotton Piece-Goods Market, 1880–1940," in *Great Britain and Her World, 1750–1914: Essays in Honour of W. O. Henderson*, ed. by Barrie M. Ratcliffe (Manchester: Manchester University Press, 1975), 309–48.

39. "War-Time Exports and Imports," *Textile World Journal* 55 (March 8, 1919): 20; Rose, *Firms, Networks, and Business Values*, 239–40; Sandberg, *Lancashire in Decline*, 197–99; Marrison, "Great Britain and Her Rivals," 309–48; and *Textile World Journal* 53 (June 22, 1918): 23.

40. Blicksilver, *Cotton Manufacturing in the Southeast*, 89–118; Scranton, *Figured Tapestry*, 323–453; Susan Benson, *Counter Cultures: Saleswomen, Managers, and Customers in American Department Stores, 1890–1940* (Urbana: University of Illinois Press, 1987); Michl, *The Textile Industries*, 96–110, 129–61; Rose, *Firms, Networks and Business Values*, 198–241; and Stephen Jay Kennedy, *Profits and Losses in Textiles: Cotton Textile Financing since the War* (New York: Harper & Brothers, 1936), 90–97.

41. Hall et al., *Like a Family*, 183–95; Vanderburg, *Cannon Mills and Kannapolis*, 47–57; and Wright, *Old South, New South*, 147–55.

9

"The Battle of Commerce Is Begun"

Building the Port of Mobile, Alabama, after World War I

MATTHEW L. DOWNS

n April 1919, Senator Oscar Underwood arrived in Mobile to campaign for reelection. The highlight of his stop was an address to an audience at the Mobile Shipbuilding Company. Introduced by Harry Hartwell, a Mobile businessman, former state senator, and longtime proponent of improvements at the port, Underwood began by praising the company for its role in the American victory overseas in the Great War. The United States had "won the great victory for the world," the senator noted, "But it would have been impossible for the American boys to win if it had not been for . . . the men in the yards who built the ships." But the United States could not afford to slow production, he argued, even as the country transitioned to peacetime: "American points must send out our commerce on ships carrying the American flag, and the people of Alabama must help to make Mobile the greatest port in the world." Underwood ended with a flourish: "The great war is at an end, but the battle of commerce is only begun."[1]

Underwood's speech touched on one of the most prominent political questions in the postwar state: economic development at the port of Mobile. Moreover, that topic spoke directly to the way that Alabama's participation in the defense effort had begun to reshape thinking about the nature of the state's economy. Mobile, a city transitioning from its long reliance on cotton, lumber, and other commodities to a more diversified economic future, represented the state and region at a crossroads, and the issue of port development helped civic and business leaders envision prosperity based on a diversified economy tapped into domestic and global trade. The United States' wartime experience presented the city and state with an opportunity, requiring an aggressive and insistent campaign so that Mobile and Alabama might overcome its regional and national rivals and secure a place in a prosperous commercial future. The success of that campaign, which resulted in industrial growth along the water-front and the Alabama State Docks, provides important insight into the way that business leaders in one southern city sought to translate the opportunity presented by the war effort into permanent economic growth.

This story of World War I–era economic development in the South and, more specifically, the role of southern boosters in mobilizing for that development have been largely overlooked by historians. Scholars have certainly noted in-dustrial growth in the war years, focused mostly on the core postwar southern industry of textiles. Most notably, George Brown Tindall's history of the South in the war years notes southern expansion during and after the war, both in terms of economic growth and the role that businessmen began to play in the political and social order of the region. Blaine Brownell, too, noted the increased role of the "civic-commercial elite" in shaping and directing southern economic growth, and while his focus is the decade before the Depression, he does note the way that boosters saw in the war an opportunity, specifically a "clear demon-stration of the possibilities and advantages" that would come with a concerted and cooperative effort by the business community to maintain growth. The seminal historians of southern economic development in the twentieth century, James Cobb and Bruce Schulman, both look beyond the Great War, focusing their efforts on the post–New Deal South and as such miss an opportunity to trace the story of economic development back to World War I and efforts by civic leaders to translate wartime growth into peacetime progress.[2]

Despite antebellum efforts to diversify the port's cotton-oriented business, civic leaders had neither the political nor the financial capital to wean their city from the cotton trade. One difficulty, which became the focus of Civil War–era efforts, was deep-water access. The channel from the mouth of the Mobile River, which housed the port infrastructure, to the mouth of Mobile Bay on the Gulf of Mexico was characterized by shallows, sand bars, and other hazards. The Battle of Mobile Bay left a number of wrecks in the waters around the city; this combined with Confederate efforts to destroy any useful infrastructure in the wake of defeat to make the port nearly unusable. While under Union control, federal officials began removing the larger wrecks and other obstructions, but clearly, only concerted effort and ample funds could address the city's needs. Desperate to revitalize the port, city leaders turned to the federal government, seeking appropriations to improve the harbor by deepening and widening the channel connecting the mouth of the river to Gulf shipping channels.[3]

On the eve of World War I, efforts to improve the channel were marginally successful. Oceangoing ships no longer had to discharge their cargo onto shallow-draft ships in the mouth of the bay or bypass the port altogether for lack of access. The individual most instrumental to Mobile's efforts to attract federal funds was John H. Bankhead, Sr., a congressman and later senator whose political influence ensured a steady stream of funds to deepen and widen the channel (about $3 million between 1890 and 1915) and to improve the Warrior River, providing nonstop shipment of coal, iron, and steel products from the Birmingham region to Mobile. By World War I, the Mobile District of the Army Corps of Engineers had spent $8.5 million on improvements to navigation in Mobile Bay. But even federal improvements had limits. In order to benefit from the deepened channel and the barges of industrial products arriving from upstate, the port of Mobile had to have facilities to handle that cargo and companies to carry those products to other ports. Mobilians understood this all too well; in fact, many Mobilians made the argument that without local and state initiative to improve the docks and the surrounding economy, federal investment would be wasted or, more worrisome, retracted.[4]

The Spanish-American War was the first "wake-up" call for post–Civil War Mobile. Despite proximity to the Caribbean theater, and despite efforts by booster organizations in the city to promote Mobile as a staging area for American efforts, the city was largely passed over in favor of competing Gulf ports at Tampa, Pensacola, and New Orleans. As a result, city leaders rededicated themselves to boosterism; in 1900, the city's various civic organizations cooperated to form the Mobile Joint Rivers and Harbors Committee to lobby for funds, particularly federal money for the channel. In the first decade of the new century, the Port City's business community intensified its efforts, traveling across the country, visiting ports that had successfully improved trade, and working to boost local investments. In the words of the president of Mobile's Commercial Club and editor of the *Mobile Register,* Erwin Craighead, boosters must "put Mobile on a parity with other deep water ports."[5]

The war and the subsequent interest in the Panama Canal led Mobile's boosters to emphasize trade with Latin America, and by 1910, the city's trade with Central and South America had increased threefold. Yet such growth was unsustainable. The city's experience with the banana trade exemplifies the problems at the port. In the decade following the Spanish-American War, Mobile emerged as a major port for the banana trade, ranking third in the country behind New York City and New Orleans. The United Fruit Company (UFC) increased operations, installing new unloading equipment on land leased from the Mobile & Ohio (M&O) Railroad. But a number of factors, including "inconsistencies in health inspections" and "quarantine procedures," caused the UFC to reconsider the Port City. By the outbreak of World War I, the company found it more economical and efficient to divert Mobile's trade to nearby New Orleans, thanks to that city's more developed infrastructure and favorable rail rates.[6]

In fact, the railroads were central to Mobile's port problems, at least in the eyes of local leaders. During and after Reconstruction, Alabama, like a number of other states, encouraged the expansion of rail networks into the interior in the hopes of boosting trade, building up and developing interior communities, and connecting southern products to a wider world. As early as the 1840s, Mobile's civic leaders began calling for a road linking the city with the Ohio River, and a group of businessmen eventually funded the M&O Railroad, which connected the city to St. Louis. As rail networks connected interior towns, cotton merchants gained access to a number of new ports, many of which were better able to handle cotton quickly and efficiently than Mobile. Eastern Alabama, long tied to Mobile thanks to the path of the state's river system, could transport products by rail to the Atlantic ports of Savannah and Charleston just as easily as sending those same products down the Coosa River. Even the M&O, which was intended to introduce new trade to the Port City, worked at cross purposes. When the road linked to New Orleans in 1870, shipping companies began diverting trade to that city's port, which had more reliable access to interocean trade. During the Spanish-American War, the railroads, benefiting from the uptick in regional commerce, expanded their footprint along the riverfront. But even as they bought up land, the companies focused on low-value commodities and continued to ship incoming goods to competing ports.[7]

Railroads had a conflicted reputation across the state. Alabamians believed railroads to be essential to economic growth, but when the post-Reconstruction state government invested heavily in railroad expansion, that involvement was marked by fraud, corruption, and bankruptcy. By the turn of the century, Alabama politics was dominated by discussion of a railroad commission with the power to regulate freight rates. In Mobile, where railroads owned much of the city's prime riverfront land, that general sentiment combined with seeming stagnation at the port to suggest that the railroads were responsible for the state of the city's economy. In fact, a survey by the Army Corps of Engineers conducted in 1922 perfectly captures the sad state of affairs at the port in the war years. Of a total 32 piers and wharves, the vast majority, 28, were privately owned, and 15 of those were owned by railroads. The railroad facilities were equipped to handle a basic level of commerce; the M&O boasted grain, banana, and general cargo capabilities, and nearly all of the rail facilities could handle lumber and coal. But their facilities were unsuited for larger oceangoing vessels, and because the rail companies could easily import and export goods through more developed ports like New Orleans, they had little incentive to improve their increasingly obsolete facilities in Mobile. At the time of the survey, the Corps of Engineers noted that "the existing dock facilities were clearly incompatible with any large-scale growth of high-grade traffic through the port of Mobile." The *Mobile Register* captured the frustration leaders felt with an editorial cartoon depicting the state of Alabama as a bottle with a cornucopia of wealth, but with its mouth "stoppered" by the railroads. In the minds of civic leaders, the private sector could not be relied upon to improve the port.[8]

World War I changed the nature of the discussion in Mobile. Nationwide, the war effort brought an infusion of federal funds for economic expansion, growth in American infrastructure, and perhaps most important, increasingly close relations between government and the private sector as President Woodrow Wilson sought to manage the wartime economy. In the South, southerners found their "horizons expanded" as boosters attracted army camps and other military installations, including naval facilities in the Gulf cities of Pensacola and New Orleans. With the United States desperate for ships to carry goods to Europe, the government encouraged shipbuilding, including facilities in Texas, Mississippi, and across the southern seaboard. As in Mobile, cities like Charleston and New Orleans saw rapid development at ports, and in many cases, those southern cities, too, embraced a development-minded ethos focused on maintaining such growth. Historian George Tindall quotes one observer who described the southern economic experience as "a kind of week-end economic debauchery," a brief period of prosperity which brought uncharacteristic growth in industry and commerce and which encouraged unreasonable expectations for development going forward.[9]

Across the state of Alabama, the war brought growth and change. At Muscle Shoals, locals turned President Woodrow Wilson's interest in the domestic production of nitrates (for munitions) into a solution for the lost potential of the Tennessee River (see below). Alabama textile mills saw elevated demand, Birmingham's mines and mills increased production, and cotton experienced its best years in recent memory. The state hosted military trainees at Camp Mc-Clellan in Anniston, at Camp Sheridan and Taylor Field in Montgomery, and at Forts Gaines and Morgan along the Gulf Coast. Like their southern neighbors, Alabamians got a "taste of prosperity" which "gave a lasting momentum" to plans for economic development.[10]

Given the growth that occurred in other parts of the state and region, Mobile's wartime experience was, as one historian noted, "perverse." The city, still reliant to a large degree on the cotton trade, was initially hit hard by the fall-off in commerce that attended the outbreak of war and the ensuing "cotton crisis" in the years prior to American involvement. Even after prices stabilized and rose during the war, Mobile struggled to regain ground lost to other ports. As American and southern trade to Britain and France increased as the war progressed, Mobile lagged behind; given the limited number of oceangoing vessels, shipping concerns chose the economy and efficiency of shipping through the port of New Orleans over the outdated, decentralized facilities at Mobile. As boom conditions appeared across the region, Mobile struggled. In 1916, one observer, attorney Frederick Bromberg, reported that "everybody in Mobile is economizing," and at the port, he lamented, the "docks are empty week days as well as Sundays."[11]

Thus, on the eve of the American entrance into World War I, Mobile's leaders watched as the first hints of a wartime boom bypassed their city. Despite a shipping channel deepened with federal funds, and despite a direct connection to the coalfields and furnaces in the northern part of the state, the city could not capitalize on existing infrastructure improvements. Instead, the limited supply of ships assured that only the most efficient and well-connected ports received trade, and because the port's facilities were largely controlled by railroad companies, much of the commerce that might have otherwise crossed Mobile's docks continued on rails to New Orleans, Savannah, Charleston, and other rival ports. Civic and business leaders realized that if they wanted to take advantage of wartime opportunities, they would need to act quickly to encourage a revitalization and reorientation at the port that would bring international commerce to an increasingly localized economy.

The boosters' strategy was two-pronged: they would encourage industrial and commercial growth at the port while improving the city's docks infrastructure to meet the demands of modern global commerce. In the first part of that strategy, the effort to encourage the growth of business at the port, Mobile's commercial-civic elite echoed (and benefited from) President Woodrow Wilson's efforts to build up a federally supported and operated American Merchant Marine. Wilson increased trade, with American manufacturing carried on American ships to markets around the world. Yet at the outbreak of the war, American ships carried less than 10% of the country's international trade—in many cases, US trade depended on the willingness of foreign shippers, particularly the British, to carry American goods to foreign ports. For planners, the war was both a revelation of the crisis in shipping and an opportunity for the country to take charge of shipping routes lying vacant as European powers focused on the war.[12]

But, as observers noted, grasping the "opportunity" of the war meant a dual-sided campaign to secure new trade routes and the ships that serviced them. The Shipping Act, passed in September 1916, called for the construction of an American merchant marine with ships built by the Emergency Fleet Corporation (EFC) and owned and overseen by the US Shipping Board (USSB). The legislation fit squarely within Wilson's vision for wartime America, establishing temporary executive control over a vital sector of the economy in order to protect American interests in a world at war; it also fit his long-term goal of establishing the United States as an international commercial power with a fleet of merchant ships carrying American goods around the globe. A furious building program, the requisition of British ships being built on American ways, and British losses in the naval war with German U-boats all combined to give the United States a comparatively "impressive" merchant marine by the time the nation entered the fighting in France. By late 1918, the EFC "presided over a small empire of shipbuilding facilities" and saw production double prewar levels. While the United States failed to become completely independent of British ships, wartime production did make a significant difference in the nation's position; by 1919, the United States' merchant fleet had grown by 60% and carried more cargo in foreign trade than in domestic.[13]

In Mobile, one of the first of the EFC shipbuilding contracts went to Alabama Dry Dock and Shipbuilding Company, or ADDSCO, in late summer 1917. David R. Dunlap, the president and general manager of Alabama Iron

Works, created ADDSCO by combining four existing companies in the hopes of "handl[ing] all branches of Marine Repair work." Within its first year of existence, ADDSCO contracted with the EFC for two ships, the US Navy for three minesweepers, and the Panama Canal Commission for two steel barges. Like other companies working on EFC contracts, ADDSCO found itself unprepared for the work and expanded rapidly to handle the wartime demand for a fleet, constructing additional dry docks and purchasing new equipment.[14]

In summer 1918, ADDSCO launched its first ship, the *Banago,* a wooden-hulled, Ferris-class steamship designed for oceangoing commerce. Given the hectic schedule of expanding facilities, finding labor, and securing the materials needed, the company was quite proud of its feat. ADDSCO's newsletter, *Fore & Aft,* crowed that "never has a body of men worked harder and more harmoniously" and included a poem, tying the work to the war effort:

> To win the war our ships must run
> To send the boys to get the Hun
> Across the pond to England and France
> Our boys will make the Germans dance.[15]

Upriver at Chickasaw Creek, another wartime shipbuilding project took shape. In late 1917, George Gordon Crawford, the president of Tennessee Coal, Iron, & Railroad, the Birmingham-based subsidiary of US Steel, announced the development of a massive shipbuilding facility to build 9,600-ton steel ships. Drawing from the steel company's production, and utilizing rail and waterway connections made possible by Senator Bankhead's work in Washington, the Chickasaw shipyard also hoped to tap into the wartime and postwar demand for American-built vessels. Crawford's vision was expansive, including a community for workers, segregated by race, that kept the labor force on site and hard at work. By 1918, work progressed on fourteen shipways by five thousand workers who lived at Chickasaw, a community that was dredged from the swamps, cobbled together in a matter of months, and tied directly to the fortunes of the shipbuilding industry; in the words of Mobile's business boosters, it was a "happy community of shipbuilders and their families."[16]

Occurring on the heels of the decline that marked the previous years, the sudden boost in shipbuilding suggested a reversal of fortune. The city's boosters looked forward to a future in which shipbuilding might anchor the port's recovery. In January 1918, the *Mobile Register* promised that visitors traveling down the Mobile River would view a "panorama . . . teeming with activity." The presence of so many growing companies would certainly insure the city's future as a site of "great development." In addition to ADDSCO and Chickasaw, the city counted a number of additional shipyards, including the F. T. Ley Company, the Mobile Shipbuilding Company, and the Henderson Shipbuilding Company, and several of the existing riverside companies grew or expanded to accommodate the possibility of increased trade. In September 1918, *Mobile Register* editor Erwin Craighead captured the city's burgeoning optimism: "the heavens opened, and the war, which threatened to extinguish Mobile, was shown to be an immense advantage."[17]

Yet just as Mobile's shipbuilding sector began growing in earnest, the Armistice took effect in France. Demand for ships slackened as the easing of tensions freed up foreign ships and allowed for the resumption of international trade. Too, Wilson, seeking the Allies' cooperation on the negotiation of a peace treaty, was hesitant to further challenge British maritime control. He was also reluctant to perpetuate such an active government program for shipbuilding, leaving his Shipping Board to finish out war work as planners decided the shape of a postwar merchant marine.[18]

As wartime contracts ran their course, Mobile's shipyards bustled well into 1919. The ADDSCO organization finished the navy's minesweepers in early 1919, and even as late as April, the company promised continuing work, warning against "grumbling busybodies" afraid of a postwar drop in employment. The company also continued to work on the improvements begun during the war, including the outfitting of facilities on Pinto Island, eventually to include a 10,000-ton dry dock, one of the largest in the South at the time.[19] At Chickasaw, though the war ended before production began, the site coasted on wartime growth, maintaining substantial payrolls and enlarging the industrial compound with concrete wharves, a powerhouse, smoke stacks, cranes, mills, and additional homes for workers. The yard built a total of fourteen cargo ships by 1921.[20]

Yet, despite the lingering effects of wartime growth, Mobile's civic leaders were keenly aware that without continued support, the shipyards would be unable to sustain production, let alone justify further growth. Citing Edward Hurley, the chairman of the EFC and a vocal proponent of American shipping, the *Mobile Register* promised postwar work "for years to come," but only if its civic leaders worked to improve the city's infrastructure, cooperated to preserve and attract industry, and encouraged future growth. At ADDSCO, company officials told workers that while construction and repair work would continue in the immediate future, the "industrial future of the Company," its ability to compete for work, depended on the willingness of workers to continue their hard work and the determination of the managers and owners to continue attracting business.[21]

The war also provided Mobile's boosters with an opportunity to push for new trade routes connecting the growing port and its products with consumers. Given that the USSB controlled the allocation of such routes, municipal and state political leaders petitioned for dedicated shipping lines and the imports and exports that would accompany them. In May 1919, Mobile's Chamber of Commerce protested to the EFC, through Alabama's congressional delegation, that although wartime growth had set the city on a path of "commercial progress," the agency had assigned ships to competing ports instead, including some ships constructed and repaired in the Port City. Senator Underwood, in particular, served as the voice of the port, given his stature in the powerful southern bloc of the Democratic Party, and civic leaders flooded his office with "voluminous data" on Mobile's wartime service and its postwar capabilities. The *Register's* editors noted that the city's "rivals" along the Atlantic seaboard received more ships, even lines to Latin American ports more proximate to Mobile, and complained that other states' representatives were better at "hustling" for business than Alabama's. As one editorial stated, "What we have been looking forward to for years is now coming to pass . . . Shall Mobile not have full part in it?"[22]

The tide slowly began to turn. In August, Mobile received an allotment of eight vessels, seven of which were transatlantic and one which shipped to Latin America. The Shipping Board's assistant director of operations, W. F. Taylor, noted that Mobile received more ships than any Gulf port, save New Orleans, and promised that the city would get as many ships as it could supply with cargo. That autumn, the Chamber of Commerce cooperated with Spring Hill College to create a vocational training program focused on preparing adult students for the "Latin American trade." The schedule of night courses was partially funded by the president of US Steel, James Farrell, and was taught by professors drawn from the chamber and its partners in the business community. It would, organizers hoped, demonstrate that Mobile was cognizant of "the commercial possibilities arising from our new position in the world."[23]

In 1920, Congress passed the Merchant Marine Act, sometimes referred to as the Jones Act, which ordered the Shipping Board to sell off its fleet and oversee a privately operated American Merchant Marine. As historian David Kennedy suggests, the removal of direct federal subsidies for shipbuilding reversed the growth of the war years, causing American control of oceangoing trade to decline in the mid- to late 1920s. Certainly, the Jones Act threatened ADDSCO and other companies that relied on federal contracts, but most Mobile businessmen remained optimistic that the city's shipbuilding industry could transition to the new environment. In fact, for much of 1920, Mobile's yards did generally better than they had in 1919, which itself was a better year than 1918. The *Register* called it the "most prosperous year in Mobile's history," with ships totaling 1.2 million tons and growing exports in iron and steel, machinery, lumber, and cotton, and imports of tropical fruits, nitrates, and ores. When the *Chickasaw City* was launched in May 1920, the first ship produced by the Chickasaw Shipbuilding and Car Company, observers saw the beginning of a "new era" for the city.[24]

The aspect of the Merchant Marine Act that truly worried Mobilians was the withdrawal of federal attention and with it, the ability to use connections in Washington to attract business. Given the long-held advantages of northern and Atlantic ports in American shipping, there was a pervasive fear that the Shipping Board would, in the interest of efficiency or economy, privilege established ports like New York City at the expense of areas like the Gulf Coast, playing "catch up" thanks to wartime gains. Mobile's leaders demanded that the Shipping Board give preference to southern ports, helping them compete for trade, especially in Latin America. For southerners skeptical of federal intervention and expansive government, this argument made for strange bedfellows, a fact not lost on the *Mobile Register*. In the midst of a string of editorials demanding federal assistance in the form of preferential treatment, the editors admitted that they normally would not favor government control of shipping, but "now that it is here, we must make the wisest use possible of it"; Mobile and other ports would "fight" to retain "what they have obtained through the equalizing actions of the shipping board." When the Shipping Board announced in 1921 that it would work to build up smaller ports as a way of avoiding congestion, Mobilians took the news as a victory.[25]

One Mobile shipper with a personal interest in the effort to direct shipping toward the Port City and Gulf Coast was John Waterman, who moved from

New Orleans to Mobile at the turn of the century in order to manage a British steamship company. He hoped to build a southern shipping concern, but pre–World War I Mobile had neither the port facilities nor the "southern capital" to do so. The war and the concerted effort to build an American merchant marine provided an opening, and in 1919, he joined with local businessmen to form the Waterman Steamship Company and applied to the Shipping Board for the right to manage ships allocated to Mobile. From the outset, Waterman blended local boosterism and patriotism in his appeal. In a letter to a USSB agent, Waterman noted that Mobile's port had been subservient to "foreign business" to carry its cargo in "foreign bottoms," but that with the demands of the war and the growth of the port during the war, that "Mobile should secure proper recognition."[26]

That same year, Waterman received his first ship, the *Eastern Sun,* and preferential rights to parts of the United Kingdom and northern France. He began compiling business and combining routes, and soon, his ships routinely plied the waters of the Atlantic and the Caribbean. Waterman consistently boasted of Mobile's cheap rates and waterway connections from the interior of the country, but he faced stiff competition from both the Atlantic seaboard and the city's neighbors on the Gulf, competition that he believed Mobile might overcome only with concerted local action and the preferential support of the federal government. He argued that Port City leaders would have to press the port's case in Washington and mobilize the "commercial interests of Mobile" to assist in the fight. Waterman actively mobilized local participation in campaigns to pressure the federal government, and along with fellow shippers eventually hired a lobbyist for the port, pressing the Shipping Board to privilege Mobile with ships and preferred routes.[27]

In the postwar years, Mobile's brokers and builders took advantage of the Wilson administration's determination to build up the American Merchant Marine. During the opportunity provided by the global crisis in shipping, Mobilians leapt at the opportunity to build ships for commerce, either for the United States or for companies looking to capitalize on the sudden decrease in foreign competition. At ADDSCO, Chickasaw, and other yards, government contracts and demand for domestic shipping helped establish shipbuilding along the Mobile River, providing the city's leadership with a blueprint for prosperity that they hoped would continue after the war. At Waterman and other steamship companies, the demand for domestic shipping led to a scramble for ships and trade routes that might boost American trade, carried in the holds of American ships. In both cases, businessmen relied on a combination of local initiative and federal support. Leaders of ADDSCO and Waterman's executives saw federal preference for American shipping as an opportunity to demand southern shipping, and specifically Mobile shipping, as the most effective way to compete against regional and national rivals. As such, the federal government was an essential partner in the effort to revitalize Mobile after World War I, and the city's leadership acted to attract and maintain that partnership.

Industrial development and federal investment were not enough to reverse the port's stagnation, however. The warehouses, wharves, slips, and docks were outdated and deteriorating, and to the great frustration of city leaders, the railroads and other private interests which controlled the vast majority of riverfront property evidenced no interest in updating facilities. Thus, Mobile's civic and business leaders focused on the possibility of public funding to modernize the docks. Yet there was a difficulty here as well. In order to build the kind of facilities needed for a modern port, capable of accommodating the ships and cargo of global commerce, boosters required a level of funding only available at the state level. However, since the Civil War, agrarian interests in Montgomery successfully limited Alabama's ability to fund statewide infrastructure improvements, which many planters associated with economic competition in the industrial and commercial sector. In the state's restrictive constitution of 1901, a conservative, segregationist Democratic government placed severe limits on the state's ability to raise funds for infrastructure improvement. In section 93, the authors specifically prevented the state government from "engag[ing] in works of internal improvement" and from "lend[ing] money or its credit in aid of such"; in section 213, the authors outlawed the accumulation of state debt except in cases of "invasion," "insurrection," or to address a small deficiency in the state treasury. Such proscriptions limited the size and scope of state government and prevented a situation in which taxes might be raised to cover a budget shortfall or fund improvements.[28]

Cognizant of constitutional limits and desperate for improvements that might help the city compete for shipping, Mobile's business community adopted two distinct strategies to improve the docks. A group of civic leaders began construction on a municipal docks project with more limited goals to fit within the city's financial capabilities. Another group planned for a publicly constructed and operated state docks facility, beginning with changes to the state constitution that would allow such a facility to be constructed. These efforts, which ended with the failure of the municipal program and the success of the state program, suggest much about the appeal of development, the role of government assistance in that development, and the determination by southern communities to compete in a national, and increasingly international, economy. Moreover, the program bridges Mobile's wartime growth and the city's efforts to expand that growth into the postwar era. The docks campaign, with its failures and successes, suggests how civic leaders understood the requirements, costs, and benefits of growth, and it shows how they "sold" that growth to the general public as a statewide good.

Given the strictures placed upon infrastructure improvement and financing by the state constitution, it is unsurprising that Mobilians first looked to the municipal government for a solution to the poor condition of the city's port facilities. Since the turn of the century, Mobile's boosters had adopted port development as a centerpiece of the city's economic prosperity, and when wartime disruptions were compounded by a powerful 1916 hurricane, civic leaders redoubled efforts to build up the port. Harry Hartwell, a state senator and a prominent booster in the city, secured the passage of a bill that gave a state harbor commission oversight of the river and the permission to acquire facilities and issue comparatively small bonds that could be applied to improvements. The Board of Commissioners also hired an engineering firm to assess the city's outdated facilities in the harbor and to draw up plans for a feasible, affordable municipal dock system. The city even convinced some landowners to sell land for port development. The next year, in an effort headed by Commissioner Harry Pillans in consultation with the new State Harbor Board, the city settled on a modest bulkhead and pier capable of handling eighteen vessels.[29]

Construction began on the "Arlington Docks" project in early 1918 with a sense of optimism, given the growth in the city and efforts to encourage trade. But fortunes soon changed. Pillans and his fellow commissioners found that the money required to purchase property, dredge the berths, and construct the pier and associated facilities outstripped the city's finances, especially as wartime inflation set in; by 1921, the city's bond was exhausted and the project was unfinished. Moreover, Pillans found himself and his project under constant criticism from the state docks facility, especially as the campaign to fund the larger project began. For supporters of the state project, Arlington was a waste of time and energy, an expensive distraction from efforts to build a port truly capable of handling domestic and international trade.[30]

In Mobile, the central figure in the push for a state docks facility was Harry T. Hartwell. The son of a Confederate veteran, Hartwell became involved in shipping concerns in the Port City, eventually partnering with Horace Turner to organize the Turner-Hartwell Docks Company in 1901. Hartwell was an active booster for the Port City: he influenced the passage of a series of tax exemptions for businesses interested in relocating to the area, and in a brief stint as state senator, he spent much of his political capital restructuring the Alabama State Harbor Commission in the hopes of building up the port. As the Arlington project floundered, Hartwell planned for a more extensive docks facility, consisting of docks, warehouses, and transportation lines, all purchased, constructed and operated by the state of Alabama. This project required the mobilization of the city and state electorate, an extensive planning and engineering program, and the cooperation of a number of business interests, including some, the railroads, who were painted as the chief source of trouble for the existing port of Mobile.[31]

Hartwell and his allies modeled their effort on the success Louisiana had in its efforts to build up the Port of New Orleans two decades earlier. In fact, Hartwell and others routinely compared Mobile to its nearest rival to impress upon others the importance of a state-supported facility able to direct the flow of Alabama trade. Encouraged by the Crescent City's business community, in 1896 Louisiana began the process of putting the Port of New Orleans under state oversight. By 1901, as Alabama's state government was drafting a state constitution severely limiting the ability to pass bonds for improvements, Louisiana took complete control of the port, extending waterfront properties and operating the docks facilities. The state went so far as to amend its own constitution for the ability to pass bonds, and by 1919, the total indebtedness was nearly $37 million. Yet when W. D. Nesbitt, the chairman of the State of Alabama Board of Control and Economy, visited the Louisiana State Docks in May 1919, he reported that the docks were a shining example of sound growth with increased tonnage and growing profits. The lesson of New Orleans was clear to Alabama's boosters: should Alabama amend its constitution and take control of its port at Mobile, the resulting facility would attract trade and grow profits.[32]

Hartwell found an ally in the fight for a state docks in the newly elected governor of the state, Thomas Kilby. A successful businessman before he entered politics, Kilby made his fortune in cast-iron pipe, eventually serving as president of the City National Bank of Anniston, Alabama, and entering state politics. At a time of entrenched political and racial conservatism, Kilby demonstrated a fairly marked progressive streak. He was, perhaps, best known for his reform efforts focused on Alabama prisons. While he was unable to end the practice of convict leasing, he did improve conditions, and while he was not a vocal proponent of women's rights or racial equality, he did seek to register women voters and prosecute lynchers. He also tried, with mixed results, to raise taxes to fund improvements, and he eventually paid off much, though not all, of the state's outstanding debt. A quintessential business progressive, Kilby sought to improve the state's economy by increasing revenue, streamlining government, and creating a positive environment for business growth.[33]

Hartwell, Kilby, and the docks boosters received an additional incentive in 1919, when Congress encouraged cities on navigable waterways (like Mobile) to provide for accessible public terminals. Moreover, Congress warned, should a city fail to provide such facilities, the secretary of war could "withhold" government funding for new or existing projects. For years, Mobile relied on federal appropriations to dredge and deepen the shipping channel to the Gulf of Mexico and to improve the Warrior River waterway connecting Mobile to the industrial products of Birmingham and its environs. As commercial and civic leaders looked to upgrade the port going forward, continued access to such appropriations would undoubtedly be essential to prosperity. The federal warning provided an important additional "prod" to the proponents of the state docks, suggesting that should Alabama fail to act, the consequences would be dire.[34]

In April 1919, the State Harbor Commission, with Kilby's blessing, launched its effort to amend the Alabama Constitution to allow the state to "employ its credit in the improvement of the harbor and navigable waters of the State." As the legislature began its deliberations on the amendment (the first step in the amendment process), William T. Donnelly, an engineer hired by the Harbor Commission, released a report underlining the need for state assistance to build a modern, internationally focused commercial port and emphasizing the broad-reaching benefits of improvements, especially when combined with industrial development. In response to Donnelly's report, the *Register* reminded readers that "private enterprise cannot be depended upon to develop economically the port system which Mobile requires if the city is to . . . become a great coaling port, a great manufacturing city and otherwise fulfill her destiny." Such pressure worked, and in early November, the amendment passed the legislature. Kilby rewarded Hartwell with a seat on the Harbor Commission in the hopes that he might steer plans for the docks project he felt to be certain.[35]

In the summer of 1920, boosters kicked off the public campaign for the constitutional amendment with a meeting of the city's Chamber of Commerce and a speech at the Elks' Lodge by Representative William Bankhead, son of the recently departed long-serving senator (and one of the most prominent supporters of federal development of Alabama's rivers and harbors) John H. Bankhead, Sr. Mobile's leading civic clubs, including the Auto Club, the Kiwanis Club, and the Rotary Club all backed the measure, as did Mobile's political delegation, including Congressmen John McDuffie and W. B. Oliver, Senator Underwood, and Governor Kilby. In September, boosters attended the meeting of the Alabama Waterways Association in Montgomery, turning the annual assembly into a massive lobbying effort for the port amendment. The meeting also inaugurated the use of a novel advertising strategy. Supporters outfitted a special theater rail car to show a film, "The Port and the People," to people along the route of the Atlanta, Birmingham, & Atlantic Railway. Boosters also kitted out automobiles in "paraphernalia" advertising the port and sent them across the state. In hindsight, this strategy focused too heavily on those areas connected to interstate commerce, the areas more predisposed to arguments about the benefits of the docks. Boosters generally ignored rural areas, distant from road and rail connections, outside the state's commercial networks.[36]

Regardless, the port's proponents remained relatively confident of their eventual success. The boosters had widespread support in the state press and pro-amendment groups were active for the amendment in a number of Alabama counties. One of the few who worried about the status of the vote was Harry Hartwell, who saw the campaign as a battle in an extended war against private interests and selfishness which had limited growth at the docks. He warned Governor Kilby of the opposition of the railroads, which he claimed were working to dampen support, and challenged the governor: "Remember the watchword at the Battle of the Marne. Thou Shall Not Pass. Don't let them."[37]

On November 2, 1920, Alabamians went to the polls to decide. The *Register* begged Mobilians to turn out for "Amendment 1," warning, "Unless we act at once it will be too late, for once commercial lanes are established they are difficult to alter." Hartwell looked forward to victory, congratulating Kilby on "another progressive idea fostered and successfully completed." The *Register* described early returns as a sign of a statewide rout, but as results trickled in, the mood soured. On November 8, an unofficial survey suggested that the amendment had failed, and a week later, the results were official: in light turnout, the amendment failed 22,000 to 35,000. Harry Hartwell, who watched the results roll in from a literal "sick bed" promised to continue fighting for his "righteous cause" against an insidious "Foe."[38]

A glance at the results suggests that Kilby's and Hartwell's statewide strategy was only partially successful. In those counties directly involved in commercial trade, counties along major waterways feeding the port and the coal-producing areas that shipped along those lanes, the amendment passed. But rural areas defeated the measure with heavy majorities against the amendment in parts of north and central Alabama and in the Wiregrass region in the southeastern corner of the state. In the words of the *Register,* there was "an innate hostility on the part of a large number of rural voters towards any change in the fundamental law of the state." At least, those voters were hostile to changes that seemed to provide no direct benefits to their communities.[39]

Boosters promised a second, more intense campaign to amend the constitution. As Harry Hartwell told the outgoing president of the Harbor Commission, "I am conceited enough to look upon the movement as my child, and no real father ever deserts his offspring." But after the initial failure, Hartwell and his fellow boosters had to reconsider their messaging. Large swaths of the electorate simply did not accept that economic development in Mobile brought meaningful benefits to far-flung communities outside the economic radius of the Port City and its tributary territory; at least, voters in those areas were unwilling to support state involvement for the project. In rural counties, still dominated by planters, infrastructure improvement was long held to be a way for industrial interests to misappropriate state funds (the very argument planters used in 1875 and 1901 to limit the state's role in funding such improvements). In a renewed campaign, port boosters would have to make clear the connections between industrial growth and statewide economic prosperity while also disavowing rural elites and their supporters of the notion that such improvement would "cost" Alabamians too much in the process.[40]

Thus, during the second docks campaign, boosters stressed the statewide benefits of the project, the soundness of the investment, and the importance of Alabama's role in a postwar, global, commercial economy. In service of this new approach, the *Register* promoted the docks with a series of quotes from national figures, including Charles Keller and Major General Lansing Beach, both of the Board of Engineers, Rivers and Harbors, and W. D. Connor of the Inland Waterways Service. The experts agreed that the development of the Mobile docks by the private sector would be disadvantageous, and that Alabamians should throw their support behind public ownership and operation. In May 1921, Governor Kilby made a highly publicized visit to the Port City, where he toured the Mobile River and the wartime shipyards in Mobile and Chickasaw. Viewing potential sites for the docks, Kilby promised that the project would be a "revelation" and admonished citizens to take advantage of the "opportunity" to "[build] up one of the greatest ports in the country, one that will attract the foreign trade of a large part of the United States, and that will make Mobile and Alabama rich in things material and give them a broader view of the world and its commerce." Mobile's congressional delegation backed a second vote and encouraged Kilby to call a special session of the state legislature. In September 1921, the legislature approved another amendment and sent it to the public for ratification.[41]

H. K. Milner, a Birmingham businessman who took over the chairmanship of the Harbor Commission in late 1921, planned a much more aggressive campaign for the election of 1922. He blamed the 1920 defeat on an underfunded effort that failed to reach all corners of the state and on postwar economic slump which made Alabama voters overly cautious of taxation and government spending, issues that many associated with amendment. So Milner and his fellow boosters met those concerns head-on. Addressing fears that the amendment would mean a tax increase to benefit a handful of Alabama businessmen in the Port City, Milner and the commission emphasized that profits from the port would be used to pay interest on and retire its own bonds. In his words, "the state will not be called upon to pay out one cent." The boosters also wanted to stress that the project would benefit Alabamians across the state, not just those in and around Mobile. Working with the governor, Milner made sure that the commission counted members from across Alabama, and he even placed Birmingham lawyer (and former congressman) Sydney Bowie in charge of the campaign.[42]

In their efforts to stress the statewide benefits of the dock, and more specifically to shore up votes in north Alabama, the group added the commission's support to another war-related development project, the government nitrate plant and hydroelectric dam on the Tennessee River at Muscle Shoals. Begun during the war to produce nitrates, the facility created a temporary boom in the Shoals region before the war ended and the withdrawal of federal funding placed the project on standby. When Harry Hartwell and a group of port boosters traveled to the Shoals in 1922, supporters of the plant and dam and their allies in Congress were trying to secure a lease of the facility to Henry Ford in the hopes that the automobile manufacturer would operate the project and spark an economic revival in the Shoals region. Hartwell delivered a speech, "Port Development at Mobile and Its Relation to Muscle Shoals and Alabama," specifically tying the fate of the two projects together. Investment at Muscle Shoals would revitalize the economy of north Alabama, which would then utilize and benefit from increased trade through a modernized, international docks facility. Of course, the visit had a practical goal: winning over the people of the Shoals to the cause of the amendment. But it also served a larger purpose. Hartwell's visit reinforced the notion that Alabamians needed to work together to maintain and expand wartime opportunities, an idea at the heart of the docks campaign and Mobile's broader work to secure industrial and commercial growth during and after the war.[43]

In September 1922, the *Register* dedicated its annual "Trades Edition" to a full-throated endorsement with letters of support from a number of prominent Alabama politicians and port boosters. The testimonials demonstrate the group's all-out effort in the weeks leading up to the vote, but they also embody the way that the campaign tied Alabama's economic future to its ability to participate in a postwar world of international trade (and national competition for that international trade). In his letter, Governor Kilby pointed to the port as the only "great project" left for Alabama to accomplish. If the state was not "awakened to its opportunities," he argued, it would effectively cede its role in global commerce to its neighbors in Georgia, Louisiana, and Florida. Milner pointed specifically to a coming shift in Alabama's economy, from agriculture to manufacturing, and argued that if Mobile was to embody its "natural" position as an outlet for Alabama's manufactured goods, it needed the kind of port that would allow goods to move to the Pacific Coast, Latin America, the Caribbean, and the rest of the world. Congressman John McDuffie called for immediate action. "We are living in a day of great industrial and commercial development," he wrote. "The hour has struck for Alabama and she cannot afford to mark time while her sister states are marching on to greater progress and prosperity."[44]

The 1922 campaign elicited relatively little open opposition, at least in the surviving published record. Leading business interests supported port development (given the obvious return on reduced shipping costs through a state-run facility), as did the state's civic elite, illustrated by the widespread support among both politicians and the major Alabama newspapers. Much of the antagonism seems to have centered on the cost of the development and specifically on the threat that the benefits of the project would not justify the costs. One opponent, calling himself "Alabamian," wrote in to the *Montgomery Advertiser* suggesting that Mobile should be responsible for building its own docks, and if Mobile could not, then the state should allow private interests to shoulder the burden or just direct the state's trade through existing, competing ports. Other opposition embodied a general distrust of changes to the constitution. As one supporter of the amendment who was working to build support in rural Jackson County reported, "The great trouble with us is men will vote against the amendment who do not understand it and do not know what it is." This latter charge, that education might prove a difference maker, was the very reason that amendment supporters were active in far-flung parts of the state, outlining the economic benefits of the docks to all Alabamians. Opposition based on fiscal conservatism was harder to answer; clearly, some Alabamians refused to accept that the state had a responsibility for or role to play in the kind of internal improvements represented by the docks. Supporters made a concerted effort to promise that the state would be conscientious and careful with the money spent. When a fiscally conservative politician named W. B. Brandon won the Democratic primary (the effective gubernatorial contest in the one-party South), he promised to support the port because it would be self-sustaining and economically constructive.[45]

On November 7, 1922, Alabama voters overwhelmingly ratified the amendment, with opposition appearing only in the counties of Lee, Henry, and Geneva. Statewide, the majority approached 80,000 votes, including support from many rural north Alabama counties that had rejected the amendment two years earlier. The *Register* praised the state for "adopting" the port of Mobile, suggesting that the victory assured a prosperous future for the port and the state. The ratification of the port aid amendment culminated a massive effort to sell state-led economic development to the people of Alabama. Moreover, it culminated Mobile's post–World War I campaign to prepare for the city's and state's entry into a new postwar economy in which Alabama could compete for international trade. Supporters of the state docks successfully convinced voters, even rural conservatives skeptical of government action, that the state should play a role in directing and supervising economic growth.[46]

The vote for the port aid amendment all but assured the construction of the state docks. Over the course of the next year, Governor Brandon set the project in motion, issuing bonds, purchasing land and clearing titles, and creating a

State Docks Commission to oversee construction and operation. In December 1923, he named William L. Sibert as chairman of the commission. Born in Etowah County, Alabama, Sibert was one of the most respected and widely known civil engineers in the country, famous for overseeing the construction of the dams and locks on the Panama Canal. As general manager of the Alabama State Docks, Sibert selected a location along the Mobile River at Farmer's Island, just north of the city; outlined plans for construction; and negotiated with the railroads, who eventually moved rail lines and cooperated to facilitate construction on the project. He also spent time showing various industrialists around the facilities under construction, working to bring in shipping and warehousing concerns, weathering a "very severe West Indian hurricane," and trying to maintain enthusiasm for the completion of the project.[47]

The Alabama State Docks formally opened on June 25, 1928. Governor Bibb Graves, who took office in 1927, hosted the opening ceremony, proclaiming a new era in the state's economy. By the end of the year, Sibert could boast a diverse collection of products moving through the port, all secured by the commission's and its municipal allies' "direct solicitation": sugar, nitrates, asphalt, newsprint, jute, marble, iron and steel products, and chemicals. The docks provided "preferential berths" to shipping concerns from Europe, the Far East and Pacific, and Central and South America, many on merchant vessels operated by Mobile's shipping companies. In an early 1929 radio address, Harry Hartwell suggested that Mobile had become one of the nation's greatest and most modern seaports, and he noted that when taken together with other industrial improvement, "[the] eyes of the industrial life of America are on Alabama."[48]

At the same time, the docks were not the outright success that boosters had promised during the port amendment campaign of 1922. In a February 1929 letter to Governor Graves, Hartwell admitted as much, noting that the docks had not yet developed the revenue necessary to be self-funding and that further investment (public and private) in the project would prove essential. In June, Sibert retired as commission chairman, even as the docks had begun to report budgetary losses. In fact, some of Sibert's efforts had proven too short-sighted; he had given several companies rate concessions, hoping to attract customers, but once he tried to raise the rates to "normal" level, concerns fled for other ports. Officials also continued to criticize railroads for fees that many in Mobile felt favored neighboring ports. By 1930, with the American economy sliding into depression, Harry Hartwell, who had entered municipal politics during the second docks campaign and was now mayor of the city, told Graves that only an immediate influx of funds would allow the state docks to "[complete] the job."[49]

Hartwell was understandably disappointed with the docks' failure to immediately turn a profit, though given the economic environment of the worsening Great Depression, that disappointment was shared by boosters across the country. Nevertheless, the work that he and his colleagues had undertaken to build up the port of Mobile was, on the whole, successful. By the 1920s, the port counted a number of operating shipyards and shipping concerns, many of which, like Waterman, ADDSCO, and Chickasaw, weathered the Depression and found renewed purpose in the defense effort of World War II. Moreover, thanks to the leadership of Hartwell, Kilby, and others, the state of Alabama had changed its constitution, and funded, constructed, and now operated a state docks facility, seeking to send its products around the world, even as it sought to bring in products from international destinations to the consumers of Alabama and the surrounding region. Mobile's boosters had hoped to position themselves to take advantage of a global economy changing after World War I, and by 1928, the rapid development of the port and its economy had arguably done just that.[50]

Speaking in 1919, Senator Underwood told the assembled workers at the Mobile Shipbuilding Company that "the great war is at an end, but the battle of commerce is only begun." He argued that Mobile could not afford to "go back to our helpless condition before 1914," but instead, had to press forward and take advantage of the opportunities presented to the city and region by the changed nature of the global economy. Mobile's business community worked to attract industry, developing shipbuilding concerns like ADDSCO and Chickasaw Shipbuilding Company. They encouraged the emergence of shipping concerns, like Waterman, and then lobbied the federal government extensively for the ships and the legislation necessary to bring those ships, and dedicated shipping lines, to the Port City. And, in one of the most pressing political questions of the 1920s, boosters put through legislation allowing the state of Alabama to begin direct operation of a publicly owned and managed docks facility. Underwood's militaristic language of campaigns and victories, of advance and retreat, fit remarkably well the "battle" for commerce conducted in Mobile, Alabama, in the years during and following World War I. The victory, even if not complete, suggests that civic leaders understood the opportunity presented by the Great War and how to use it to position Alabama for a more prosperous and stable future.[51]

NOTES

1. Quoted in "State Must Pull Together for Mobile, Says Underwood," *Mobile Register,* April 6, 1919, 1A.

2. George B. Tindall, *The Emergence of the New South, 1913–1914* (Baton Rouge: Louisiana State University Press, 1967), 53–63, 95–101; Blaine A. Brownell, *The Urban Ethos in the South, 1920–1930* (Baton Rouge: Louisiana State University Press, 1975), 142; James C. Cobb, *Industrialization and Southern Society, 1877–1984* (Lexington: University of Kentucky Press, 1984); and Bruce Schulman, *From Cotton Belt to Sunbelt: Federal Policy, Economic Development, and the Transformation of the South, 1938–1980* (Durham, NC: Duke University Press, 1994). Cobb's history of southern industrialization does mention the influence of "business progressives" in state governments in the 1920s. See Cobb, 30–31.

3. Harriet E. Amos, *Cotton City: Urban Development in Antebellum Mobile* (Tuscaloosa: University of Alabama Press, 2001), 212–13, 221.

4. John S. Sledge, *The Mobile River* (Columbia: University of South Carolina Press, 2015), 171–81; Christopher MacGregor Scribner, "Progress versus Tradition in Mobile, 1900–1920," in Michael V. R. Thomason, ed., *Mobile: The New History of Alabama's First City* (Tuscaloosa: University of Alabama Press, 2001), 158–59); and D. Gregory Jeane, with Bruce G. Harvey, *A History of the Mobile District Corps of Engineers* (US Corps of Engineers, Mobile District, 2002), http://cdm16021 .contentdm.oclc.org/cdm/ref/collection/p16021coll4/id/138 (accessed January 13, 2017), 95, 98. For fears concerning ongoing federal investment, see, for example, "Vote for the Port Amendment," *Mobile Register,* October 25, 1920, 4; and "Port Development the Issue," *Mobile Register,* April 3, 1921, 6.

5. Quoted in David Ernest Alsobrook, "Alabama's Port City: Mobile during the Progressive Era, 1896–1917," (PhD diss., Auburn University, 1983), 94–98. Alsobrook suggests that Mobile's boosters, the "commercial-civic elite," emerged during the pre–World War I period as the preeminent force in city politics, just as the port of Mobile was undergoing an economic transformation. See ibid., 358–59.

6. Alsobrook, "Alabama's Port City," 3, 89–95; Sledge, *The Mobile River,* 165, 227–28.

7. Edward L. Ayers, *Promise of the New South: Life after Reconstruction,* 15th anniversary ed. (New York: Oxford University Press, 2007), 59–63; Gavin Wright, *Old South, New South: Revolutions in the Southern Economy after the Civil War* (Baton Rouge: Louisiana State University Press, 1997), 39–43; Amos, *Cotton City,* 207; Don H. Doyle, *New Men, New Cities, New South: Atlanta, Nashville, Charleston, Mobile, 1860–1910* (Chapel Hill: University of North Carolina Press, 1990), 76–79; William Warren Rogers, Robert David Ward, Leah Rawls Atkins, and Wayne Flynt, *Alabama: The History of a Deep South State* (Tuscaloosa: University of Alabama Press, 1994), 178–79.

8. "Look Alive for the Port," *Mobile Register,* December 29, 1918, 6; Waterman to Hempstead, July 27, 1926, Box 3, Folder 3, John B. Waterman Papers, Doyle Leale McCall Rare Book and Manuscript Library, University of South Alabama (hereafter Waterman Papers); Earle L. Rauber, "The Alabama State Docks: A Case Study in State Development" (Federal Reserve Bank of Atlanta, January 1945), 3–5, in Special Collections, Mobile Public Library, Mobile, Alabama; Scribner, "Progress versus Tradition in Mobile, 1900–1920," 156, 158–60; "History Reviewed," *Mobile Register,* November 12, 1922, 6; Sledge, *The Mobile River,* 165. See Alsobrook, "Alabama's Port City," 99–100. For the state of the docks, see also Jeane, *A History of the Mobile District Corps of Engineers.* James F.

Doster's *Railroads in Alabama Politics, 1875-1914* (Tuscaloosa: University of Alabama Press, 1957) is the classic account of the political fight over railroads and influence in Alabama politics during the period leading up to World War I. See also Martin T. Olliff, *Getting Out of the Mud: The Alabama Good Roads Movement and Highway Administration, 1898-1928* (Tuscaloosa: University of Alabama Press, 2017), 25–27.

9. David M. Kennedy, *Over Here: The First World War and American Society* (New York: Oxford University Press, 1980), 128–35, 139–41; Tindall, *Emergence of the New South*, 33–36, 44–53, 56. Tindall's chapter on World War I in the South is subtitled "Southern Horizons Expand." Paul Koistinen has suggested that the close relationship between business and the government during the war serves as an early example of what would later become known as the "military-industrial complex." See Koistinen, "The 'Industrial-Military Complex' in Historical Perspective: World War I," *Business History Review* 41, no. 4 (Winter 1967): 378–403. Blaine Brownell notes the growth of a number of cities during and after the war, including Nashville and Charleston, commenting that the latter city's chamber of commerce was "aggressive," even invasive in efforts to seek out opportunities for growth. See Brownell, *Urban Ethos*, 24–25, 31.

10. Wesley Phillips Newton, "'Tenting Tonight on the Old Camp Grounds': Alabama's Military Bases in World War I," in Martin T. Olliff., ed., *The Great War in the Heart of Dixie: Alabama during World War I* (Tuscaloosa: University of Alabama Press, 2008), 41–65; Tindall, *Emergence of the New South*, 56–61. For the Muscle Shoals development, see Matthew L. Downs, *Transforming the South: Federal Development in the Tennessee Valley, 1915-1960* (Baton Rouge: Louisiana State University Press, 2014).

11. Scribner, "Progress versus Tradition in Mobile, 1900-1920," 176; Michael V. R. Thomason, "Mobile in World War I," in Olliff, ed., *The Great War in the Heart of Dixie*, 123–24; Alsobrook, "Alabama's Port City," 4, 292.

12. Kennedy, *Over Here*, 299–303. Wilson was equally concerned about a shortage of ships, to the point that he proposed purchasing German ships stuck in US ports. Alabama's Senator Underwood was a key voice in Wilson's efforts to solve the shipping crisis. See M. Ryan Floyd, *Abandoning American Neutrality: Woodrow Wilson and the Beginning of the Great War, August 1914–December 1915* (New York: Palgrave Macmillan, 2013).

13. Kennedy, *Over Here*, 304–5, 326–37; Arthur S. Link, *Wilson: Confusions and Crises, 1915-1916* (Princeton, NJ: Princeton University Press, 1964); Richard Sicotte, "Economic Crisis and Political Response: The Political Economy of the Shipping Act of 1916," *Journal of Economic History* 59, no. 4 (December 1999): 861–84.

14. Thomason, "Mobile in World War I," in Olliff, ed., *The Great War in the Heart of Dixie*, 127–28; C. E. Watson, "Our Organization," *Fore and Aft* 2, no. 1 (August 2, 1919), 3, in Box 1, Folder "Vol. 2," Alabama Dry Dock and Shipping Company Collection, Doyle Leale McCall Rare Book and Manuscript Library, University of South Alabama, Mobile, Alabama (hereafter, ADDSCO Collection).

15. "On Time," *Fore and Aft* 1, no. 6 (August 24, 1918): 2; Box 1, Folder "Vol. 1"; and "The Banago," *Fore and Aft* 1, no. 7 (August 31, 1918): 1, Box 1, Folder "Vol. 1," ADDSCO Collection.

16. Sledge, *The Mobile River*, 187; Thomason, "Mobile in World War I," 128–29; "Chickasaw near Mobile, When Completed Will Be a Model Industrial City," *Mobile Register*, 78th Trade Edition,

September 1, 1918, 3C; "Mobile's Piers in the Bridge to France," *Electric Railway Journal* 51, no. 25 (June 22, 1918): 1185–1186. The official and semi-official announcements about the progress at Chickasaw failed to mention conflict and controversy, so the voices of workers at Chickasaw have largely gone unheard. A careful reading of the existing material, though, suggests that promoters made a concerted effort to segregate the facility by placing the two worker villages on either side of the main road into the town, and planners consistently stated their intention to make workers "happy" by providing amenities like schools and community buildings. Clearly, the company was worried about the possibility of unrest. See "Chickasaw near Mobile" and "Mobile's Piers in the Bridge to France."

17. "Passing Year Brings Biggest Concerns Here," *Mobile Register,* January 5. 1918, 1; "Industrial Hive of Ship Building on Mobile River," *Mobile Register,* January 5, 1918, 1; "Mobile Enterprise," *Mobile Register,* January 13, 1918, 4; Craighead, "The New Dawn Is Here!" *Mobile Register,* 78th Annual Trade Edition, September 1, 1918, 1; Thomason, "Mobile in World War I," 129–30.

18. Kennedy, *Over Here,* 330–38.

19. "Peace Parade!" and "The War after the War," *Fore and Aft* 1, no. 17 (November 16, 1918): 1–2, Box 1, Folder "Vol. 1"; "Sit Steady," *Fore and Aft* 1, no. 39 (April 25, 1919): 2, Box 1, Folder "Vol. 1"; and "Dry Dock and Woodworking Department," *Fore and Aft* 2, no 1 (August 2, 1918): 8, Box 1, Folder "Vol. 2," ADDSCO Collection.

20. Thomason, "Mobile in World War I," 129–30; "Chickasaw, the Fairy City," *Mobile Register,* May 25, 1919, 6; "Chickasaw Shipyard, Chickasaw, Alabama," GlobalSecurity, http://www.globalsecurity.org/military/facility/chickasaw.htm (accessed July 28, 2017); "New Homes for Employees," *American Shipping,* August 10, 1920, 28.

21. "Of Vital Interest: An Editorial," *Mobile Register,* November 3, 1918, 1; "The War after the War," *Fore and Aft* 1, no. 17 (November 16, 1918): 2, Box 1, Folder "Vol. 1," ADDSCO Collection.

22. "Mobile Shippers Protest," *Mobile Register,* May 25, 1919, 6; "Mobile to Get Relief in Allocation of U.S. Vessels," *Mobile Register,* May 25, 1919, 1A; "Our Port and So, America," *Mobile Register,* June 8, 1919, 6; "Some Mobile's Rival Ports Fare Better in Allotments," *Mobile Register,* August 3, 1919, 1A, 3A; and Editorial, *Mobile Register,* August 4, 1919, 4.

23. "Eight Vessels Allocated Here for the Month of August," *Mobile Register,* August 10, 1919, 1A, 2A; "A Training in Trade," *Mobile Register,* September 8, 1919, 4. Moreover, Taylor suggested that the nature of shipping, with vessels stopping at multiple ports, made it difficult to compare numbers of allotted vessels.

24. "A Letter to Our Employees," *Fore and Aft* 2 (September 4, 1920), Box 1, Folder "Vol. 3," ADDSCO Collection; "Figures Show Shipbuilding Is Permanent Mobile Industry," *Mobile Register,* January 4, 1920, 1A, 2A; "Chickasaw City Sailing Marks New Era for Port of Mobile," *Mobile Register,* May 9, 1920, 1A; "Most Prosperous Year in Mobile's History Closes," *Mobile Register,* January 2, 1921, 1A, 2A.

25. "Southern Ports and Shipping," *Mobile Register,* December 28, 1919, 4; "The U.S. Shipping Board," *Mobile Register,* November 14, 1920, 6; "Shipping Board Will Build Up Smaller Ports," *Mobile Register,* August 7, 1921, 1.

26. John B. Waterman to George J. Santa Cruz, Division of Operations, Emergency Fleet Corporation (EFC), United States Shipping Board (USSB), May 16, 1919, Box 11, Folder 1A; Waterman

to Oscar Underwood, June 15, 1919, Box 11, Folder 1A; and Waterman to R. B. Chandler, *Mobile Register,* October 9, 1938, Box 12, Folder 8, Waterman Papers; and Sledge, *The Mobile River,* 188.

27. Waterman to "Mr. Roberts," July 26, 1926, Box 3, Folder 3; Waterman to R. B. Chandler, *Mobile Register,* October 9, 1938, Box 12, Folder 8; Waterman to Earnest Ladd, President of Merchant's Bank, April 9, 1924, Box 11, Folder 1B; Waterman to W. B. Keene, Vice President of the Emergency Fleet Corporation, April 26, 1924, Box 11, Folder 1B; and Arledge to Waterman, April 10, 1925, Box 6, Folder 6.9, Waterman Papers; "Mobilians Seek Endorsement for Ship Subsidy Bill," *Mobile Register,* April 16, 1922, 1A. Mobile was not alone in its hopes that the government would prefer smaller, southern ports. See "Makes Plea for 'Delivery' of Southern Ports," *Mobile Register,* March 26, 1922.

28. The Constitution of Alabama, 1901, http://alisondb.legislature.state.al.us/alison/codeofalabama/constitution/1901/CA-245628.htm (accessed March 14, 2016). This prohibition against state-funded improvements dated back to the "Redemption" constitution of 1875, in which Black Belt planters enshrined their own agrarian interests, prevented industrialists from assuming control of state finances, and repudiated the Reconstruction-era government's failed attempt to partner with railroads (which the Black Belt planters charged as "corruption" in the development of state transportation networks). See Rogers et al., *Alabama,* 266–68, 350–51; and Harvey H. Jackson III, "White Supremacy Triumphant: Democracy Undone," in Bailey Thomson, ed., *A Century of Controversy: Constitutional Reform in Alabama* (Tuscaloosa: University of Alabama Press, 2002), 18–19.

29. Alsobrook, "Alabama's Port City," 289–90, 292–93; Mobile Board of Commissioners, Minutes for May 23, 1916 (593), January 2, 1917 (56), April 3, 1917 (81–83), Minutes of the Board of Commissioners, 1911–1984, in Record Group 6: Records of the Board of Commissioners of the City of Mobile, 1911–1985, Mobile City Archives, Mobile, Alabama (hereafter Board of Commissioners Minutes); and Kelly Kazek, "Vintage 1916 Photos Show when Alabama Experienced Its Second-Highest Hurricane Storm Surge," July 5, 2016, al.com, http://www.al.com/living/index.ssf/2016/07/vintage_1916_photos_show_when.html (accessed January 13, 2017).

30. Mobile Board of Commissioners Minutes for August 14, 1917 (119–20), February 12, 1918 (184–85), December 26, 1918 (290–91), March 11, 1919 (315), June 24, 1919 (350), February 22, 1921 (545–46), March 15, 1921 (552–53), April 12, 1921 (560), Board of Commissioners Minutes; "Arlington Dock Main Municipal Project for 1918," *Mobile Register,* January 20, 1918, 1; "Mobile Begins Building of Additional Port Facilities," *Mobile Register,* March 17, 1918; "Ten Years—Arlington Docks," *Mobile Register,* September 4, 1921, 6; "Tomorrow," *Mobile Register,* September 11, 1921, 6. See also Thomason, "Mobile in World War I," 126–27.

31. Thomas McAdory Owen, *History of Alabama and Dictionary of Alabama Biography,* vol. 3 (Chicago: S. J. Clarke Publishing Co., 1921), 764; Alsobrook, "Alabama's Port City," 100–102, 295–97; "Golden Era Opens for Mobile," *Mobile Register,* August 29, 1915, 6; Sledge, *The Mobile River,* 171–81.

32. Chairman W. D. Nesbitt, State of Alabama Board of Control and Economy, to Kilby, May 9, 1919, 1, 2, Roll 20; and Hartwell to Kilby, January 11, 1919, Roll 20, in Governor Thomas Kilby Papers, SG031372, Alabama Department of Archives and History, Montgomery, Alabama (hereafter Kilby Papers). Nesbitt reported that tonnage had doubled from 4 million to 8 million tons since 1901 and that the facilities covered all bond interest payments with an additional surplus of $700,000 per year. In the following years, Georgia, too, set in motion plans for a state-operated port, at Savannah. Though Georgia did not create a port authority until after World War II, news of the plans served

as another prod for Alabama to act. See "The Georgia Port Plan," *Mobile Register*, May 21, 1922, 6; and Henry E. Barber, "Georgia Ports Authority," in *New Georgia Encyclopedia*, http://www.georgia encyclopedia.org/articles/business-economy/georgia-ports-authority (accessed July 25, 2016).

33. Rogers et al., *Alabama*, 415; Michael A. Breedlove, "Thomas E. Kilby, 1919–1923," in *Alabama Governors: A Political History of the State* (Tuscaloosa: University of Alabama Press, 2001), 166–69. Kilby's progressive support for business did not extend to labor. He opposed unionization, and during the 1919 coal strike, he called out the National Guard to protect non-union miners.

34. Rauber, "The Alabama State Docks," 8; "Thomas' Words of Warning," *Mobile Register*, June 8, 1919, 6; "Shall It Be Progress," *Mobile Register*, July 18, 1920, 6.

35. A. G. Ward to Kilby, April 18, 1919, Roll 20, Kilby Papers; William T. Donnelly, "Report of William T. Donnelly to the State Harbor Commission, Relative to Port Development at Mobile," July 29, 1919, Roll 9, Governor William Brandon Papers, SG003675, Alabama Department of Archives and History, Montgomery, Alabama (hereafter Brandon Papers); "Development of Harbor by State Is Urged by U.S.," *Mobile Register*, October 5, 1919, 1A, 2A; Hartwell to "Bill" (Darden?), Thursday, ca. October 18, 1919, Roll 20; Kilby to R. V. Taylor, November 7, 1919, Roll 20; Kilby to Hartwell, November 7, 1919, Roll 20; and Kilby to J. H. Webb, ca. November 8, 1919, Roll 20, Kilby Papers; "Executive Takes Stand Facilities Belong to State," *Mobile Register*, November 9, 1919, 1B, 2B. Kilby also restaffed the Harbor Commission to include more members from outside the Mobile region in the hopes that it would help make a "statewide" case for the port. See A. G. Ward et al. to Kilby, February 8, 1919, Roll 20, Kilby Papers.

36. "Campaign for Port Amendment Will Be Launched Tuesday," *Mobile Register*, July 25, 1920, 1A; "For Alabama and the Port," *Mobile Register*, July 26, 1920, 4; "Mobile Sends Large Delegation to Port Aid Convention," *Mobile Register*, September 12, 1920, 1A, 2A.

37. "Boosting This Port," *Mobile Register*, September 5, 1920, 6; Hartwell to Kilby, October 7, 1920, Roll 20; Hartwell to Kilby, "Sunday 1920" (no date), Roll 20; and Kilby, Unnamed Press Release, October 1920, Roll 20, Kilby Papers; "State Press on the Port," *Mobile Register*, October 24, 1920, 6.

38. "This Day, Mobilians!" *Mobile Register*, November 2, 1920, 4; Hartwell to Kilby, telegram, November 3, 1920, Roll 20, Kilby Papers; "Nearly Complete Count Shows Port Amendment Safe," *Mobile Register*, November 6, 1920, 1; "Unofficial Vote Would Indicate Port Aid Is Lost," *Mobile Register*, November 8, 1920, 1; "Port Aid Amendment Appears Lost by Large Majority," *Mobile Register*, November 14, 1920, 1A, 2A; Hartwell to Murray Brown, November 8, 1920, Roll 20, Kilby Papers. Ironically, the one county in which Hartwell predicted railroad malfeasance that would undermine support, Calhoun, produced a majority for the amendment. See "Majorities on Amendment," *Mobile Register*, November 14, 1920, 2A.

39. The *Mobile Register* published a useful chart showing majorities for and against the amendment on a county-by-county basis. See "Majorities on Amendment," *Mobile Register*, November 14, 1920, 2A; "Port Aid Amendment Appears Lost by Large Majority," *Mobile Register*, November 14, 1920, 1A, 2A; "The Port, First and Last," *Mobile Register*, November 7, 1920, 6. Such voters were not completely adverse to change; in that same election, Alabama voters approved a bond for state road projects.

40. "Gen. Connor Will Recommend Mobile Terminal," *Mobile Register*, September 27, 1920, 1; Hartwell to Murray Brown, November 8, 1920, Roll 20, Kilby Papers; "[Coal Terminal?] Available

for Port Facility," *Mobile Register,* November 12, 1920, 1; "Port Aid Amendment Appears Lost by Large Majority," *Mobile Register,* November 14, 1920, 1A, 2A; "Mobile Business Interests Unite to Secure Coal Terminal," *Mobile Register,* November 28, 1920, 1A; Hartwell to Murray Brown, February 14, 1921, Roll 20, Kilby Papers. The vote reflects V. O. Key's classic analysis of local politics in Alabama. As in other southern states, county-level politics reflected the interests of local elites—so-called "courthouse rings." See V. O. Key, Jr., *Southern Politics in State and Nation,* A New Edition (Knoxville, University of Tennessee Press, 1984): 52–55.

41. "Port Development the Issue," *Mobile Register,* April 3, 1921, 6; "Keller Declares City Ownership of Terminals Essential," *Mobile Register,* April 3, 1921, 1A, 2A; "The Community's Duty," *Mobile Register,* April 17, 1921, 6; "For Port Freedom," *Mobile Register,* April 24, 1921, 6; "Governor Kilby Urges Public Ownership of Port Terminals," *Mobile Register,* May 8, 1921, 1A; "The Governor and Mobile," *Mobile Register,* February 21, 1921; Kilby to McDuffie, May 26, 1921, Roll 12; McDuffie to Kilby, May 31, 1921, Roll 12; W. B. Oliver to Kilby, June 1, 1921, Roll 12; Underwood to Kilby, June 10, 1921, Roll 12; and Kilby to Frederick Thompson, September 2, 1921, Roll 12, Kilby Papers.

42. "See Benefit for All Alabama by Development of Port," *Mobile Register,* October 2, 1921, 1A; Milner to Kilby, January 28, 1922, Roll 20; H. K. Milner, President, State Harbor Commission, to Gordon Smith, Mobile Chamber of Commerce, April 18, 1922, Roll 20; Milner to Kilby, May 15, 1922, Roll 20; and Milner to Kilby, May 15, 1922, Roll 20, Kilby Papers.

43. "Mobile Interest in Shoals," *Mobile Register,* May 21, 1922, 6; "Shoal Delegates Leave Today for Three Day Meet," *Mobile Register,* May 21, 1922, 1A. For the debate over the Muscle Shoals development and its relationship to the prospects of ongoing industrial development in the South, see Downs, *Transforming the South.*

44. Draft, article for *Mobile Register,* Kilby, undated (September 1922), Roll 20, Kilby Papers; "Leaders of State Endorse Seaport Amendment: See Great Opportunity Alabama's Development," *Mobile Register,* 82nd Annual Trade Review, September 1, 1922, 2A, 3A.

45. "Unequivocal Approval Given Amendment by Next Governor," *Mobile Register,* September 17, 1922, 1A; "Why Don't We Do It?" *Mobile Register,* October 29, 1922, 6; J. B. Hackworth, Scottsboro, to Kilby, November 1, 1922, Roll 20, Kilby Papers.

46. "Every Vote Will Count," *Mobile Register,* November 5, 1922, 6; "Port Amendment Is Overwhelmingly Ratified," *Mobile Register,* November 8, 1922, 1, 2; Milner to Kilby, November 18, 1922, Roll 20, Kilby Papers; "The New Year and Mobile," *Mobile Register,* January 1, 1923, 4.

47. Sledge, *The Mobile River,* 191–92; "Seaport Legislation to Be Presented Both Houses This Week," *Mobile Register,* January 14, 1923, 1A; George Crawford, President of TCI, to Brandon, October 29, 1923, Roll 9; Sibert to State Docks Commission, Report for 1924, December 22, 1924, Roll 9; Brandon to Sibert, March 21, 1924, Roll 9; Brandon to Underwood, April 21, 1924, Roll 9; Governor's Office, Report of the State Docks Commission, March 12, 1925, Roll 9; Harry Hartwell (Mobile Commissioner) to Brandon, January 15, 1926, Roll 9; Sibert to Brandon, March 24, 1926, Roll 9, Brandon Papers; C. J. Schexnayder, "William Sibert," *Encyclopedia of Alabama* (http://www.encyclopediaofalabama.org/article/h-3371; accessed May 26, 2016). As early as 1919, supporters of a state docks floated Sibert's name as a potential candidate to oversee the project.

48. Graves to Miles C. Allgood (Washington, DC), May 29, 1928, Box SG21154, Folder 29; J.W. White to Sibert, December 11, 1928, Box SG21154, Folder 29; and Hartwell, "Alabama and Its Only

Seaport," January 25, 1929, Box SG21155, Folder 4, Governor Bibb Graves (1927–1931 term) Administration Files, Alabama Department of Archives and History, Montgomery, Alabama (hereafter Graves Administration Files).

49. Hartwell to Graves, February 1, 1929, Box SG21155, Folder 4; Horace Turner to Graves, June 28, 1929, Box SG21154, Folder 29; and Hartwell to Graves, April 4, 1930, Box SG21155, Folder 1, Graves Administration Files. Sibert's solicitation did bring in business, including newsprint from Canada, bagging from India, cork from Spain, and bauxite from British Guiana. Nevertheless, in order to compete against rival ports and private shippers, the Docks Commission had to offer rates too low to offset the cost of operating the docks and liquidating the associated debt. See Rauber, "The Alabama State Docks," 35–36, 51–53. The position of mayor was held by a commission member selected to serve as mayor by his colleagues.

50. Earle Rauber, an economist with the Federal Reserve, compiled a report investigating the profitability of the port by 1945. Despite its early problems with funding, Rauber concluded that the state docks were successful in bringing new business to the city and state and allowing Mobile to compete for trade. Nearly everyone, "city officials, chamber-of-commerce representatives, railroad and steamship executives, bankers, businessmen, and stevedoring companies," would agree that "the state docks have been the making of the city [of Mobile]." See Rauber, "The Alabama State Docks," 51.

51. Quoted in "State Must Pull Together for Mobile, Says Underwood," *Mobile Register,* April 6, 1919, 1A.

CONTRIBUTORS

ANGELA JILL COOLEY is an associate professor of history at Minnesota State University, Mankato, where she teaches US Constitution and Civil Rights. She previously completed a postdoctoral fellowship at the Center for the Study of Southern Culture at the University of Mississippi, a PhD at the University of Alabama, and a JD at the George Washington University Law School. She is the author of the book *To Live and Dine in Dixie: The Evolution of Urban Food Culture in the Jim Crow South* (University of Georgia Press, 2015), as well as of numerous journal articles and book chapters.

ANNETTE COX grew up in North Carolina, where her father, mother, and numerous other relatives worked in textile mills. Educated at University of North Carolina–Greensboro and University of North Carolina–Chapel Hill, she is the author of publications on the southern textile industry in the *Journal of Southern History, Business History Review,* and the *North Carolina Historical Review.*

MATTHEW L. DOWNS is chair of the Department of Social and Behavioral Sciences and associate professor of history at the University of Mobile. He is the author of *Transforming the South: Federal Development in the Tennessee Valley, 1915–1960* (Louisiana State University Press, 2014), which won the James B. Sulzby Award for best book on Alabama history. He also serves as the editor of the *Alabama Review.*

M. RYAN FLOYD is an associate professor of history and the coordinator for Secondary Social Studies Education at Lander University in Greenwood, South Carolina. He is the author of *Abandoning American Neutrality: Woodrow Wilson and the Beginning of the Great War, August 1914–December 1915* (Palgrave Macmillan, 2013). He has also written articles on the history of the American

South, on US foreign relations, and on history education in the *Alabama Review,* the *Proceedings of the South Carolina Historical Association,* and various online publications.

KEITH GORMAN is assistant dean for Special Collections and University Archives at University of North Carolina–Greensboro. Gorman leads the department's efforts in collection development, instructional services, digital initiatives, community engagement, and donor relations. Trained as a historian, Gorman received a PhD in history from the University of Wisconsin–Madison. After a ten-year teaching career at Simmons College, he left the classroom to pursue a career in archives. He received his MLS (archives concentration) at Simmons College. His research areas include the impact of archives on a community's shared memory, incorporating primary sources in K-12 curriculum, and the politics of commemoration.

JAMES HALL is a doctoral candidate in twentieth-century US history at University of North Carolina–Greensboro. The son of a career Air Force serviceman, he currently resides in Winston-Salem, North Carolina.

FRITZ HAMER is curator of history and archivist for the South Carolina Confederate Relic Room and Military Museum in Columbia, South Carolina. Prior to this, he served as curator of history for the South Carolina State Museum. He has written on a wide variety of topics in various publications, including *Forward Together: South Carolinians in the Great War* (History Press, 2007), and, most recently, he co-edited a set of articles entitled *South Carolina in the Civil War and Reconstruction Eras* (University of South Carolina Press, 2016).

JANET G. HUDSON is two-time winner of the Stephen L. Dalton Distinguished Teacher Award and author of the prize-winning book *Entangled by White Supremacy: Reform in World War I–era South Carolina* (University Press of Kentucky, 2009). Her project on African American soldiers from North Carolina who served in World War I can be found at http://blacksoldiersmattered.com and in a chapter in *North Carolina in the Great War* (University of Tennessee Press, forthcoming). She is also founder of XCEL Quest Coaching & Consulting, coaching idealistic professionals to tame the chaos so they can make meaningful contributions.

LEE SARTAIN is senior lecturer in American Studies at the University of Portsmouth, England. His books include *Borders of Equality: The NAACP and the Baltimore Civil Rights Struggle, 1914–1970* (University Press of Mississippi, 2013), and *Invisible Activists: Women in the Louisiana NAACP and the Struggle for Civil Rights, 1915–1945* (Louisiana State University Press, 2007), which won the Jules and Frances Landry Award for the best book on a southern topic. He also co-edited *Long Is the Way and Hard: One Hundred Years of the National Association for the Advancement of Colored People* (University of Arkansas Press, 2009).

KATHELENE MCCARTY SMITH holds the faculty position of instruction and outreach archivist at University of North Carolina–Greensboro, serving both as the coordinator of and as a teacher in the instructional program of Special Collections. Smith earned an MA in art history from Louisiana State University and an MLS in Library and Information Studies from UNC–Greensboro. Her research interests include the role of academic libraries in fostering life-long learning, volunteer programs in special collections and archives, social activism on college campuses, and the mobilization of North Carolina's women's colleges during World War I.

INDEX